CHRISTIANITY AND SOCIAL SERVICE IN MODERN BRITAIN

In the daily clamour for leadership, for faith, for a new heart or a new cause, I hear the ghost of late Victorian England whimpering on the grave thereof.

(G. M. Young, *Victorian England: Portrait of an Age*, 1936)

Christianity and Social Service in Modern Britain

The Disinherited Spirit

FRANK PROCHASKA

OXFORD
UNIVERSITY PRESS

OXFORD

UNIVERSITY PRESS

Great Clarendon Street, Oxford OX2 6DP

Oxford University Press is a department of the University of Oxford.
It furthers the University's objective of excellence in research, scholarship,
and education by publishing worldwide in

Oxford New York

Auckland Cape Town Dar es Salaam Hong Kong Karachi
Kuala Lumpur Madrid Melbourne Mexico City Nairobi
New Delhi Shanghai Taipei Toronto

With offices in

Argentina Austria Brazil Chile Czech Republic France Greece
Guatemala Hungary Italy Japan Poland Portugal Singapore
South Korea Switzerland Thailand Turkey Ukraine Vietnam

Oxford is a registered trade mark of Oxford University Press
in the UK and in certain other countries

Published in the United States
by Oxford University Press Inc., New York

British Library Cataloguing in Publication Data

Data available

Library of Congress Cataloging in Publication Data

Data available

Typeset by Newgen Imaging Systems (P) Ltd., Chennai, India
Printed in Great Britain
on acid-free paper by
Biddles Ltd., King's Lynn, Norfolk

ISBN 0–19–928792–9 978–0–19–928792–5

1 3 5 7 9 10 8 6 4 2

To
Bernard and Maxine Semmel

Preface

This book springs from a longstanding scholarly interest in the history of Christianity. While I have no personal religious faith, my research has left me with a respect for the religious temper and its role in society and politics. In a study of British Christianity, which concentrates on Protestant traditions in particular, I hope I will be forgiven for not including more material on other faiths. The evolution of religion in British society is a phenomenon with many creeds, not all of which can be encompassed in this book. Jews have a strong tradition of social reform, for example, which in many ways is comparable to Christianity. But the Jewish community, although influential, has never constituted as much as 1 per cent of the population of Britain. Similarly, there were only an estimated 23,000 Muslims in Britain in 1951, though they now make up about 3 per cent of the population and play an increasingly important role in the nation's religious life. Between November 1996 and November 2001, the Charity Commissioners registered 385 Islamic and Muslim societies. The role that institutions of Jewish, Muslim, and other faiths play in the future will be well worth watching.

This is an interpretive study, which seeks to contribute to the history of social service, religious decline, and democratic traditions. It makes no claims to have exhausted the subject of Christian charity in modern British history, which is inexhaustible in any case. The thinking behind this book has been influenced by the rediscovery of civil society after the collapse of the Soviet Empire in 1989, which has reshaped the context in which voluntary institutions are seen and studied. The rethinking of politics after the events of 1989 made me more sensitive to the relationship of Christian societies and democracy in Britain. This issue interested the Victorians, who admired the democratic nature of self-governing institutions, but it faded in the twentieth century with the growth of government and the decline of religion, trends that were not unrelated to each other. The effect of state provision on Christianity and its associated institutions is a principal concern of this book. So too is the issue, raised by Alexis de Tocqueville, among others, of the historic relationship between religious associations and freedom in Anglo-American democracy. For the historian, such matters are worth revisiting in their own right. They also resonate in the current debate on the future of British social democracy.

Though my focus has shifted, the research for this project began years ago when I was working on my first book, *Women and Philanthropy in Nineteenth-Century England* (1980). Chapters 4 and 5 draw on articles published in *History* (1989) and *Historical Research* (1987) respectively. I would like to thank the many librarians and archivists in England, most notably those at the British Library, the Institute of Historical Research, and the National Archives, who have made my research so congenial over the years. Since my arrival at Yale, the staff of the Sterling Memorial Library, the Beinecke Library, and the Divinity School Library, whose British collections are exceptional, have been most supportive. In particular, Susanne Roberts, the Librarian for European History, has given unstinting attention to my many enquiries. My colleague John Harley Warner kindly invited me to give Chapter 5, 'Nursing', to his seminar on the History of Medicine at the Yale Medical School, which elicited much stimulating comment.

Many individuals have given me assistance and advice, not least my students, who have enlivened my thinking on British social policy. I would especially like to thank my friends George Behlmer, who read the manuscript in its entirety with his customary acumen, Robert Whelan, who generously helped with detailed points of research, and James Sheehan, who helped shape my views on Christian decline while we were on holiday together in London. Oxford's expert readers provided just the sort of comment needed to bring the book into sharper focus. Christopher Wheeler, my editor, steered the manuscript through the Press with proficiency. Kay Rogers, Jeff New, and

Matthew Cotton moved the publishing process along seamlessly. My daughter Elizabeth, formerly of the Oxford University Press, has been a knowledgeable guide and critic. As ever, my greatest debt is to my wife Alice Prochaska and to our children, who have been unfailingly charitable in encouraging another of my manuscripts. My family support me in dedicating the book to two dear friends.

New Haven
2005

Contents

1

Background

Christianity must be maintained at any cost in the bosom of modern democracies.

(Alexis de Tocqueville, *Democracy in America*, 1840)

We are no friends to benevolent despotisms in this land of ours. We like, in most ways and as far as may be, to administer ourselves. So private charity is with us an all-important agency.

(Revd Archer Gurney, *Loyalty and Church and State*, 1872)

In the spring of 1810 Sarah Martin, a 19-year-old seamstress, attended a sermon at the New Meeting-House in Great Yarmouth. The text was 2 Corinthians 5: 11: 'Knowing therefore the fear of the Lord, we persuade men.' 'It was then', she said in later life, 'that the Spirit of God sent a ray of light upon my guilty soul, slave of Satan, "fast bound in misery and iron".' 'Looking unto Jesus', she wished 'the Lord to open privileges to me of serving my fellow creatures, that happily I might, with the Bible in my hand, point others to those fountains of joy, whence my own so largely flowed.'[1] She dedicated the rest of her life to good works, most notably prison visiting, for which she became celebrated as a model of the charity of the poor to the poor. Her story, retailed in the religious press for decades after her death in 1843, testified to the transforming power of evangelical Christianity, the faith that did so much to set the moral tenor of Victorian Britain.

Today Sarah Martin is long forgotten, an oddity from a distant and different age. In turn, she would find contemporary Britain odd and unfamiliar. In the mid-nineteenth century over half the population attended church regularly. At the end of the twentieth century only 8 per cent did.[2] Over the same period government took over primary responsibility for social provision, with the blessing of the Church of England. Such trends reveal a momentous shift in values, which point to a dramatic decline in Christianity and its traditional role in social service. In a secular culture, in which rights take precedence over duties, people no longer look to voluntary institutions but to government. Christian societies are no longer ubiquitous in the social and charitable landscape. What happened to the world of Sarah Martin, of Sunday schools and ragged schools, of Bible and missionary associations, of visiting and temperance societies, of mothers' meetings and Dorcas societies, and the many other institutions that tended to the needy and benighted and played such a prominent part in the day-to-day lives of the faithful?

In modern Britain, we can barely conceive of a society that boasted millions of religious associations providing essential services and a moral training for the citizenry, a society in which there were more scripture readers than scientists in the workforce.[3] Reading our secular selves into history, it is questionable whether we can fully understand the motives of the faithful in the past, even when we admire their energy and accomplishments. In an increasingly mobile and materialist world, in which culture has grown more national, indeed global, our intellects no longer relate to the lost world of parish life. To most people in Britain today, the very idea of Christian social reform has a quaint, Victorian air about it. As we reject the pieties and social hierarchies of our ancestors, we tend to forget that benevolence and neighbourliness, self-help and helping others, were among the most urgent of Christian values. We also tend to forget that much of Britain's idealism and democratic culture grew out of these values. That a majority of the nation's citizens no longer accept the veracity of Christian doctrine should not blind us to the truth of such generalizations. Much turns on improbable metaphysics.

The Victorians, who believed that Britain's greatness rested on Christian foundations, assumed that religion and the public good were inextricably linked.[4] It was axiomatic, as one social campaigner declared in 1800, that charity could only be effectively exercised under the influence of 'sacred principle'.[5] Not all Christians were charitable, of course. Nor were all Britons Christian. But few dissented from the view that any faith was better than none. Most believers thought of themselves as derelict in their duty without a new heart or a new cause. For the great majority of those who imbibed the social gospel of vital religion, belief without active benevolence was inexplicable. As one female campaigner put it in 1815, 'uncharitableness is that which strikes at the foundations of Christianity'.[6] She would probably have agreed with her contemporary John Adams, the second American president, who in a critique of Mary Wollstonecraft's book on the French Revolution argued that the principle of human equality was 'founded entirely in the Christian doctrine that we are all children of the same Father, all accountable to Him for our conduct to one another, all equally bound to respect each other's self love'.[7]

Needless to say, Christians, whether British or American, often failed to live up to such ideals. With their contorted emotional lives, evangelicals, in particular, were prone to humbug and 'stringent piety'. But given religion's capacity to enthuse, it more often than not encouraged the expression of public spirit and voluntary service, what William Wilberforce called 'Practical Christianity'. Evangelical doctrine did not assume that good works guaranteed salvation, but the faithful often regarded charity 'as the only sure evidence of a true conversion'.[8] The Victorian man of letters Edmund Gosse, who endured an evangelical childhood of the most puritanical type, observed that in the nineteenth century Christians of all classes raised good works to a new status. 'It is extraordinary how far-reaching the change has been, so that nowadays a religion which does not combine with its subjective faith a strenuous labour for the good of others is hardly held to possess any religious principle worth proclaiming'.[9]

Today, the voluntary work of the faithful is often called 'spiritual capital', a religious variant of what political scientists refer to as 'social capital', which includes diffuse patterns of social interaction outside the family, from dropping in on a neighbour to the work of illustrious charities.[10] In the nineteenth century such activity was more likely to be called good works, public spirit, or simply charity. But whatever it is called, the timeless tradition of religious social service has trickled away in Britain since its Victorian heyday. Today, advocates of active citizenship may wonder where the public spirit or social capital of the future will come from when the British 'Sea of Faith', as Matthew Arnold divined in 'Dover Beach', has receded, with 'its melancholy, long, withdrawing roar'. On visiting a parish church today, how many of us wonder, like Philip Larkin, 'who will be the last, the very last, to seek this place for what it was'?[11]

It may be worth investigating a few of the institutions that gave expression to religious spirit in the past. They not only made life more bearable and human, but propelled those traditions of free association that are thought to be essential to the creation of a vibrant democracy. Voluntary bodies gave a voice to those who were excluded, or felt excluded, from the political nation: minorities, dissenters, women, and the working classes. Through associational culture, the most obscure sects prospered in their own enclave of belief. Whatever the faith or the cause, self-governing institutions could achieve their ad hoc purposes without being stifled by ritualized conventions or enmeshed and consequently immobilized by politics. The fluid, instrumental traditions of voluntary association made a rigid, monopolistic political system less likely to develop in Britain. The very density of free associations, catering to all manner of maladies and aspirations, thwarted the revolutionary theorists, who anticipated the collapse of the social order.[12]

The Puritan sects, it is routinely said, left a legacy of free associations and democratic ideas that was transmitted to the nineteenth century. When the Victorians looked to the past for inspiration they found it as often as not in the Puritan revolution. As the prolific historian G. P. Gooch wrote in 1898, 'modern democracy is the child of the Reformation'.[13] The Puritan principles of the priesthood of all believers and the duty of free inquiry unleashed centrifugal forces that encouraged the emergence of competing Christian sects. 'The spiritual independence of the Puritan', as one writer put it, 'made an immeasurable contribution to the democratic and religious freedom of society.'[14] 'The freedom of the religious sect', as another writer observed, 'turned into the ideal of the freedom of associations.'[15] As the movement of religious association expanded, it gave voice to minority and majority opinion alike. By encouraging participation, charities and other forms of voluntary association acted as 'schools of citizenship' for those both inside and outside the political nation.

Anglo-Saxon Protestantism supplied a powerful engine for the expression of public spirit in what is nowadays called civil society, the separate sphere of voluntary institutions that provides a 'moral space between rulers and ruled'.[16] Classical, early Christian, and neo-Roman authors had little notion of civil society as a buffer against government, a halfway house of free associations between the state and society. They equated public spirit with political or military service. In seventeenth-century Britain the Commonwealth fused ancient ideas of republican citizenship with Christian notions of benevolence and social justice. In the eighteenth century an important ideological shift was taking place over the application of civic virtue. In an era of democratic stirrings, the idea of public spirit moved on among the politically articulate. As atavistic conceptions of nobility and aristocratic hauteur weakened, there emerged the idea that moral values applied to actions, that privilege entailed responsibility to the less fortunate.

Under the influence of authors such as the Scottish theologian and social thinker Thomas Chalmers (1780–1847) and the poet Samuel Taylor Coleridge (1772–1834), the movement of ideas was giving shape to a vision of citizenship that found expression in voluntary, non-governmental institutions. Industrial and urban growth, which led to a concentration of poverty and distress, propelled the massive expansion of charitable institutions and societies for mutual aid that was taking place at the time. Gradually, traditional forms of benevolence, which were thought to be inadequate in an industrial age, gave way to the collective effort of worthy societies, what Alexis de Tocqueville, the great interpreter of civic democracy, called 'the habit of association'. Successive waves of revivalism inside and outside the Church of England gave the 'habit' momentum. So much so, that the democratizing effects of religious revival became a staple of Whig history, at once Protestant and progressive.

In the movement for social reform, evangelicals provided a vanguard. They believed mankind fallen, yet felt a need to alleviate human suffering through voluntary effort. They did not exaggerate the moral potential of politics, nor the capacity of the state to reduce poverty. Inspired by that central doctrine of the Atonement, they recoiled from Caesar. Nonconformists had good historical reasons for distrusting the power of the state. Until 1828 they were excluded from full participation in civil government by the restrictions imposed by the Test and Corporation Acts passed in the seventeenth century. Their emphasis on the freedom of religious sects evolved naturally in the direction of voluntary associations, jealous of their independence. Associational culture gave them opportunities for public service that they were denied elsewhere. Among Nonconformists generally, the ideological and structural links with voluntarism were intimate in both mutual aid and charity.[17]

The attitude of voluntarists to the state in the nineteenth century has been likened to the revulsion felt by the curly-haired boy in *Nicholas Nickleby*, as his mouth opened before Mrs Squeers's brimstone and treacle spoon.[18] To most Victorian Christians, the state was an artificial contrivance, useful in punishing sinners, but incapable of redemptive action. Inclined to attribute the source of social problems to individual failings, they concluded that the remedy must be found in personal reformation, assisted by discretionary charity. Steeped in an individualist and familial ethic, Christians believed that government action in the social sphere obstructed the free development of home and community life. As a result they were reluctant to seek state assistance except in an enabling role and were apt to think that government regulation led to bureaucratic administration. Institutional autonomy acted as an antidote to standardizing bureaucracy; it also helped to heal social divisions, for at its best it encouraged class cooperation. The individual, not as ratepayer but as fellow-sufferer, was responsible for the cares of the world.

Such attitudes were in keeping with the shift in theology that took place in the late eighteenth century, which focused religious energy on voluntary institutions. By the end of the eighteenth century many evangelicals, including William Wilberforce and John Wesley, would have agreed with St Bernard: 'take free will away from man and there is nothing to save.' As Wesley put it, predestinarianism destroyed charitable zeal, particularly the 'saving of souls from death'.[19] As evangelicals discarded the Calvinist straitjacket, they adopted the view that salvation was conditional and provisional. The result was an elevation of works, particularly those of a missionary character, in the daily lives of evangelicals. Their 'heartburning', harangues, and supplication suggest that their needs were as great as the needs of those they wished to serve. When they were looking into the souls of fellow-sinners, they were nursing their own souls and fortifying themselves against the terrors of self-examination. The psychic turmoil that resulted from Christian self-examination predisposed the faithful to charitable conduct and animated piety.

Christianity is not simply a theory of past and future events, but something that actually happens to people. In the great public baptism of evangelicalism, sin, conversion, and the ministry of works were often experienced as real events, bringing with them a measure of emotional instability. Not all denominations were obsessed with sin. The Wesleyan Methodists, among others, emphasized the assurance of forgiveness. But in many of the religious autobiographies of the time—Sarah Martin's writings were typical of the genre—good works followed closely upon spiritual vacillation, an immediate, deeply felt struggle with Satan. As an Anglican diarist tormented by her lapses in charitable effort wrote in the 1860s, 'the devil is a roaring lion that walketh about seeking whom he may devour'.[20] Few things did more to shape society in nineteenth-century Britain than spiritual vacillation, tempered by evangelical discipline.[21] Charitable institutions benefited mightily from a consciousness of sin and a sense of moral embattlement. As the Edwardian educational reformer Rachel McMillan observed, the religious temper is 'forged in red caverns of love and hate . . . with seeing eyes and conscious choice'.[22] She did not comment on the future should the 'red caverns of love and hate' cool and the consciousness of sin subside.

The evangelical intensification of religious belief led to a vast expansion of charitable associations with social, educational, and missionary purposes. Paradoxically, these institutions coexisted with the fatalistic attitude toward poverty that marked economic thinking after Malthus. But unlike liberal economists, Christian campaigners looked beyond material life to eternity. The source of their vitality turned on imaginative richness and the belief that life had ultimate meaning. Moreover, the individualist ethic and sectarian rivalry that marked British Protestantism was in tune with laissez-faire doctrine. As the sociologist Max Weber argued, a similarity of outlook developed between Protestantism and free enterprise, an 'elective affinity' between spiritual and material interests that deeply influenced institutional culture and social structure.[23] Indeed, the free enterprise of associational religion provided the human face of capitalism, addressing the social and individual ills that capitalism created.

In the communion of Christianity and commerce, religious virtues resembled those of successful businessmen, with an echo of the Protestant suspicion of wealth, which encouraged giving some of it away. Wesley exhorted Christians to gain and save, but also to give, for there was a danger of money sinking them 'to the nethermost hell'.[24] By such calls on the faithful to practice frugality and 'divine charity', evangelicalism harnessed social conscience to liberal doctrine. The individualism that marked liberalism had its foundation in a Christian conception of personality, and much of Britain's associational life may be seen as liberalism turning its mind to social conditions under religious pressure. But in the alliance of religion and liberalism, which would become increasingly troubled from the late nineteenth century onwards, the decidedly older and senior partner was religion. By contrast with Christianity, 'liberalism happened along'.[25]

In a culture that was profoundly voluntary, free associations became an essential sphere of local democracy and civic pride, of individual hope and aspiration. The associational ideal was particularly suited to missionary purposes in an urban and industrial age, for 'it offered ordinary men and women the real attractions of a divine social activity, the genuine possibility of meaningful self-improvement and the ultimate sacred goal of personal salvation'.[26] Associational culture also offered a pragmatic training ground in citizenship and politics. Church and chapel societies prepared many a Liberal and Labour leader for secular office. For their part, friendly societies, which had strong links with Nonconformity, were 'highly principled, democratic organisms whose members were required to be active and conscientious practitioners of civic virtue and public spirit'.[27] Of course, many voluntary bodies were not inspired by a faith in democracy; and some of them, run by autocrats, had little enthusiasm for the participation of the membership.[28] Yet self-governing institutions, which embodied what has been called 'subscriber' democracy, supplied the growing points of personal and social initiative.

The historian Arthur Schlesinger's belief in the central importance of voluntary associations to American democracy could be applied to Britain. (Much of America's charitable culture had its origins in British Protestantism.) Voluntary societies, he argued, provided the people with their greatest school of self-government. 'Rubbing minds as well as elbows, they have been trained from youth to take common counsel, choose leaders, harmonize differences, and obey the expressed will of the majority. In mastering the associative way they have mastered the democratic way.'[29] In centralized welfare states, it is easy to forget that a nation's political condition depends to a large extent on the creative chaos of its associational life, on the myriad actions, typically unexceptional and little publicized, undertaken in local communities by self-governing churches, charities, mutual aid societies, clubs, and other institutions that operate outside the state.

The scope for democratic participation is proportional to a nation's associational life. Take the practice, once common among British charities, of electing beneficiaries by the vote of subscribers. Such institutions, often called 'voting charities', sharpened the significance of participation and had the merit of making personal bonds between the giver and the receiver of assistance. Like other associational forms, they brought people together while reducing the chasm between the social classes. Typically, a committee drew up a list of candidates eligible for relief, and all the subscribers then voted, each casting his or her vote proportional to the amount of his or her subscription. The practice may have been, as Florence Nightingale complained, 'the best method for electing the least eligible', but it embodied a democratic process, however corrupted by electioneering, in which negotiation and compromise were essential.[30] For many benefactors, particularly women, they were the only elections in which a vote could be cast.

Democracy comes in different forms, and the Victorians often thought it inherent in institutions. Most charities, whether they had votes to distribute or not, encouraged the habits of association and may be seen as an expression of democracy in the sphere of social and moral reform. To the liberal mind, the diffusion of power was a guarantor of freedom. Institutional self-government, it was argued, provided a check on the mechanisms of the central state—and the tyranny of the majority. It also acted as a check on the vicissitudes of the market, for it encouraged peaceful competition and solidarity based on shared interests. Philanthropy was a form of enlightened self-interest. John Stuart Mill elaborated its political significance in the *Principles of Political Economy* (1848): 'The only security against political slavery, is the check maintained over governors, by the diffusion of intelligence, activity, and public spirit among the governed.' Without the habit of spontaneous voluntary action, he added, citizens 'have their faculties only half developed'.[31]

It was a Victorian commonplace that society was most likely to flourish through local self-government and individual effort. National progress, it was argued, was the result of individual energy, not the institutions of government. 'The highest patriotism and philanthropy', wrote Samuel Smiles in *Self-Help* (1859), 'consists not so much in altering laws and modifying institutions, as in helping and stimulating men to elevate and improve themselves by their own free and independent individual action. . . . No laws, however stringent, can make the idle industrious, the thriftless provident, or the drunken sober. Such reforms can only be effected by means of individual actions, economy, and self-denial, by better habits, rather than by greater rights.'[32] Such views, widely circulated in the popular press, permeated political life in mid-nineteenth-century Britain, from Tory paternalists to Chartists and Owenites.[33]

Such views also cut across the denominations, which were arguably more important in the development of a social consensus than political affiliations. Clearly, they fuelled the idealism of charitable campaigners, whose dislike of government interference and centralization had deep roots in British culture. Under Christian influence, charity bridged the divide between individualism, so marked a feature of the nineteenth-century temper, and the collective needs of the community. The Revd Archer Gurney, a former English Chaplain in Paris, put the religious-cum-political case for charity in 1872: 'We are no friends to benevolent despotisms in this land of ours. We like, in most ways and as far as may be, to administer ourselves. So private charity is with us an all-important agency.'[34] It was widely assumed that in serving good causes voluntary associations served the wider cause of religious and civil liberty.

Societies proliferated in a liberal society splintered by religious, class, and local allegiances. Of course, many voluntary institutions in the eighteenth and nineteenth centuries did not have a specifically religious purpose, from trade unions to philosophical societies. But the boundaries between religion, philanthropy, and mutual aid were less marked in the past. Societies for the reformation of manners and the spread of the gospel, for example, were among the earliest voluntary institutions in Britain. Anglican charities such as the Society for Promoting Christian Knowledge (1698) and the Society for the Propagation of the Bible in Foreign Parts (1701) 'discovered that love of God could not be separated from service to man'.[35] The eighteenth-century charity school movement, as we shall see, owed a huge debt to the SPCK.[36] Societies for the spread of Christianity administered relief, visited prisons, trained teachers, and assisted the children of the poor. Their influence on other institutions that worked with the destitute suggested the considerable overlapping of proselytism and social work.

Charitable campaigners held a holistic view of human life in the past. They rarely made distinctions between religious and social welfare. Institutions whose objects were educational or recreational had underlying moral, if not spiritual, purposes and were part of a pattern of benevolence often seen as having a welfare element. Much charitable effort took place in areas that fitted ill with a materialistic view to welfare inherited from the state. In a time when medicine dealt with prognosis and could do so much less for the body, the needs of the soul demanded more attention. The missionary character of much charity must be seen in light of the limitations of the available health and social services. Before the twentieth century human suffering was commonly seen through a religious lens. Religion made sense in a world in which life was uncertain but the leaving of it was likely to be torment. This helps to explain why Christian belief was so widespread, even among the poor, who customarily turned up at church for baptisms and funerals, if not ordinary Sunday services.[37]

The religious disposition was inseparable from charity in the Christian mind, the word charity itself synonymous with the conduct of Christ. All religious denominations stressed the importance of public spirit and personal service. But none gave greater importance to it than evangelicals. Their dynamic ethic of private asceticism and public activism may have been 'morally tidy', as Dickens put it, but it was difficult to ignore. There was a tendency to equate 'philanthropist' with 'evangelical' in the nineteenth century, but evangelicals did not invariably promote charitable organization, for many of them preferred spontaneous giving to regular subscriptions.[38] Yet evangelicals ran perhaps as many as three out of four voluntary societies in the second half of the nineteenth century.[39] Whatever the precise figure, 'British philanthropy, like Victorian society as a whole, became tinctured with the evangelical spirit'.[40] Even non-Christians, who felt uncomfortable with religious societies, were susceptible to its influence. Righteousness so permeated British society in the hundred years or so before the First World War that the period has been called the 'Evangelical century'.[41]

In an era of sectarian rivalry, different denominations had different charitable emphases. Anglicans favoured anti-slavery and Bible societies; Unitarians and Quakers promoted educational causes; Baptists and Congregationalists were well represented in the temperance movement.[42] Methodists spread their charitable net widely and were pioneers of district visiting. Catholics made up only about 5 per cent of the population of England in 1851.[43] But their role in the cause of British voluntarism should not be overlooked, for they founded innumerable associations that mirrored Protestant ones, if only to counter proselytizing evangelicals. But whether high church or low, Methodist, Baptist, Unitarian, Quaker, or Catholic, all competed for converts and custom through their respective societies. In the missionary atmosphere of the time, the competition for bodies and souls created considerable overlapping of rival institutions, which could be counter-productive and would eventually serve as a point of criticism to those who looked to the state to provide solutions to social problems.

Social ills had great immediacy in a little-administered world. When government had little interest in social policy beyond the Poor Law and sanitary reform, the pressures were on the individual, and the public saw few alternatives beyond benevolence and self-help. In the familiarity of the community, whether rural or urban, the creation of local associations was a moral obligation and a test of faith. It found expression in the best of times as in the worst, which helps to explain why the prosperous mid-Victorian years saw the luxurious growth of civic and charitable enterprise. The results were sometimes disproportionate to the need of the recipient, but proportionate to the need of the giver. Before the twentieth century, a sense of duty to the community prevailed over any assertion that the deprived had a right to national assistance. But charity would prevail over state assistance only so long as moral reformation was thought to be the best remedy for indigence. In other words, only so long as Christianity provided a compelling explanation for the ills of society—and the capacity and commitment to combat them.

In keeping with a church- and chapel-going people, parishes, congregations, and religious societies served as centres for the expression of good works and grass-roots participation. The British have always been most interested in what happens around their homes and streets, despite the sporadic outpouring of public sympathy for national causes or foreigners in distress. And they did not have to read Samuel Smiles to know that propping up the family and the parish with good works and a little self-help was often the only way of preventing the deterioration of those vital social institutions. Traditionally, much charitable activity was informal, centred on families and neighbourhoods. But alarmed by social conditions and aroused by religion, they increasingly sought solutions in a philosophy of social reform expressed through associations. The desire to reinvigorate the bonds of civic life was perhaps inevitable in a time of religious enthusiasm and urban decay. The ideal of a Christian commonwealth of stable communities grew in proportion to the pains of an industrial society. The needs of the community bound the citizenry together in a web of obligation and expectation, though not untouched by hypocrisy and deception.

Mr Casaubon, a scholar little known to charity, conceded in George Eliot's *Middlemarch* (1871–2) that philanthropy was 'a wide field'.[44] Institutions were under way for virtually every human ill, individual or social, moral or physical, many of them associated with the increasingly urban and industrial environment. The historian G. M. Trevelyan described a culture so overrun with philanthropy that 'not even the dumb animals were left unorganized'.[45] James Stephen, writing in the 1840s, called the period the age of charitable societies: 'For the cure of every sorrow . . . there are patrons, vice-presidents and secretaries. For the diffusion of every blessing . . . there is a committee.'[46] 'In no other kingdom under the sun . . .' the *Nonconformist* proudly declared in 1842, 'is there such a periodical gathering of benevolence and piety.'[47] In such an atmosphere, the financial resources of philanthropy expanded each year. In the mid-Victorian years charitable revenues far exceeded the gross expenditure on poor relief in England and Wales.[48]

Social historians may sometimes share Walter Bagehot's melancholy doubt 'whether the benevolence of mankind does most harm or good', but they do not dispute that Christian campaigners were ubiquitous in nineteenth-century Britain.[49] Despite reservations about the organization and results of voluntary effort, the phenomenal growth of charitable funds and societies suggests that most citizens thought philanthropy a valuable hedge against misfortune and indispensable to social progress. Charity turned privilege into virtue and propelled people into good works who had little goodness in them. But as so much unpleasantness resulted from the best of motives, it was only just that social betterment sometimes issued from the worst. For those earnest Christians who set the tone of Victorian Britain, duty turned to privilege. Elizabeth Barrett Browning, who honoured their code of service and self-sacrifice in *Aurora Leigh*, put it simply:

> After Christ, work turns to privilege;
> And henceforth one with our humanity.[50]

Octavia Hill, one of Britain's more remarkable philanthropists, saw all humanity linked by a great chain of Christian service. In her annual 'Letter to My Fellow-Workers' in 1898, she turned her mind to charitable campaigners past and present: 'For surely we may believe that in our desire to help the poor, to better the earth our Father made, we are bound into one great fellowship, not only with friends here, not only with those scattered in various places, not only the living, but with the great company that has gone before, whom we are passing on to meet when we are needed here no more.'[51] In harking back to those who had 'gone before', she reminded her readers of one of the great strengths of Christianity: a history both ancient and protean that exercised a prodigious power over generations of the faithful, bringing each in turn into communion with a venerated past.

Lest we forget, the duties of volunteers like Hill's 'fellow-workers', who ministered to the poor in city slums and tenements, factory towns and rural hovels, could be decidedly unpleasant. There was more to face-to-face charity than bountiful ladies passing out peppermints. So many people lived in such squalor, ignorance, and ill health that expectations of moral reformation and improved family life were often premature. Given the pressures of population growth and the dislocations created by industrialization, the supply of charitable relief struggled to keep up with demand. This helps to explain why there was a fixation with feigned distress and distinctions between the deserving and undeserving poor in the nineteenth century. Ingenious swindlers dressed up in ragged clothes and touching lies fostered such distinctions. It was reported in the 1830s that imposters wrote a thousand begging letters a day in London alone.[52] The funds they extracted from the unsuspecting were desperately needed elsewhere.

Charitable reports, memoirs, and social investigations are full of the most heart-rending scenes:

W.K. and his family were in the utmost distress, when a member of the Committee first visited their wretched habitation; two children lay dead on the same table; another child was dangerously ill; the poor man disabled by severe rheumatism; and his wife in a state of distraction, occasioned by a long series of affliction and painful privations. (Spitalfields, 1820)[53]

W.L.—aged eighteen years.—Had not slept on a bed for upwards of three years, neither had his clothes off during that time—except when he got wet, and then lay naked, in a hole under the stairs of an empty house in St. Herman's Hill. He had no recollection of ever seeing his parents, he being left at the door of Westminster workhouse when he was two years old. (London, 1849)[54]

In visiting a slum in the North of England, our officers entered a hole, unfit to be called a human habitation—more like the den of some wild animal— almost the only furniture of which was a filthy iron bedstead, a wooden box to serve for table and chair, while an old tin did duty as a dustbin. The inhabitant of the wretched den was a poor woman, who fled to the darkest corner of the place as our Officer entered. (late nineteenth century)[55]

The Salvation Army rescued this poor woman. It was an institution that knew more about human misery than most, and pioneered some of the most original relief schemes of the time, including city colonies, cooperative farms, and the poor man's lawyer. Its reports were stunning indictments of the conditions of life in the slums, conditions that led the scientist Thomas Huxley, once a medical officer in London, to declare that the savages of New Guinea lived a more decent existence than the population in the East End.[56]

The cases attended to by Christian campaigners called on all their reserves. By today's standards the poverty was so profound, the disease and hardship so overwhelming, that abstract debates about the value of charity were often out of place. That many volunteers died of disease as a result of their labours and several were killed on their rounds suggests a remarkable level of commitment. Unlike social scientists and political economists, who rarely left their armchairs, charitable campaigners had to clean up the mess. Confronted with a scale of pain, dying, and death nowadays unimaginable, they were not going to be reasoned out of their humanity by promises of Utopia tomorrow. If their charges were not attended to by charity, many of them would not have been attended to at all. General William Booth, the founder of the Salvation Army, had nothing against Utopianism, collectivist or individualist, but he did not have the patience to wait for an overhaul of the social structure or the emergence of a welfare state. 'In the meantime, here is John Jones growing more impatient than ever because hungrier, who wonders if he is to wait for a dinner until the Social Revolution has arrived.'[57]

Re-creating the world of nineteenth-century charity is difficult because so many of the societies, once so familiar, are part of the lost, little-remembered voluntary culture. Many have left not a trace behind. But the more deeply one looks into the subject, the richer it becomes. The array of institutions, often interrelated and mutually supportive, varied from place to place. Richly endowed with wealthy individuals and societies, London provided much of the impetus behind the national institutions with their myriad branches across the country. The great missionary societies were perhaps the most adept at enlisting provincial auxiliaries. The British and Foreign Bible Society had 2,349 subsidiary associations to dispense the Bible by 1830.[58] Aspiring citizens outside the capital put their own institutions on the map, often using charity as a means of consolidating their local influence. By mid-century most large towns and cities could boast of voluntary hospitals, infirmaries, asylums, visiting societies, homes, and orphanages, often the products of the new wealth created by industry. The local middle-classes were usually in charge, though aristocrats and working men sometimes turned up as governors.[59]

Whether they were auxiliaries of great societies or not, most charities had considerable autonomy. The myriad parish societies, often centred on the vestry, had membership numbers that varied from under ten to hundreds. Women were very well represented in these institutions, which reflected their high level of religious observance. For their part, working-class women were more likely to be caught up in religious institutions than their menfolk, who had wider opportunities for social life in sport and public houses.[60] In the late Victorian and Edwardian years women outnumbered men at Sunday services by a ratio of roughly two to one, with modest differences between the denominations and localities.[61] By that time the contribution of women to charity, which was widely recognized and often criticized, can hardly be overemphasized.[62] Those institutions serving the needs of women and children were often under female management, or had a mixed management of men and women.

Moral reform was among the great campaigns in which women served in the vanguard. Reformers could be found in pubs and beerhouses, at dogfights and gambling dens, at factory gates and dockyard dining halls, with needlewomen in sweatshops and miners at the coal face. They invaded army barracks and boarded Royal Navy ships, as ever armed with godly literature. Tracts were not in short supply, for the Religious Tract Society alone published over 15 million a year by the 1840s.[63] The preoccupation with sin and antisocial behaviour was common to many institutions, and many communities had their own societies devoted to moral reform, often in association with national charities such as the Vigilance Association, the Social Purity Alliance, and the White Cross Army. The Reformatory and Refuge Union, which acted as a clearing-house of information for societies dealing with outcast children, assisted over a thousand local charities by the end of the nineteenth century.[64] The Girls' Friendly Society, which sought to bring the working classes under the moral supervision of middle- and upperclass ladies, had about 200,000 members in 1,749 branches in England and abroad by 1914.[65]

Elsewhere, the moral education of the young was richly served by charity schools, Sunday schools, ragged schools, Bible classes, and Bands of Hope. The number of students who attended Sunday schools in England, Scotland, and Wales grew like Topsy from the late eighteenth century onwards, and in the 1880s reached nearly 6 million, a remarkable figure in a population of 26 million.[66] Juvenile branches of the missionary or Bible societies were a major industry, not least because they raised large sums of money from the young.[67] The Church Missionary Society alone had nearly a thousand juvenile associations by the end of the century.[68] The Children's Scripture Union, which had 700 branches in the 1880s, reminded children of the source of their inspiration.[69] Nor were children excluded from the organizations of adults, for if Christianity and the habits of association were to be passed from generation to generation it was necessary to set an example to the young.

In the mid-Victorian years most communities would have boasted various schools for the poor, visiting societies, working parties, mothers' meetings, and temperance societies, which met in homes, churches, or chapels, or in mission rooms rented for the occasion. Soup kitchens, maternity charities, crèches, blanket clubs, coal clubs, clothing clubs, boot clubs, medical clubs, lending libraries, and holiday funds expanded the expression of Christian service. Such associations are particularly revealing of the grass roots and take us deeper into those ideals of neighbourliness that sought to bring the nation's classes into closer contact. Meanwhile, innumerable penny banks, savings banks, provident clubs, goose clubs, slate clubs, and pension societies, often attached to city missions, mothers' meetings, and other charities, reflected the Victorian obsession with thrift and mutual aid. They were part of the makeshift economy in poor neighbourhoods, where strategies for survival were all too often touched by desperation.

We should not assume that associational democracy was a form of democracy that excluded most of the population. Given the level of immediate need, charity was a necessity in poor neighbourhoods and took various forms, from providing shoes and Sunday dinners to deprived children to setting up a visiting society or a missionary association. As Mrs Pember Reeves noted in her classic study of the London district of Kennington before the First World War, the 'respectable poor live over a morass of such intolerable poverty that they unite instinctively to save those known to them from falling into it'.[70] The charity of the poor to the poor was, according to various observers, startling in its extent.[71] Friedrich Engels, invariably hostile to middle-class philanthropy, remarked that 'although the workers cannot really afford to give charity on the same scale as the middle class, they are nevertheless more charitable in every way'.[72] He did not consider that this expression of working-class solidarity might work to prevent a revolution.

Few charitable campaigns went without working-class support. The statistical information for working-class charity, while fragmentary and patchy, is suggestive. A survey of rather more prosperous working-class families in the 1890s showed that half of them contributed funds to charity each week and about a quarter of them made donations to church or chapel.[73] The hospitals were among the charities favoured by working men and women. Well over half the income of several hospitals in the North of England came from 'workmen'.[74] Miners provided for others in South Wales.[75] The Saturday Fund, founded in 1874, merged charity with what many contributors saw as a scheme of medical insurance. In the 1890s it raised about £20,000 a year through workshop, factory, and street collections.[76] The League of Mercy, founded in 1899, raised £600,000 from artisans, tradesmen, and humble subscribers for the voluntary hospitals of London before they were nationalized in 1948.[77]

The financial impact of working-class contributions should not be exaggerated, for weekly wages, at least before mid-century, prohibited subscriptions of any size.[78] But contributions from the less well off did not go unnoticed. Evangelicals were among the most appreciative. 'Poor contributions', announced the *Christian Mother's Magazine* in 1845, 'whether we consider the proportion which they bear to the whole wealth of the givers, or their aggregate amount, are, in effect beyond all comparison the most important.'[79] Along with hospitals and Sunday schools, the foreign missions were among the most successful at extracting donations from the labouring classes. The Methodist Missionary Society raised millions of pounds from humble subscribers in the nineteenth century, largely through its sophisticated network of local associations.[80] The *Evangelical Magazine* pronounced at mid-century: 'The pecuniary offerings of the pious poor, both with respect to their aggregate amount and the sacrifices they involve, ought to be regarded as the most precious portion of the funds raised for the spread of the gospel among the heathen.'[81] No matter how impoverished the Briton, the heathen overseas could be made to look more wretched.

The availability of records of wealthy, middle-class institutions has distorted our understanding of charitable experience. In any study of organized charity, the contribution of the working classes is likely to be underplayed, for so much of it was informal and unrecorded, unostentatious and uncelebrated, often merging with mutual aid. But the relative dearth of evidence for organized working-class benevolence should not lead us to underestimate its extent. Working men and women established their own Sunday schools, charity schools, soup kitchens, wash-houses, temperance societies, Salvation Army shelters, boot and clothing clubs, servants' institutions, navvy missions, sick clubs, mothers' meetings, and visiting societies.[82] When they cooperated with their wealthier neighbours, as in hospital provision, education, or foreign missions, their philanthropy acted as a springboard into the existing social system. When the poor contributed to unemployment funds, established Chartist Sunday schools, or passed the hat round for the Tolpuddle martyrs, their actions may be seen as an expression of radical politics through private benevolence. Such forms of self expression were particularly important before the advent of universal suffrage.

The respectable working class, often identified with church and chapel, was particularly noticeable in its charitable activity. Evangelical dissent, with its strength outside the wealthier strongholds of Anglicanism, was especially attractive to the upwardly mobile. Philanthropy was a test of respectability, and one had to be far down the social ladder, on poor relief or a recipient of charity, to be altogether free from social obligation. Many a sermon sent out the message that if the poor walked humbly and acted charitably they were promised 'the same earthly inheritance' as the God-fearing rich. As a labourer from Northumberland remarked in the 1850s, 'the penalty for not helping one's neighbour is death, for it is a sin against God'.[83] Such sentiments were part of a Christian's spiritual baggage and resulted in considerable working-class support for religious and other causes. While social superiors and employers extracted some of this support through pressure—household servants were particularly vulnerable—it was in keeping with the impulses and aspirations of respectable working men and women.

Participation in charitable causes was a passport to social status and social integration, but it was also a part of the pattern of working-class education and leisure. To many, it was as important as the training picked up in schools or mechanics' institutes. In encouraging skills and a wider social outlook, it was not unlike the education on offer in mutual aid societies, trade unions, or benefit clubs, which, it should be said, often had a charitable dimension. Whether in their own charities or working for middle-class institutions, humble men and women honed a basic education and often developed skills in bookkeeping, secretarial work, fund-raising, and general administration. In voluntary societies, unlike the wider world over which they had little control, working-class campaigners could make decisions that had meaning for their own lives and those around them. In the context of the political transformation taking place in the nineteenth and early twentieth centuries, the view that charitable work represents a 'nursery school of democracy' is especially apt.[84]

Associational philanthropy saturated people's lives in the past, both givers and receivers, to an extent that is nowadays unimaginable. A glimpse of the Rothschild Buildings in the East End of London in the late nineteenth century is a case in point. Apart from the extensive network of casual benevolence performed daily by the residents, organized societies luxuriated, a tribute to the congruence of Judeo-Christian traditions. Run mostly by women, with the assistance of the poor of the tenements, they included: the Sick Room Helps Society, Jews' Lying-in Charity, Israelite Widows Society, Whitechapel Children's Care Committee, Soup Kitchen, Boot Club, Clothing Club, Children's Penny Dinner Society, Ragged Schools' Union, Bare Foot Mission, Children's Country Holiday Fund, and a Savings Bank run by St Jude's School. This concentration of 'charity, thrift, and paternalistic interference in the lives of the respectable working class', remarks the historian of the buildings, 'was to steal its way into every pore' of the residents.[85] This would not have happened, it should be added, if the 'respectable working class' had not cooperated or had not reaped some benefit from the charitable world that engulfed them.

Carrow Works in Norwich, the manufacturing centre of Colman's mustard, was a world away from the East End tenements, but its example typified the way in which charitable provision often operated in provincial centres of industry. Caroline Colman, the wife of the wealthy manufacturer and Liberal MP for Norwich James Colman, set about her good works promptly upon her marriage in 1856. Guided by her religious conscience, she initiated various schools attached to the works. She provided technical classes for up to 200 men and sewing and cooking classes for the women. She taught the children herself in the Sunday school. Through such institutions, she not only encouraged residents and employees to identify with their communities, but also supported various national charities, including the London Missionary Society and the Royal Society for the Prevention of Cruelty to Animals. This was typical of the way in which the provincial associations provided the financial wherewithal for the campaigns of larger, national societies.

Mrs Colman overlooked few aspects of the employees' lives at Carrow Works. With her husband's encouragement she promoted the local hospital, hired sick visitors and nurses, provided a blanket and parcel distribution, and at Christmas distributed hampers and works' almanacs. She established or oversaw a home for girls, a lending library, refreshment rooms at the factory, a milk scheme for children, a mothers' meeting, a medical club, a sick benefit society with 500 members, a clothing club with 960 members, and almshouses for pensioners. Here was virtual cradle-to-the-grave coverage. It proved a shrewd and effective combination of charity and sound business, which in the nineteenth century were so often intertwined. Mrs Colman's aim was 'to raise the moral as well as the commercial standing of the firm'.[86] The concentration of charity and self-help left few people in Carrow unaffected.

The role of charities in promoting social cohesion and integration has not always been appreciated.[87] But as the example of Carrow Works suggests, charitable institutions had the great merit of encouraging men and women in obscure places to feel part of the moral and social economy, and to meet their local needs free from the constraints of a centralized state. One should keep in mind that Britain was administratively less uniform and centralized than continental countries, at least those conquered by Napoleon. In the nineteenth century local authorities provided a multiplicity of goods and services that would astound many of today's local-government officials, whose powers have been reduced so drastically by parliament. Cities and towns in the four distinctive nations were jealous of their autonomy and proud of the local traditions. As Mr Thornton, the northern manufacturer in Elizabeth Gaskell's novel *North and South*, (1854–5) declared: 'We hate to have laws made for us at a distance. We wish people would allow us to right ourselves, instead of continually meddling, with their imperfect legislation.'[88] The leading municipal and voluntary institutions in the provinces were pre-eminent symbols of public spirit and independence from London.

By the late nineteenth century philanthropy was not only a sign of Christian worth and civic virtue but of national standing. Indeed, the Victorians equated their civilization with the proportion of national activity given over to benevolent causes, just as a later generation would equate it with the welfare state. When Podsnap boasted to his foreign guest in *Our Mutual Friend* that 'there is not a country in the world, sir, where so noble a provision is made for the poor', he was trying to show his country to best advantage. When *The Times* announced in 1885 that London's charitable receipts exceeded the budgets of several European states, it was a source of national and imperial pride.[89] Ten years later the Charity Commissioners gloried in their report 'that the latter half of the 19th century will stand second in respect of the greatness and variety of Charities created within its duration, to no other half-century since the Reformation'.[90]

As such historic reference implied, Christianity underpinned Britain's culture of social service in the nineteenth century. But self-advertising reports of charitable growth, however accurate and well meaning, did not equate with charitable effectiveness. Rising contributions raised expectations of their successful application. From the late nineteenth century the persistence of poverty became increasingly embarrassing in a society of obvious wealth that prided itself on social improvement. As Christian commitment faded in the twentieth century, the ministries of state gradually displaced the ministries of religion as founts of hope and charity. In contemporary Britain Christianity may be in crisis, as many historians and sociologists contend, but one should not assume that it is dead.[91] There remains a goodly measure of belief, not least among Catholics and the expanding Pentecostal churches.[92]But Christian belief is much less often expressed in church membership or in belonging to voluntary societies.[93] To both believers and unbelievers today, the Victorian assumption that competing religious institutions could stem the tide of social distress is baffling.

Views on the causes of secularization abound, from urbanization to the cultural revolution of the 1960s, from the effects of scientific rationalism to social diversity, from modernization to Sunday shopping.[94] Whatever one thinks about the ongoing debate on secularization, the role of charity in the equation remains something of a mystery. So too does the advance of government responsibility for education and welfare that resulted from the extension of the franchise and worries about national efficiency. A look at the rise and fall of several distinctive forms of voluntary provision in the following chapters—schooling, visiting, mothering, and nursing—should illuminate some of the difficulties confronting Christianity from the late nineteenth century onwards, while shedding light also on the interrelated problems facing charitable institutions. Those problems were often at their most immediate in church and chapel associations, which served as the focus of religious life for so many Christians.

The relationship between Christianity and state social provision is particularly relevant to both religion and charity. What changes in Christianity made accommodation with the state palatable? For decades Britons have looked primarily to government—to the social services and the National Health Service—to address both social and physical ills. The contrast with the mid-Victorian years, when the only agent of central government much seen in British neighbourhoods was the post-office clerk, could not be more striking.[95] What role did the churches play in the rise of state provision, and did the erosion of Christian belief encourage the expansion of government? In turn, did the growth of state provision diminish religion? Did the rival denominations have the flexibility to deal with changing social and political attitudes? In particular, did the Church of England, with its social hierarchy and ancient rituals? The comparison with America, with similar religious traditions but no state church and modest government welfare provision, springs to mind.

The contribution of religion to the growth of associational culture in the past raises important questions. Can public spirit flow from a citizenry without religion? Can a nation generate social or spiritual capital without the institutional support of the churches? Can a secular state provide a basis for public morality? Can it replace or co-opt voluntary institutions without a loss of freedom? Before the end of the nineteenth century most Christians would have answered these questions with an emphatic no. For them religion was the fount of morality and indispensable to the vitality of civic life. Thomas Chalmers argued in *The Christian and Civic Economy of Large Towns* (1821–6) that active citizenship was not a feature of public assistance but of religious charity, which, if wisely administered, was 'so beautiful a part of man's relations with man'.[96] Thomas Stephenson, the founder of children's homes, put the case uncompromisingly in 1869: 'good citizens can only be found in good Christians.'[97]

Such beliefs were in keeping with the views of Tocqueville, who argued in *Democracy in America* that 'Christianity must be maintained at any cost in the bosom of modern democracies'.[98] Tocqueville is a touchstone for Britain as well as America. For him Christianity was not an opiate, nor a morality of slaves, but a religion of self-discipline and personal service that answered social and political needs. In his little-known 'Memoir' on pauperism, written in 1835 after a visit to England, he observed that one of the merits of Christianity was that it made charity a 'divine virtue'. In turn, a merit of charity was that it directly involved the giver in the fate of those relieved, creating moral ties between rich and poor.[99] In so doing, Christian associations encouraged not only benevolence but also citizenship and civility.

To Tocqueville, as to Max Weber, there was a connection between voluntarism and personality. In a culture in which free associations prospered, individuals had to prove themselves resolute and responsible in their dealings with others. This was in sharp contrast to an authoritarian culture, however benign, which encouraged docility and indecisiveness in its citizens.[100]

Like countless Victorians, Tocqueville believed that freedom was a corollary of faith. Religion, he insisted, must ally itself with liberal institutions in freedom-loving nations to offset the harmful effects of democracy, and its tendency to promote egalitarianism at the expense of liberty. Political liberty required attachments to a variety of institutions, including the family, the churches, and civic institutions. Without a culture of association, democratic nations became prey to overbearing government prone to a benign form of despotism, in which the citizenry exchanged freedom for benefits: 'Such a power does not destroy, but it prevents existence; it does not tyrannize, but it compresses, enervates, extinguishes, and stupefies a people, till each nation is reduced to nothing better than a flock of timid and industrious animals, of which the government is the shepherd.'[101]

If Tocqueville were alive today, he would find contemporary Britons decidedly sheepish. Representative democracy has proved to be a poor servant of Christianity, or of associational culture. Since the Second World War most Britons have been content to sacrifice the traditions of Christian service in exchange for rights and entitlements from government. But as their elected ministers vacillate and stumble, political cynicism has grown and faith in the shepherd has become more tentative.[102] Across the party spectrum, politicians now concede that the state has failed to elevate the principle of social duty and have adopted the mantra of balancing rights with personal responsibility.[103] But what are the springs of personal responsibility and public spirit in a society whose religious moorings have been largely swept away? Is Tocqueville's prophecy of a democratic form of despotism, built on class resentments and justified in the name of welfare, an issue today, not in America but in Britain?

2

Schooling

Train up a child in the way he should go,
And when he is old, he will not depart from it.

(Proverbs 22:6)

The Godless, non-Bible system, is at hand . . . Our nature is
nothing, the heart is nothing, in the estimation of these zealots
of secular knowledge. Everything for the flesh and nothing for
the soul; everything for time and nothing for eternity.

(Lord Shaftesbury, 1870)

A Godless education was virtually non-existent in Britain, as elsewhere in Europe, before the Enlightenment.[1] The philosophical
framework largely ruled out a secular alternative to Christianity, and
the schools reflected the religious temper of the time. In a society in
which learning had a redemptive purpose, an education without religious instruction would have been seen as a form of deviancy. As long
as education was seen as a religious issue rather than a political one,
government showed little interest in it. Those children lucky enough
to attend school, from the lowliest dame school taught in a back room
to an illustrious grammar school like Westminster, did so thanks to
private provision or philanthropy. Before the eighteenth century destitute children were very lucky indeed to receive any formal education,
apart from a vocational training, and then it was all too often picked
up in a workhouse, which had schools attached beginning in the

1690s. As elsewhere in the instruction of the poor, workhouse children were 'to have the fear of God before their eyes'.[2]

By the early eighteenth century traditional forms of educating the poor, such as endowed parish schools overseen by trustees or the vestry, were thought to be inadequate. Many such schools persisted, but in a society growing more urban and industrial the hallmark of elementary education was increasingly the result of collective effort rather than individual benefaction. In the eighteenth and nineteenth centuries benevolent citizens, parishes, churches and chapels, and national societies founded tens of thousands of voluntary schools, often representing competing denominations. These various institutions—charity schools, Sunday schools, and ragged schools—were expressions of a Christian associational culture, typically financed by subscriptions and managed by local committees. They did not provide a balanced curriculum but imposed a syllabus that centred on the Bible. The children of the poor and dangerous classes were to be rescued from idleness and pointed down the 'right channel of Christian Benevolence' towards productive labour and a higher, risen life.[3]

In the eighteenth century the nation's rulers assumed that education was essential to both the dissemination of the Gospel and the maintenance of the social order. Queen Anne wrote to the archbishops of Canterbury and York in support of the foundation of charity schools in 1711: 'the pious Instruction and Education of Children is the Surest Way of Preserving and Propagating the Knowledge and practice of True Religion.'[4] When Jacobites still threatened the Protestant succession, few doubted the meaning of 'True Religion'. As a churchman observed in the early eighteenth century, children who had learned the Anglican catechism 'would never stoop to beads and Latin charms, nor bow their necks to the dark slavery of Rome'.[5] To Puritans, early training mattered, for they had Rome to fear in this life and hellfire in the next. But as the sermons of the day enjoined, divine law offered succour, and with effort in the Lord's vineyard, redemption. As the Day of Judgement loomed, the mind attuned to scripture turned, as one of the faithful reminds us, to 'CHARITY, without which we shall certainly perish among the reprobate'.[6]

Such fears and assumptions propelled the movement for the provision of charity schools for the poor in the early eighteenth century. Charity schools, observed the essayist Richard Steele, were 'the greatest instances of public spirit the age had produced'.[7] Though benefactors had established such schools in the past, it was the Society for Promoting Christian Knowledge (SPCK) that provided the sponsorship and support that rallied to the cause of educating the poor in England and Wales. Its interest stemmed from 'the visible decay of Religion in this Kingdom, with the monstrous increase of Deism, Prophaness, and Vice'.[8] The SPCK did not provide finance or management, but promoted locally controlled, parish-based schools paid for by subscriptions and special sermons. These institutions introduced new methods of philanthropic organization and finance; they also provided instruction to girls, who were excluded by the endowed grammar schools. Unlike the grammar schools, the charity schools did not offer a classical education. They were ' "pious nurseries" for godly discipline', which provided a basic level of literacy to children of artisans, labourers, domestic servants, and paupers.[9]

The figures for the charity school movement are fragmentary, but by 1730 it was said that 1,419 schools were in operation in England with 22,503 pupils. In Wales, where the movement developed somewhat later, there were nearly 3,500 schools founded between 1737 and 1761, with 150,000 pupils.[10] The schools were thinly distributed in much of the country, and the Anglicans did not have the field to themselves, for Nonconformists, Methodists, and Quakers established their own institutions, in which poor children in their communions learned to read the Bible and sometimes to write and do sums. In Presbyterian Scotland, which enjoyed a reputation for education, a system of parish schools provided the rudiments of learning. But the Highlands and Islands were regions poorly served. There the Scottish SPCK, founded in 1709, took action. By the mid-eighteenth century it had charge of 150 charity schools in the Highlands and Islands, with over 6,000 pupils. In 1809, the centenary of the Scottish SPCK, the number had risen to 189 schools, in which about 13,000 children received instruction.[11]

Wherever established, the charity schools have commonly been criticized for the narrowness of the education on offer. The curricula and teaching methods were typically inflexible, with religion the centrepiece of instruction. But the scriptures provided a literary form and a critique of social conditions to those who wished to find it. To Puritans, the Bible was truth revealed, part poetry, part radical handbook, which left its readers with a love of language and a hatred of injustice. As a leading authority on eighteenth-century schooling remarked in the 1930s: 'Historians who are surprised by the rapid reception of radical thought in the early nineteenth century, show themselves ignorant of New Testament ethics and unaware of the innumerable charities bestowed for the express purpose of teaching the poor to read.'[12]

Few now deny that 'New Testament ethics' helped shape 'radical thought' and associational life in Britain. Anti-Catholicism itself might be seen as a great radical cause, which permeated other causes, for it runs like a thread through the Puritan-evangelical tradition and progressive Whig history. In the early eighteenth-century charity school movement, Anglicans and Nonconformists found a common enemy in Catholicism, which they believed 'oppressive to the liberty and the souls of men'.[13] That the Protestant parties also turned on each other only stimulated the emergence of further schools. 'Prejudices are very precious things in Church matters', remarked the novelist Charlotte Yonge, a devout Anglican who taught a Sunday school class for seventy-one years.[14] Sectarian rivalry and factional politico-religious struggle beset the charity school movement from its beginnings, but gave it life. That so many poor children in Britain learned to read was in no small measure due to religious intolerance.

For all the inadequacies of the charity schools—the narrow curriculum, limited resources, and deficient teaching—they were pioneers of the associational Christian charity that was emerging in Britain. Few other eighteenth-century institutions, apart from societies for the promotion of the Bible, did more to heighten social awareness or to develop the parish or congregation as a centre of Christian activity. In organization and fund-raising, the schools provided the model for many other voluntary agencies that were to follow, including visiting societies, Sunday schools, and missionary associations. They expanded the opportunities for the expression of personal service and served as a principal agency by which the middle classes were brought into the work of social reform. In so doing, they provided, as their historian Agnes Jones observed, 'an invaluable training ground for democratic government'.[15]

Sunday schools provided a similar training and trajectory.[16] It was the loss of momentum of the charity school movement that provided an opening for the Sunday schools, which carried forward the aims and methods of the charity schools on a one-day-a-week basis.[17] Examples of Sunday schools can be found in the early and mid-eighteenth century. But their rapid development at the end of the century is usually identified with Robert Raikes (1735–1811), a printer in Gloucester, who opened his first school in 1780.[18] Through his newspaper he gave publicity to his 'little experiment' and other schemes. With a talent for propaganda, Raikes turned what had been local initiatives into a national enterprise. 'In those parishes where the plan has been adopted', he wrote in the *Gloucester Journal* in 1783, 'we are assured that the behaviour of the children is greatly civilized. The Barbarous ignorance in which they had before lived being in some degree dispelled.'[19] This was a clarion call to respectable citizens across the country, alarmed by the antics of undisciplined children roaming the streets. In Scotland, where Sunday schools spread rapidly in the 1780s, it was hoped that they 'might decrease the rate of burglary during the hours of divine service'.[20]

In 1785 various Anglicans and Nonconformists founded the Sunday School Society based on Raikes's plans. Within twenty-five years the society claimed to have established 3,350 schools with 275,000 enrolled.[21] This was but a fraction of the overall activity, for many schools were initiated locally without connection to the society. The schools sought out the 'deserving poor', or 'persons employed in the manufactures'. The indispensable text, as in the weekday charity schools, was the Bible, though catechisms, primers, and hymn-books supplemented it. Such materials were thought sufficient to give a rudimentary education to children in employment, on farms or in textile factories, who could not attend school without interruption to their work. The fact that Sunday school scholars did not have to take time off made the schools acceptable to factory-owners. Indeed, they proved particularly popular in the manufacturing districts of England, where child labour was exploited.[22]

The rapid expansion of the Sunday school movement was given momentum by political events after 1789. There is a grain of truth in the saying that when the French became republican the English became religious. French principles invigorated both piety and paternalism in Britain and were a great stimulus to charitable organization. Few in Britain advocated the French Jacobin dictum that education should be 'universal, compulsory, gratuitous, and secular'. To a conservative generation of Britons, such ideas looked decidedly dangerous. An educated working class might simply create labour unrest and social instability. To the commercial mind, there was little point in raising taxes for educational reform without the assurance that it would bring immediate results. Moreover, obligatory schooling would require state control, which was deeply suspect in Britain. In a nation in which religious freedom had been hard won, compulsory secular education was seen as an attack on individual liberty and conscience.[23] Voluntary schools, each reflecting local religious leanings, was a British alternative.

In deepening the religious hue of British philanthropy, the French Revolution revitalized parish life and put Sabbath schools, along with other schools, on the front line of homeland defence. As the British ruling class saw it, Sunday school instruction would reform the behaviour of the lower orders through inculcating patriotism, piety, and industry. In the heightened political atmosphere, Anglican reformers like Hannah More and Sarah Trimmer saw the education of the poor as part of a strategy for national survival, a means of checking the spread of irreligion among the labouring population. The poor, More argued, should be instructed 'with a view to check the spirit of insubordination'.[24] Meanwhile Mrs Trimmer sought royal favour in the

Sunday school campaign, in the knowledge that royal patronage would bring immediate benefits. Having secured Queen Charlotte's blessing for her own schools, she wrote: 'Her example will cause them to be universal: they will soon be extended over the whole kingdom.'[25]

An effect of the French Revolution was to intensify sectarian divisions, making cooperation between Anglicans and Nonconformists more difficult. In the battle for the souls and minds of the young, many Anglican churchmen worried that schools unconnected with the Church of England would excite radical ideas. To many of them, the teaching of writing and arithmetic was potentially dangerous. As Hannah More insisted: 'He who is taught arithmetic on a Sunday as a boy, will, when a man, open his shop on a Sunday.'[26] The bishop of Rochester, among others, inflamed denominational divisions by denouncing Methodist Sunday schools as conventicles for the spread of 'atheism and disloyalty'.[27] He need not have worried. Methodists were often hostile to traditional doctrines stemming from the Reformation, but they were not enthusiastic about French principles. If the French historian Élie Halévy is to be believed, the evangelical revival led by Wesley spared England from violent revolution.[28]

Sectarian rivalries ensured that no one class or denomination had a monopoly on Sunday schools. Indeed, radicals and Chartists established a small number of 'alternative' Sunday schools, a tradition that would have appalled Hannah More.[29] In the early years undenominational schools were common, but with the growth of political and social tension and the withdrawal of Methodists from the Church of England the Sunday school movement became more sectarian in outlook.[30] In the competitive religious atmosphere, the rival denominations worshipped themselves; they believed it imperative to teach their children the tenets of their faith and to inculcate social discipline. Sunday schools became a crucial ingredient in denomination survival, which helps to explain their popularity. The Nonconformist sects that most encouraged Sunday schools proved highly successful in disciplining their children and passing on the faith to the next generation. The Wesleyan Methodists called their schools 'the nursery of the church'.[31] They endorsed what the Book of Proverbs enjoined: 'Train up a child in the way he should go, and when he is old, he will not depart from it.'

With the years, the Sunday schools became increasingly sophisticated in their methods, with texts and techniques suited to the different age-groups in attendance. When so many children died before their conversions could take place, there was a premium on reaching children as early as possible. Thus, infant classes, which the educational reformer Robert Owen pioneered at New Lanark, became attached to Sunday schools beginning in the 1820s. The primary object of the classes was to instil religious principles and awaken tender minds to a sense of sin. Children as young as eighteen months learned to count by holding their toes and lifting their feet alternately as they recited their numbers. Being unable to read, they learned the facts of the Bible by the use of scripture prints. At the other end of the age spectrum there were 'senior classes', in which the scholars did advanced work in scripture and committed hymns and catechisms to memory. On their departure from school, they were solemnly presented with a Bible.[32]

One of the great advantages of the Sunday school—and a reason for its rapid expansion—was that one could be set up on a shoestring, often by the simple device of a special sermon.[33] As with voluntary association generally, new schools could be launched with a minimum of interference or contractual obligation. All that was needed was a teacher, pupils, a Bible, a few primers, and a room. Many teachers volunteered, while institutions, including the Religious Tract Society (1799) and the Sunday School Union (1803), provided cheap reading matter. Classes often met without charge in houses, chapels, vestries, and mission rooms. In rural areas they sometimes met in barns, in the manufacturing districts in factories.[34] Wherever they were held, it was common for the scholars and their teachers to attend church or chapel for religious services after class.

The founders and organizers were usually middle class—clergymen and their families could hardly avoid the work—but the schools were inexpensive enough for the poorer classes to establish them as well. The denominations with the most proletarian adherence, Catholics and Primitive Methodists, made relatively little use of Sunday schools.[35] But there is evidence that labourers, weavers, blacksmiths, and other humble men and women founded or helped to organize schools.[36] Sarah Martin held a class before taking on prison visiting.[37] Agnes Weston, celebrated for her mission work among sailors, 'had a good committee of working-men' around her in the 1860s when she allied her Sunday class to the temperance campaign.[38] Travers Madge, a Sunday school teacher in Hulme, a suburb of Manchester, left a moving record of humble worshippers in religious communities that 'never find any place in the formal catalogue of sects', who held their services and taught their children 'in little upper rooms in back streets . . . aiming at something nearer to their ideal of what a church of Christ should be, than their members have been able to find in the larger ecclesiasticisms of the religious world'.[39]

   Whatever the sect or social setting, working for a Sunday school was not only evidence of respectability and local standing but provided valuable skills to those involved. In common with other institutions, they were a training ground in administration, a model of local associ-ation that offered opportunities in self-government. The rules and orders could be elaborate and the meetings remarkably democratic.[40] Whether dealing with parents, inspecting schools, administering applications, drumming up subscriptions, running committees, or punishing miscreants, those who operated Sunday schools honed practical and negotiating skills. For those working-class men and women who founded schools, or worked with their social superiors in running them, it was experience that was relatively easy to come by, for volunteers were always needed. The schools, however humble, played a role in extending traditions of associational democracy across the classes and denominations.

The role of Sunday schools in elementary education was profound. Before the coming of state education in 1870, the schools taught more children how to read and write than any other educational institution. The overall number of Sunday schools built or founded in England and Wales by 1811 has been put at 4,687, rising to 23,135 in 1851.

About 45 per cent of them belonged to the Church of England.[41] The number of children enrolled in the schools rose prodigiously, from 425,000 in 1818, to about 2.6 million in 1851. Put differently, about 75 per cent of children between 5 and 15 in England and Wales attended a Sunday school in the 1850s, a percentage that rose further in the decades to follow.[42] The teachers, whose numbers rose to 250,000 by 1851, were increasingly volunteers and former scholars, many of them women, who were usually drawn from the socio-economic class of the providing denomination.[43] Many were young and untrained. Charlotte Yonge joined her mother's Sunday school in 1830, at the age of 7, and was a teacher within weeks. 'It was a mistake, for I had not moral balance enough to be impartial, and I must have been terribly ignorant', she noted in her autobiography.[44]

But why did children join Sunday schools in such numbers? They were, of course, under pressure to do so from ministers and mill-owners, but especially from parents. Charlotte Yonge's experience was typical of countless middle-class children: 'Mamma took me to her Sunday School.'[45] The more practical the education, the more working-class parents were likely to approve of the schools. The ability to read was increasingly a sign of prestige in poor neighbourhoods, and if children came home better dressed and disciplined as well, it was all to the good. The demands of the industrial revolution made literacy increasingly useful, and those who wished to get on in life were wise to take advantage of any opportunity to get an education. A large number of Sunday school pupils received no other education. For those children who toiled long hours in factories, it was their only opportunity to receive a scrap of formal schooling before the Factory Act of 1833 introduced two hours of compulsory education each day.

Most Christian parents would have commended an early nineteenth-century handbill: 'Ten reasons why I love to go to my Sunday-school.' They included: 'Because I am ignorant and want to be taught'; 'Because I shall get no good by spending the time in idleness and play'; 'Because good boys and girls love to go there'; 'Because there my mind is improved, and I learn my duty to God and man'; 'Because I wish to go to Heaven when I die, and at the Sunday-school I shall learn the way thither'; and 'Because God commanded us to keep holy the Sabbath-day'.[46] This last reason had an irresistible logic to it, for as Edmund Gosse lamented in *Father and Son*, there was nothing to relieve the gloom in 'the unbroken servitude of Sunday'.[47] In *Little Dorrit*, Dickens spoke for generations of children through the character of Arthur Clennam, who recalled the dreary Sundays of his youth, with their indigestible sermons and Spartan dinners. When a child could be punished for playing in the street or drawing a picture on the Sabbath, the opportunity to mix with other children in a schoolroom could provide a measure of relief.

To the delight of children, whatever their age, the schools increasingly provided amusements and distractions that were in short supply elsewhere, including teas and treats, summer outings, parades, football and cricket matches, lantern lectures, musical events, school prizes, and Christmas festivities. Such events were all the more memorable in evangelical circles, which placed restrictions on dress and amusements. Teachers and parents sponsored the entertainment on offer to children, but much of it was in conjunction with the foreign missions, which saw Sunday schools as a rich field for development. Visits to Sunday schools from foreign missionaries, often with a regenerated heathen in tow, helped to fill out enrolments and inspire the children. As early as 1808 the British and Foreign Bible Society and the Church Missionary Society received funds from Sunday school collections.[48] With the years, all the major missionary societies published children's periodicals and hired special agents to organize children's events and raise funds.

Sunday schools and their juvenile associations enriched the coffers of the missionary societies. Children were ideally suited to extract the 'widow's mite', a halfpenny from an artisan or cottager, or, failing all, a contribution from their own parents. The Baptist and Methodist Missionary Societies had a large enough following among the labouring classes to diminish the problem of soliciting funds in poor neighbourhoods. Children placed missionary boxes in homes and hotels, churches and chapels, railway stations and other public places. Opening them often called for a celebration, introduced and closed by prayer. To provide a climax to such activities, the missionary societies organized great annual children's meetings. In 1842, for example, between 5,000 and 6,000 Sunday school children attended the London Missionary Society's annual celebration at Exeter Hall, at which missionaries brandished fallen idols and paraded converts saved from the jaws of hell.[49] By such means, the missionary societies raised millions of pounds from children and their collections in the nineteenth century.[50]

Highly adaptable, Sunday schools became part of the network of local welfare agencies outside the Poor Law. Bringing together children, teachers, parents, and local worthies, the schools were ideally placed to serve the community in an era that desperately needed social services. Like other charities, to which they were commonly attached, the schools often came to the rescue of needy families in times of personal calamity, illness, or bouts of unemployment. They commonly provided meals, clothing, shoes, and money, sometimes with the help of other local associations. By the 1830s many a Sunday school had a savings bank, sickness, burial, or clothing club attached. The Sunday school in Cockermouth, Cumberland, offered sick benefits, a clothing club, and a funeral society that provided a coffin for a weekly contribution of a halfpenny.[51] By the end of the nineteenth century the Harborough Congregational Sunday School in Leicestershire, founded in 1796, had a Young Men's Institute, a Young Men's Bible Class, a gymnasium, a debating society, a Band of Hope, a Christian Endeavour Society, football and cricket clubs, and a sick fund.[52]

Just as the Sunday schools were expanding in the early nineteenth century, population growth and industrial change increased demands for a revival of the older charity school tradition. The confident middle classes, convinced of their moral superiority, wished to share their religious convictions with their social inferiors. Meanwhile, bands of radical working men and their middle-class allies sought to extend educational opportunities to poor children as a preparation for citizenship and social improvement. In the counter-revolutionary years of the French Revolution and the Napoleonic wars, conservative churchmen, who often saw the Established Church and the state as part of one indivisible body, found an opportunity to buttress their campaign against irreligion by the provision of new day schools. But schooling was costly and contentious, and the success of earlier charitable efforts reinforced the conventional wisdom that education was a field for voluntary action rather than a responsibility of the taxpayer.

In the early nineteenth century two new institutions took up the cause of primary education, and built on the tradition of the eighteenth-century charity schools. First in the field was the British and Foreign School Society (1808), formerly the Lancasterian Schools Association. It reflected a wide spectrum of opinion, and included evangelical Anglicans, Nonconformists, and utilitarians. A rival charity, the National Society for Promoting the Education of the Poor in the Principles of the Established Church (1811), soon emerged. It was a linear descendant of the SPCK, and many of its schools started life in association with that institution. Both the BFSS and the National Society used the associational model and raised funds from subscribers in their respective congregations, but they required modest payments from parents to help cover costs. In the view of promoters, fees had the additional advantage of making parents identify more closely with the schools. Religion was central to both institutions. The BFSS enforced Bible reading, but typically 'without note or comment', while the National Society instilled the liturgy and catechism of the Church of England. There was no love lost between them.

Over the years other sectarian bodies also established voluntary schools, including the Catholic Poor School Committee, the Wesleyan Education Committee, and the Congregational Board of Education. The charitable constituencies of these voluntary bodies raised considerable sums, though with more significant funding the BFSS and the much larger National Society set the pace of elementary education.[53] Though little noted, royal patronage gave a tremendous boost to Anglican education. By means of 'Royal Letters', which were read out in churches across England and Wales, the National Society raised £185,000 between 1823 and 1852.[54] But for all the generosity of churchgoers and subscribers to charitable schools, many localities, particularly the cities, remained without adequate provision. As the problem of educating the poor became more conspicuous, the government felt obliged to intervene, if only timidly. In 1833, it voted the sum of £20,000 for the building of schools to be shared between the BFSS and the National Society. This marked the beginning of government interest in education.

When the government intervened in 1833, the total number of pupils in unendowed day schools was about 1 million, by which time there were more than a million in Sunday schools.[55] The statistical record suggests that between 67 per cent and 75 per cent of the British working class had achieved a basic level of literacy by 1840, which was in large measure due to the efforts of the day schools and the Sunday schools.[56] The effect of schooling on the condition and behaviour of poor children was increasingly evident. The strategy of indoctrinating children through religious education, which had widespread appeal across the sectarian divide, did not convert the working classes en masse, but it did lead to a more literate, disciplined, and respectable working class. Without the Sunday schools and charity schools, millions of children would have grown up without any formal instruction. In addition to raising levels of literacy, the schools had the merit of keeping children out of mischief.

In the first half of the nineteenth century commentators often noted that the populace was growing more respectable, and they attributed the improved state of the common people to the civilizing effects of schooling. In 1816 one witness observed a 'great alteration in the moral condition of Spitalfields' since the establishment of Sunday schools. 'You never hear of any attempt to riot there.'[57] Lord Mahon noted in his *History of England*: 'Among the principle means which, under Providence, tended to a better spirit in the coming age, may be ranked the system of Sunday schools.'[58] Francis Place, radical tailor and founder-member of the Lancasterian Schools Association, remarked in 1829: 'I risk nothing when I assert that more good has been done to the people in the last thirty years than in the three preceding centuries . . . they have become wiser, better, more frugal, more honest, more respectable, more virtuous than they ever were before.'[59] In his autobiography, the freethinking Francis Place relates how his own Christian training in a London day school left him fortified against evil.[60] Education was an essential means by which evangelicalism, to use the words of G. M. Young, that most perceptive historian of Victorian England, became 'secularized as respectability'.[61]

By enlarging the number of respectable and literate poor, the work of the charity schools and Sunday schools drew attention to those left behind. Indeed, the schools increased the chasm, often noted by contemporaries, between the rough and respectable poor. Despite the efforts of Christian campaigners, there remained a great many children who were beyond the reach of a teacher. These were the juvenile outcasts, unkempt and unruly children out of the pages of *Nicholas Nickleby* and *Oliver Twist*, whose parents were dead, drunk, or negligent. Increasingly, social investigations threw up details of these degraded victims of abuse and neglect, children who had, as one Christian witness put it, mastered 'the arts . . . of imposture, lying, begging, stealing'.[62] When juvenile crime was on the rise, the Victorian public came to see such wayward youths, in the words of the social reformer Mary Carpenter, as the 'children of the perishing and dangerous classes'.[63]

The lowest of the poor, who were often in and out of reformatories and workhouses, had little opportunity for conventional schooling. When they did, it often left them disillusioned. One pauper child, who had spent time in a workhouse, remembered his return to Sunday school with horror, as his schoolmates mocked his clothes and branded him a 'workhouse brat'.[64] He was one of the lucky ones, for a kindly teacher sent him to a school that specialized in distressed children. Such institutions came to be known as ragged schools. It is impossible to identify the first ragged school, for there was little distinctive about giving a religious education to troublesome youth. As an official of the Ragged School Union put it, 'even mediaeval England knew the ragged school as an ancient institution'.[65] But the idea of the modern ragged school probably dates to the late eighteenth century.[66]

John Pounds (1766–1839), a crippled Portsmouth cobbler, is often seen as the leading promoter of the ragged school. In 1818 he first took into his Sunday school wild and delinquent children neglected by the local authorities. Over a period of thirty years he rounded up 500 or so waifs and strays and trained them in holiness and knowledge, though rather more in the way of holiness, as Pounds had little knowledge himself.[67] The evangelical belief that destitution and sin went hand in hand led to an ever-widening concern for slum children. In the capital, isolated ragged schools appeared in the 1830s, several of them founded by the agents of the London City Mission, a district visiting society. An early published reference to ragged schools appeared in the *City Mission Magazine* of 1840, which mentioned five schools 'formed exclusively for children raggedly clothed' by city missionaries in the 1830s.[68] Their object was to rehabilitate degraded children and return them to society as useful citizens acting on Christian principles.

On first visiting a ragged school in 1843, Dickens wrote to the philanthropist Angela Burdett-Coutts: 'I have very seldom seen, in all the strange and dreadful things I have seen in London and elsewhere, anything so shocking as the dire neglect of soul and body exhibited by these children.'[69] Personal details of individual ragged children tell a tale of gross neglect that all too often led to a life of crime:

D.F., aged 14.—Mother dead several years; father a drunkard and deserted him about three years ago. Has since lived as he best could; sometimes going errands, sometimes begging and thieving. Slept in lodging houses when he had money, but very often walked the streets at night, or lay under arches or door steps.[70]

J.W.—No home; sleeps at Mrs. B's lodging-house when he has money; pays threepence a night for his bed; when no money, sleeps in carts or on landing about four nights a week. Father deserted mother fifteen years; mother dead two years. Occasionally employed as an errand boy.[71]

Not surprisingly, such children tried the patience of ragged school teachers, who sought to temper firmness with Christian kindness in the classroom. School histories are full of tales of riotous behaviour, fistfights, and petty depredations. When a pious visitor told a class of London ragged children that the all-seeing Lord was watching over them, one young boy looked up at the ceiling and with an expression of incredulity said, 'Blest if I see Him'. Mary Carpenter retails the experience of a London schoolmaster, who recorded shrill cries of 'Cat's meat' while he was reciting the Lord's Prayer.[72]

Mary Carpenter and Charles Dickens raised public awareness of the work of ragged schools, but no one did more to extend the movement than the great Tory paternalist Lord Shaftesbury, who had been instrumental in factory reform in the 1830s. His first direct experience was in 1843, when he replied to an appeal in *The Times* in aid of Field Lane Sabbath School in Saffron Hill, London. Given his longstanding interest in the cause of outcast children, it was not surprising that he revelled in the squalor and rallied to the work. The following year he became president of the newly formed Ragged School Union, a position he held until his death in 1885. With Lord Shaftesbury on board, the union flourished. In 1861 it could claim 176 schools, with an average day attendance of 25,000.[73] By 1865 there were over 600 schools affiliated across the country, which provided rudimentary instruction for over a quarter-of-a-million children.[74] In their unwillingness to accept any child as lost, the schools were far ahead of anything on offer to delinquent children elsewhere. Ragged schools, as an authority on the history of child abuse remarks, 'may be regarded as one important precursor of the campaign against cruelty to children'.[75]

As the secretary of the Ragged School Union put it, the schools were 'Great Gospel Machines'. All other objects were to be 'subordinated to the chief end of bringing neglected and ignorant children within the reach of the doctrine of Christ'.[76] To many in the movement, the schools were essentially part of Victorian missionary enterprise, turned to children on the home front. To others, they were an antidote to revolution, which had engulfed Europe in 1848.[77] Whatever the reasoning behind the movement, nothing was to interfere with the religious purpose of the schools, certainly not an education as commonly understood today. This was a point of principle to Shaftesbury, who believed that 'religion must be the alpha and omega of all education given to the poorer classes'.[78] His admonition to the schools 'to stick to the gutter' had serious limitations as an educational policy. But education as such was not the issue to Shaftesbury, whose social pity did not extend to supporting the development of a child's mind.

Arguably, the ragged schools contributed far less to education than to social welfare. As with Sunday schools and other local charities, a web of interconnected institutions provided opportunities for self-help and advancement. Ragged children who were asked to do little more in the classroom than read the Bible and recite the Ten Commandments, benefited from an array of services that including day schools, night schools, Sunday schools, refuges, clothing clubs, country holidays, homes for orphan children, parents' meetings, and emigration schemes. In 1862 there were eighty-eight night schools, eighty-one Sunday schools, forty-two penny banks, forty-one clothing clubs, and forty-five industrial classes attached to ragged schools in the two districts of the Ragged School Union to the south and west of London.[79] Three years later most of the 600 schools in the Union had links to clothing clubs, industrial and sewing classes, temperance societies, working-men's clubs, and flower shows.[80]

Industrial schemes, which were also common in workhouse schools, became a popular means of transferring ragged children from a criminal class to a productive one. Boys were taught tailoring and shoemaking, carpentry and mat-making. The girls, as elsewhere in schools for the poor, had to settle for sewing, knitting, and embroidery. Whether they learned a skill or not, various means were tried to give the children a start in life. One scheme was the rag-collecting brigade, in which the boys salvaged household rubbish for a modest wage. More colourful was the shoeblack brigade, founded at the time of the Great Exhibition in 1851. Ragged school pupils pocketed £500 by polishing over 100,000 shoes! Soon shoeblack societies expanded across London—and eventually spread abroad—providing humble employment, and ideally greater discipline, to boys whose future was on the streets.[81]

For all their efforts and successes, the ragged schools failed to reach many outcast children, while distancing the ones they did recruit from other children who had claims to respectability. Some critics, including the journalist and social investigator Henry Mayhew, thought they did more harm than good, for they simply produced more sophisticated criminals, who could now read the price on the stolen articles.[82]

Clearly, the ragged schools did little to improve the quality of primary education in Britain. But the desire to reform behaviour rather than develop the mind was not exceptional. Most people agreed that education should have religion at its heart, though there was disagreement on which denomination best met the requirement. As the historian of Victorian respectability put it: 'Only eccentrics thought that education had something to do with developing the talents and capabilities of individual children, or with enhancing the quality of the human resources of society.'[83]

In the first half of the nineteenth century the mantras of local self-government and religious liberty remained powerful and told against any notions of greater government involvement in education. In 1856 William Gladstone warned of the risks posed by state aid to schooling: 'the day you sanction compulsory rating for the purpose of education you sign the death-warrant of voluntary exertions.'[84] The voluntary Christian culture had kept any prospect of a more uniform and comprehensive system at bay. Whenever radicals proposed that government should take a leading role in education, Anglicans, Nonconformists, and Catholics saw their own narrow interests at stake. The Chartist William Lovett lamented that, when any reform of education came forward, 'bigotry at once commenced its ravings from every church and conventicle in the kingdom, declaring all light to be impious and godless, unless it were kindled at their particular altar'.[85]

It was against this background of religious competition that critics started to see England's class-conscious, Bible-centred schools for the poor as a brake on progress and national efficiency. (Education in Scotland also needed reform because of an insufficient number of schools in the growing cities, but it had adapted rather better to the demands of industrialization and suffered less from class divisions.)[86] When full-time formal schooling was becoming the norm for males of the higher classes, the patchy, partial, and precarious education of poor children stood in stark relief. By comparison with much of Europe, which had taken to system building in education, schooling in England looked increasingly peculiar and out of step. In the mid-nineteenth century over four-fifths of the publicly inspected schools were run under the auspices of the Church of England.[87] But for the state to take over a greater responsibility for education, the Victorians would have to divest themselves of the idea that the church was indivisible from the state.

At mid-century the British government had little control over education beyond a responsibility for workhouse, prison, army, and navy schools, the allocation of grants to societies like the BFSS and the National Society, and a duty of school inspection introduced in 1839.[88] Educational reform was much debated in the middle decades of the century, but sectarian opposition ensured that the House of Commons had become 'a great cemetery of deceased Education Bills'.[89] Voluntarists opposed state education as a threat to political liberty and parental responsibility. The idea of rate-aided schools had little charm for religious leaders, who argued that it would 'have dried up all the sources of voluntary effort, and ultimately would have handed all the schools of the country to the Secularists'.[90] In 1855 Shaftesbury opposed a scheme that would raise local rates to maintain education, for he assumed that ratepayers would soon rid the schools of religion. He wrote in his diary: 'Such a plan is a death-warrant to the teaching of Evangelical religion. *It had better be called "a water-rate to extinguish religious fire among young people".*'[91]

In the 1860s the influence enjoyed by the denominations over education waned as external factors began to shift public opinion in favour of a more comprehensive system of education. But to an ever-growing number of people, voluntary provision was simply too thinly spread and poorly funded to meet the nation's needs. The SPCK, which continued to provide grants to Church of England schools, estimated that as many as a quarter of all children attended 'no school at all'.[92] Abroad, Prussia's military victories suggested that nations with compulsory elementary education provided superior soldiers.[93] Meanwhile, British manufacturers faced stiffer competition and now felt the nation needed to invest in a better-educated labour force. At home, the rapid growth of the urban population had strained the ancient parochial system, exacerbating the deficiencies of the existing schools. The deficiencies, in turn, heightened concerns about the danger to society of so many children growing up without any schooling whatsoever. The Christian sects would pay a price for not having converted the working classes en masse. A secular education, rather than a religious one, was beginning to be seen as the remedy for social and political unrest.[94]

The 1867 Reform Act, which added nearly a million working-class voters to the electorate, pointed to the inadequacies of education, not least the large number of poor children who remained unschooled. During the debate over the Bill, the MP Robert Lowe, a former vice-president of the Committee of Council on Education, voiced a growing worry that power would be transferred to the ignorant masses. A new era of centralization had arrived, he declared, and it was now necessary to compel 'our future masters to learn their letters'. And he added tellingly: 'this question is no longer a religious question, it has become a political one.'[95] For political as well as social and economic reasons educational reform became a matter of urgency. Gladstone's Liberal government, formed at the end of 1868, was thus in a strong position to carry out reforms, despite the opposition of religious leaders. W. E. Forster, who introduced the Elementary Education Bill in parliament, declared: 'On the speedy provision of elementary education, depends our industrial prosperity, the safe working of our constitutional system, and our national power.'[96]

The Education Act of 1870 was a compromise, but it brought the government into the field of education as never before.[97] It did not apply to Scotland or Ireland, which were specifically excluded from its provisions, nor did it make schooling free or compulsory. But it did eliminate many of the deficiencies of the existing religious schools. A primary purpose was to provide an elementary education for the many children who were beyond the reach of the voluntary schools.[98] (Secondary education would have to wait, if only because demand could not be proven until elementary education had taken hold.) The Act established school boards in areas of recognized need paid for out of the rates. These democratically elected board schools were to complement the existing voluntary schools, not replace them, which in practice created a dual system of board and voluntary schools in competition with one another. By 1880 the school boards had built or acquired 3,400 schools, with an average daily attendance of over 750,000 children.[99]

As the board schools expanded, they set in motion a process of social engineering that would have serious repercussions for both Christianity and associational charity. The religious day schools had long undergone government inspection, but educational provision before 1870 had been voluntary for organizers and parents alike. Poor parents were free to send their children to a local Sunday or charity school or withhold an education from their children altogether, as many did for economic reasons. With the advent of state education, the government gradually imposed minimum standards and set the curriculum, including limits on religious instruction, leaving parents with only the choice of deciding how much schooling a child received. The 1870 Act thus marked a 'great divide for the parental consumer'.[100] Not least of its effects was to dispose parents to feel that the education of poor children would in future be a responsibility of government, not of voluntary institutions as in the past.

The issue of religious instruction in the new state schools was acutely sensitive. As G. M. Young put it: 'No party would have dared to turn the Bible out of the schools, and no two parties could agree as to the terms upon which it should be admitted.'[101] By 1870 the politicians had moderated their view that all education should be hallowed by religious influence. A school system paid for out of taxation could hardly be seen to favour one denomination over another. Many Liberals who voted for the Education Act supported rate-aided public education because they objected to subsidizing religious instruction. Prime Minister Gladstone wrote to Shaftesbury that the reform must not give ammunition to those who feared that the state would 'become entangled in theological controversy'.[102] Thus, a provision of the Act prohibited the teaching of any 'religious catechism or religious formulary distinctive of any particular denomination', a clause that effectively kept ministers of religion out of state schools. Religious education, if it was given at all, was to be non-denominational in the board schools.

To many committed Christians, the Act sounded the death-knell for religious teaching. They feared that rate-aid would also destroy the subscription system of schooling and with it the tradition of self-government in education. Once education was free there would be no turning back, even if rate-aid failed to achieve the desired results. Churchmen were particularly unhappy with the clause in the Act that enforced non-denominational instruction in the new board schools. Would religion wither in the calm of universal agreement? Canon Robert Gregory, who became dean of St Paul's Cathedral in 1890, argued that non-denominational teaching 'was one in which nobody believed'.[103] The Revd Richard Burgess, an official of the National Society, took the view that 'the surest way to undermine religious convictions and Christian principles is to persuade men that modes of faith are matters of indifference and that to adhere to any particular creed is the sign of a narrow mind'.[104] Shaftesbury, though not hostile to state education in principle—as long as it was religious—gave the Act a chilling rebuff: the new schools, he wrote, 'founded on rates and fierce hatred of "denominational" teaching' would prove to be, in nine cases out of ten, vast factories for Infidelity'.[105]

The rival denominations could only look on, fearful that Christianity, and more specifically their particular version of it, would suffer with the advance of state education. The Timetable Conscience Clause in the Act, which restricted the amount of time that could be devoted to religion in the school day, was an especial worry. The bishop of Lincoln feared that the clause would breed generations of infidel teachers and pupils.[106] Anglicans generally disapproved of the board schools, which they took to be bastions of godless education. They soon felt under siege, knowing that their schools were at a disadvantage in the competition with rate-aided board schools. Catholics, whose schools had risen in number in the mid-Victorian years, also felt threatened (there were 34,750 children in Catholic schools in 1850).[107] Nonconformists were unhappy with the survival of the Church of England schools, but felt somewhat easier about the new system, for they did not have such a large stake in charity schools, and the only alternative to a board school for their children was often an Anglican school.

The Education Act of 1870, despite its compromises, established the principle that every child in the nation had a right to be educated. In 1880 Mundella's Education Act enforced compulsory attendance across the country for children between 5 and 10, though with mixed results because of parental resistance and difficulties in prosecution. In 1891 the Fee Grant Act virtually established free elementary education. The prospect of free education at point of use was a potent weapon in the campaign for educational reform. The rate-aided schools had a decided advantage in an era when schools needed new equipment and improved facilities. In the 1870s and 1880s the voluntary schools persevered. Indeed, they expanded in number until 1890, when decline set in.[108] In the end, they lacked the resources to finance the buildings and facilities required by government.[109] Increasingly, parents discontinued their subscriptions to the voluntary schools and rallied to the board schools, a trend not unconnected with the rise in taxes. By 1900 the board schools had taken over more than 1,000 voluntary schools.[110]

The secularizing effects of the Education Act should not be overestimated in the short term, for thousands of religious schools survived. (The number of Catholic schools rose from 400 in 1871 to 1,000 or so in 1900.)[111] Moreover, most of the school boards provided religious lessons, albeit non-denominational, with their scale and content varying from one institution to the next.[112] Furthermore, most parents wanted their children taught religion, if only because they thought morality could not be taught without it. But what had previously been a near monopoly of Christian responsibility for education, grounded in religion, came to an end in 1870. When the Education Act excluded parsons from the board schools, it introduced a culture in education in which religion became a subject like any other. At the time critics said that public morals would suffer if the schools taught religion like arithmetic or grammar. Once teachers treated the Bible as just another book, it would lose its power over the imagination.[113]

The inability of Anglicans and Nonconformists to set aside their differences came at a price for Christianity. In effect, sectarian divisions contributed to the gradual marginalization of the churches in education and religion in the schools. 'The Act of 1870', as one Anglican lamented, 'opened the door to the progressive secularization of English Education. . . . The price of disunity was that a system of education, voluntarily organized by several Christian denominations, now found itself challenged by a rival system, neutral even towards Christianity itself, and with all the material advantages of complete support from taxation.'[114] The very divisions within Christianity, which had led to the proliferation of religious schools in a hierarchical, pre-democratic age, ultimately contributed to the decline of Christian education in the maelstrom of an emerging representative democracy. In education, the ideal of the Godly Commonwealth was giving way to the reality of the secular state.

Democracy did not kill off religious education, but it contributed to its decline. Was the democracy of one man one vote compatible with the voluntary tradition that had Christianity at its core? Shaftesbury, like many of his co-religionists, believed not. He dreaded a future in which the enfranchised masses no longer feared the Lord. 'We have now come to a period in the history of our country', he said in 1870,

when there has just been granted to the people almost universal suffrage. Is this the time to take from the mass of the population, in whom all power will henceforward reside, that principle of internal self-control, without which there can be no freedom, social or political? . . . Is this a time to take from the mass of the people the checks and restraints of religion? Is this a time to harden their hearts by the mere secularity of knowledge, or to withhold from them the cultivation of all those noble and divine influences, which touch the soul?[115]

As an emergent democratic society expected state education to widen, it placed less and less value on evangelical learning. Whether secular knowledge hardened the heart or not, the impetus given to it by government would ultimately compromise religion, while leaving the tradition of subscriber democracy in education behind.

The ragged schools were clearly left behind. The reforms set in motion by act of parliament in 1870 undermined the voluntary day schools, but they devastated the ragged schools and their distinctive tradition of Christian teaching. Shaftesbury wrote in his diary at the time: 'The godless, non-Bible system is at hand; and the Ragged Schools, with all their Divine polity . . . must perish under this all-conquering march of intellectual power. Our nature is nothing, the heart is nothing, in the estimation of these zealots of secular knowledge. Everything for the flesh and nothing for the soul; everything for time, and nothing for eternity.'[116]

After 1870 the ragged schools, as Shaftesbury lamented, were a 'dying Patient'. The school boards took over buildings that had been paid for by subscriptions and adapted them for the needs of state education. Still, the Ragged School Union survived.[117] In 1893 it changed its name to the Ragged School Union and Shaftesbury Society. (Today it is simply the Shaftesbury Society.) Many of its former schools became missions and shifted their focus to the care of the handicapped, vocational training, and social work, areas in which the government had, as yet, little interest.[118]

In 1902 the Conservative government, with the issue of national efficiency in mind, passed another Education Act, which would have further repercussions for Christianity. The Act abolished the school boards, made county councils responsible for elementary education in England and Wales, and set up new secondary schools. It retained the dual system of state and voluntary schools and extended rate-aid to voluntary schools, measures that Anglicans and Catholics largely welcomed. Nonconformists, however, objected to Anglicans and Romanists receiving money from the taxpayer. The adversaries of the Church of England need not have worried, for the additional funds gave only temporary respite to church schools. The demands soon made upon them by the Board of Education exacerbated their long-standing financial problems. The result was a further decline in their number. In Newcastle, for example, the number of voluntary school places dropped by nearly 50 per cent between 1903 and 1914.[119]

Under the 1902 Act the state schools retained non-denominational teaching. But as many religious commentators had anticipated, secular subjects continued to squeeze out Christian instruction. By law, parents had the right to withdraw their children from religious lessons in state schools. In a market-driven and increasingly materialist society, parents and teachers could be forgiven for taking the view that religious instruction was a frill. As state education took hold, Christian campaigners had less and less control over the moral training of schoolchildren. The limits imposed on religious instruction in state schools was a portent of things to come. So too was the decline of the denominational conflicts of the past. The waning of those once powerful rivalries was itself a sign of Christian weariness. Eventually, the churches turned their minds to cooperation. As one of the official reports of the Church of England observed in the 1940s: 'The invasion by the State of spheres of life which hitherto have been the preserve of religious and philanthropic organizations is yet another incentive to the Churches to work more closely together and to heal their divisions.'[120]

It had been assumed that state schools would provide some degree of non-denominational religious worship without being required to do so. Christian teaching in the state schools persisted, but the religious commitment of teachers and staff could not be taken for granted. Meanwhile, the churches continued to struggle to afford the financial costs of their schools, which led them to frustrate an attempt by the Labour government of 1929–31 to raise the school-leaving age to 15.[121] When the Education Act of 1944 did so raise it and created the structure for the post-war educational system, it made a daily act of non-denominational worship compulsory. But this gesture to religion was arguably too little too late. It did not reflect stronger Christian belief; rather the reverse. It suggested that the Christian devotion of parents and teachers could no longer be relied upon. As the historian A. J. P. Taylor observed in his discussion of the 1944 Act: 'Christianity had to be propped up by legislative enactment. The British people were, however, to show that they were more concerned with this world than with the next.'[122]

Christianity in education continued its slide into irrelevance after the Second World War. In a society becoming more worldly and multicultural, its devotees lacked conviction. In many schools what passed for religious lessons became 'barely distinguishable from civics or general or social studies', which reflected the steady encroachment of secularism in the 1960s and 1970s.[123] In a paper published by the National Society in 1984, the authors said that 'the Christian teacher must be profoundly grateful that he is able to share common ground and he will resist the temptation to claim for his own practice a Christian distinctiveness in which his secular colleagues cannot share'.[124] In those schools with a high intake of children from non-Christian backgrounds, the daily exercise of compulsory Christian worship became increasingly awkward, carried out perfunctorily or not at all.

A survey of head teachers carried out in 1994 showed that 70 per cent of heads were not holding the daily act of worship required by law and that 60 per cent could not deliver the curriculum on religious education.[125] In 2000, Church of England and Catholic schools still accounted for 35 per cent of all primary schools and 15 per cent of all secondary schools in England.[126] But half the heads of the church schools thought the requirement for broadly Christian daily services and religious lessons 'unacceptable'.[127] One Anglican who taught religious education in a comprehensive school in the 1990s observed: 'I had never heard of anyone who said that Christianity could be taught as true.'[128] Just as the Victorian opponents of secular education had predicted, God, at least the Christian God, had become a stranger in the schools.

In the decades following the 1870 Education Act, the Sunday schools fared little better than the voluntary day schools and the ragged schools. Enrolments, at least, remained high because Anglicans and Nonconformists, unsettled by the decline of their day schools, rallied to Sunday schools as the nursery of their denominations. But with the arrival of board schools and compulsory elementary education, the educational purpose of Sunday schools, like the ragged schools, became superfluous. Without adequate classrooms and equipment, how were they to compete with rate-aided schools? According to one Methodist pastor, the 1870 Act had transferred 'the religious training

of the young . . . purely on the Christian Churches'.[129] As a consequence,
Sunday schools intensified their religious instruction, but with largely
untrained teachers. Increasingly, however, religious instruction looked
less and less relevant in a commercial society that looked with favour
on a state system of education with ever-widening provision. As early
as 1899, a speaker at the National Sunday School Convention said,
rather harshly, that Sunday schools 'were merely a temporary panacea
against ignorance and overwork in the early days of the factory
system'.[130]

As such a remark suggests, the decline in Sunday schools can be
dated from the late Victorian years. Sunday school enrolments for all
denominations in England, Scotland and Wales dropped from over
5.8 million in the 1880s (19 per cent of the population), to 5.2 million
in 1921 (12 per cent of the population), to 3.6 million in 1941 (8 per
cent of the population).[131] Teacher numbers dropped significantly in
the Church of England, from 212,000 in 1909[132] to 126,000 in
1939.[133] Whether this deterioration in teacher and pupil numbers can
be linked directly to a loss of faith in organized religion is unclear.
Most British churches showed modest declines in church membership
in the early decades of the twentieth century.[134] The figures for church
attendance were more startling. In York, for example, adult attendance fell from 35.5 per cent of the population in 1901 to 17.7 per
cent in 1935.[135] As parents deserted their churches, it seems likely that
children would tend to desert their Sunday schools. The decline in
Sunday schools was regional, but as far as one can tell from the available statistics, it was not out of step with the decline of Christianity
generally.

Like other religious institutions, Sunday schools had great difficulty adapting to a mobile and material culture that offered more and
more distractions. By the late nineteenth century better wages,
reduced working hours, and cheap public transport undermined
Sabbatarian principles.[136] As early as the 1870s there were at least five
national societies campaigning to 'reduce Sunday gloom'.[137] Even
clergymen, freed from 'Puritanical moroseness', began to support
Sunday games.[138] As Sabbatarianism waned, the schools, like the

churches, had to compete for the time and attention of members. The institutional diversity of Sunday schools intensified in the more relaxed atmosphere. But outings, plays, and lectures looked tedious when compared to the many secular entertainments appearing in the early twentieth century, such as professional sport, cinema, and wireless. With its moral seriousness, evangelical Christianity was not a lot of fun at the best of times. By the First World War, the Sunday school, which offered little in the way of excitement or educational purpose, was beginning to look old fashioned.

Whether the Great War 'unleashed a pagan flood which swept away many a sacred sanction' and drove the nation into a 'devil's brew' of vice, as one overheated writer put it in 1938, is doubtful.[139] But the war clearly shook any vestiges of Victorian optimism and demoralized the churches. As the dean of Durham Cathedral observed at the time: 'organised Christianity does not come well out of the world crisis.'[140] Adam's temptation and fall from grace, as a more recent authority observes, 'had not prepared generations of men and women for the sort of evil experienced during 1914–1918'.[141] Given the demands and sacrifices of war, many people got out of the habit of Sunday observance, and consequently Sunday school attendance. As mentioned, the number of Sunday school scholars and teachers fell in the interwar years, which the levels of inflation, unemployment, and mass poverty did nothing to allay. Nor did the movement of people to the expanding suburbs assist the Sunday schools. As one West London resident put it: 'So many families have moved out of the more central districts, that the teachers in those areas find it difficult to maintain their classes.'[142]

The Second World War accelerated the deterioration of the Sunday schools, as it did the churches and voluntary culture generally. The calling-up of teachers, the evacuation of children, and the commandeering of school buildings by the authorities for civil defence led to a suspension of activities and a loss of morale. In the first year of the war the Church of England reported a massive decline in voluntary contributions to Sunday schools.[143] Aerial bombing was catastrophic. Sheffield lost thirty-two schools in the first raid, a pattern that was repeated across many parts of the country. In London, bombs destroyed the headquarters of the Sunday School Union, with the loss of its library and publishing and business offices. As the social work and elaborate youth programmes of Sunday schools struggled to survive, government intervention intensified. Meanwhile, the relaxations of Sunday observance laws during the war made it more difficult to honour the Sabbath. With the churches distracted, schools closed, staff missing, and the parochial system in disarray, a crisis ensued.[144] The notion that Sunday schools served as a nursery of religion was no longer tenable.

After the war there appears to have been a brief resurgence in Sunday school attendance, but the climate soon deteriorated. State welfare provision made their social work seem unnecessary. Meanwhile sport, the cinema, television, and eventually Sunday shopping offered alluring alternatives to Christian observance. Abstentions increased as fewer and fewer parents, no longer church members themselves, encouraged their children to attend Sunday school. In 1957 a survey carried out by the Free Church Federal Council asked children why they were deserting the schools in such numbers. They replied: 'Bored', 'not learning anything', or as one child bemoaned, 'everybody said I was a sissy'.[145] As the youth culture changed in the 1960s, Sunday school attendance was decidedly for sissies. Sunday school statistics were by then fragmentary, but a steady decline in enrolments had set in, dropping to just 4 per cent of the population by the end of the century.[146] The Sunday school, as one writer put it at the millennium, 'is close to disappearing as a significant institution'.[147] So too is Christianity, by some accounts, and the collapse of Sunday schools has played its part in the process. They had, after all, supplied the churches with new members for over 200 years.

In 1910 the writer G. K. Chesterton quipped that a time would come when people would burst into laughter when told that men once 'thundered . . . against Secular Education'.[148] And so it has. The remarkable transformation in British education has had powerful repercussions for British culture. In the mid-Victorian years an education without

Christian teaching at its heart was rare. A century later, Christianity in the classroom was more often than not an embarrassment to teachers and pupils alike. Before 1870 the great majority of schools in England and Wales were voluntary and self-governing, largely paid for by subscriptions and local collections. A century later education was overwhelmingly provided by the state, free at point of use, and the remaining private schools were subject to government regulation. Charity schools, ragged schools, and Sunday schools, which once had a near monopoly over the education of the poor, are now largely of historical interest, curious reminders of Victorian class distinctions and confining pieties. The Bible, once the 'alpha and omega' of instruction, had been consigned to the dustbin of history.

Christian schooling suited a voluntary society with powerful local allegiances, low taxes, and class distinctions. Its impulse to inculcate morality suited an era when personal reformation was thought essential to social stability. But as education became an issue of mental training rather than moral improvement, the emphasis on religious instruction showed its limitations. In any case, evangelicalism could not keep pace with the number of sinners in need of regeneration. Nor did it have an answer to the growing worries about national efficiency and commercial competition. In an advanced industrial society, economic imperatives were replacing religious ones. As schooling became part of a national debate, a secular education rather than a religious one emerged as a solution to the problems of the state. Once education became politicized, notably at the time of the 1867 Reform Bill, the government felt obliged to address the patchy, ill-coordinated voluntary system of denominational education. The decline of Christianity may have had more to do with the extension of democracy than with Darwinism or the higher criticism. Ironically, representative democracy eroded the grass-roots democratic training encouraged by associational Christian education.

The pressures of representative democracy unsettled both charitable associations and denominational Christianity. In state schools the taxpayer replaced the subscriber, and the minister of education replaced the minister of religion. As an education based on Christian charity gave way to comprehensive secular provision, the government crafted a fig-leaf of religion in the schools as a gesture to the clerics and a nod to the past. Few outside the churches cared that denominational traditions and self-government suffered in the transformation of education, certainly not the civil servants in the capital, who thrived on regulation and centralization. Few outside the churches worried about the loss of civility that a secular education might encourage. There was no going back to Christian discipline, much less Christian 'truth'. As the schools discarded the fictions of Bible learning, religion surrendered its responsibility as an instrument of moral education. But with the triumph of secularism, from where would moral training come? Christianity was always more than a source of moral discipline; it was, as Nietzsche observed, 'a large treasure-trove of the most ingenious means of consolation'.[149] But with the death of God, from where would consolation come?

3

Visiting

I was a stranger, and ye took me in; naked and ye clothed me: I was sick, and ye visited me.

(Matthew 25: 34–6)

The State is under the moral law of God, and is intended by Him to be an instrument of human welfare.

(Resolution of the Bishops, Lambeth Conference, 1948)

Of all the forms of charitable activity established in Britain, none was more important than district, or household, visiting. It is little remembered today, except as the forerunner of social casework. But from the late eighteenth century until well into the twentieth it represented the most significant contribution made by organized religion to relieving the ills of society. The visiting society may be seen as the principal institution reflecting that parochial idealism which grew in proportion to the pains of an urban, industrial society. It should also be seen against the background of opinion that was suspicious of government intervention, hostile to mounting poor rates, and anxious to preserve local autonomy. Enjoying enormous public support, visiting charities were so widespread in Victorian Britain that few of the nation's inhabitants could have been unaware of their existence, certainly not the poor whose homes or hovels were canvassed, sometimes invaded, so assiduously. The simple doctrine that informed district visiting for much of its history was that impoverished and benighted souls could be saved by the agency of another human being, who cared enough about them to be interested in their survival and spiritual well-being.

The custom of visiting the poor had very old traditions in Britain. Casual visiting remained powerful, particularly in the countryside, but the emergence of district visiting societies added system and coordination. Geared to cities, the visiting societies were often based on parish boundaries. In Victorian London, for example, a typical parish would have from 4,000 to 6,000 inhabitants, but the poorest parishes often had twice these numbers. Dividing the neighbourhoods into districts, the societies assigned visitors to specific streets and households, ideally one visitor to every twenty to forty families.[1] With weekly visits, more often if the need arose, visitors brought the face-to-face charity of the country village to city slums. Armed with the tools of their trade—Bibles, tracts, clothes, blankets, food and coal tickets, domestic advice, medical assistance, friendship, and love—these foot soldiers of the charitable army went from door to door to combat the evils of poverty, disease, and irreligion.

By the end of the eighteenth century visiting societies were well established in Britain. John Wesley's experience as a sick visitor in the 1740s resulted in much regular visiting by members of his fellowship.[2] Non-denominational institutions emerged somewhat later, though it is difficult to determine which organization was first in the field. The beginning of district visiting on a significant scale is probably best dated from 1785, when a Methodist, John Gardner, established the Benevolent, or Strangers' Friend Society in London.[3] As with so many charitable campaigners, it was Gardner's first-hand experience of death and hardship that jolted him into action: 'I had been visiting a poor man dying of fistula. He lay on the floor covered with a sack, without shirt, cap, or sheet, and in a dull, despairing tone exclaimed, "I must die without hope".'[4] Gardner returned home, rallied his wife and neighbours, and the charity was born. It grew rapidly, and by 1802 sponsored 110 volunteers working throughout the capital, attending to 'the destitute sick poor without distinction of sect or country'.[5]

By the early years of the nineteenth century there were Strangers' Friend Societies in Bristol, Birmingham, Manchester, Liverpool, Sheffield, Leeds, York, and Hull.[6] They joined one of the fastest-growing forms of institutional philanthropy of the day. The pace and extent of visiting varied from place to place, in part determined by the existence of a resident middle class and the degree to which the societies employed working-class visitors. By mid-century Manchester was 'awash with scripture readers, tract distributors . . . and district visitors of all shapes and sizes', but parochial and congregational associations only developed a comprehensive system of domestic visiting from the 1860s onwards.[7] By that time, few poor families in Britain's cities were free from the dutiful attentions of domestic visitors. While the response of the poor could be indifferent and sometimes hostile, the extent of neighbourly visiting vastly increased the interaction between the classes.

With the years visiting became a feature of city missions, hospitals, homes, temperance societies, and settlement houses. The largest single type was connected to churches and chapels. Whatever their affiliation, they instructed the ignorant, nursed the sick, comforted the dying, and 'glorified God in all things'. Some, like the West Street Chapel Benevolent Society in London, were set up by the poor to relieve their poor neighbours.[8] Others specialized in tract distribution, lying-in, or sick visiting. There were forty-five visiting charities to the blind by 1889, which were the pioneers in social work among the blind.[9] Other societies extended visiting practices beyond the home, to fire stations, post offices, restaurants, and bus stations.[10] All in all, they played an increasingly prominent part in the provision of social services. Though limited in what they could provide, they were cheap and preventive, and proved especially useful in rapidly expanding cities short of medical facilities. Like the casual visiting that persisted into the industrial age, they bolstered that network of relations between the classes which contributed to Britain's high degree of self government and social order in the nineteenth century.

There were as many types of visiting society as there were denominations and distresses, but the evangelicals set the tone. Visiting contributed mightily to the evangelical influence over respectable culture, up and down the social order. Certainly, as a contemporary reminds us, evangelicals were on the alert to 'check . . . the insidious approaches of our Jesuitical foe'.[11] The rivalry was intense among the visiting charities, for, among others, Anglicans, Methodists, Roman Catholics, Baptists, and non-denominational visitors were active, often in the same neighbourhoods. Jewish communities established their own visiting agencies, in part to counteract the proselytizing of evangelicals.[12] The Bradford Town Mission, founded in 1850, claimed to be unsectarian, aiming 'not to proselytize, but to evangelize', but it eventually felt the need to counteract secular and socialist opinion through meetings and lectures.[13]

By the mid-Victorian years there were hundreds of visiting societies in Metropolitan London alone. Some of them were large and richly endowed, like the General Society for Promoting District Visiting, which 'tenderly examined' the 'temporal and spiritual condition' of all the poor families it could reach.[14] The London City Mission carried out about 2 million visits a year on a budget of between £20,000 and £40,000 annually.[15] At the other extreme there were societies with only a couple of visitors and scant resources. The great majority of London's 250 parish churches and nearly 100 Episcopal chapels sponsored a visiting society by 1850. The few that did not were in rich neighbourhoods where charitable workers were little in demand.[16] In the last quarter of the century the Metropolitan Visiting and Relief Association, which promoted Church of England visiting societies by grants to London clergy, oversaw the activities of over 200 of these parish charities, with 2,200 visitors.[17]

It is uncertain just how many of the roughly 300 dissenting chapels in London supported visiting societies, but judging from their general enthusiasm for missionary and charitable work, it seems likely that the majority of them did. Across the Christian divide, scores of Catholic societies and religious communities carried out household visiting and helped to swell the number of visitors in the country at large. Sisters of Charity, Sisters of Mercy, Sisters of Nazareth, and the Society of St Vincent de Paul were active. One band of French Catholic peasant women, 'the little sisters', begged and lived off scraps themselves to visit the poor of Hammersmith.[18] Complementing their work in the capital was an association called the 'Ladies of Charity', made up of women serving their local Catholic churches in much the same capacity as the women who formed visiting societies in the Church of England. In the Archdiocese of Westminster, for example, the Ladies of Charity could boast twenty visiting societies, most of them founded in the 1840s and 1850s.[19]

As the many references to sisters, deaconesses, and ladies' societies suggest, women provided the great majority of visitors, and without their devoted service the movement would have been a pale shadow of itself. Despite the prejudice against them in some quarters, women showed, from the earliest years of visiting, a greater willingness to volunteer than men. It was often said that visiting was best done by women, because they had wide sympathies, a knowledge of domestic management, and could more freely enter homes in which men were rarely found at visiting times.[20] There were charities, such as the London City Mission that used only paid male visitors, but they were exceptional. (If a society required full-time male visitors it was probably necessary to pay them.) The evidence suggests that by the mid-nineteenth century there were about three women volunteers for every man, a figure that was on the rise. One commentator, writing in 1887, remarked that 90 per cent of the visitors to the East End were women.[21] It was not uncommon by that time for commentators to lament the shortage of male volunteers, especially gentlemen, and use the pronoun 'she' when referring to visitors.[22]

The total number of visitors from all faiths working across the country was considerable. Precise statistics are not available for all denominations, but in its first official count in 1889, the Church of England announced that there were 47,112 district visitors, mostly female, working in 12,000 of the 15,000 parishes in England and Wales, a figure that rose to 74,009 in all the church's parishes in 1910.[23] A few years later it was reported that 85,000 district visitors served in the Anglican Church, of whom 75,000 were women.[24] It has been estimated that if all the visitors from across the religious landscape were added to these figures, the nationwide visiting force at the beginning of the First World War would have reached nearly 200,000 in a population of 36 million.[25] Whatever the precise figure, the number of visitors was impressive. There were only 168,000 established civil servants in Britain in 1914.[26]

While the number of visitors varied from institution to institution, there was considerable uniformity in the constitutions that governed the various societies. Like the eighteenth-century charity schools, most visiting charities supported themselves from voluntary contributions, largely subscriptions, and were managed by a committee elected annually by the members, who were often required to contribute a guinea a year. Clergymen dominated the parish societies, but the larger institutions could boast an array of officers, including a president, vice-president, secretaries, treasurers, perhaps a surgeon or a nurse, and, at the bottom of the hierarchy, a team of visitors. Typically, the committee outlined and organized the districts to be canvassed. The larger societies often appointed sub-committees to oversee the administration in the particular neighbourhoods. This division of authority, it was argued, had the advantage of keeping the management in touch with local conditions. Those societies that could afford it published reports, which included aims and statistics, funds received and expended, lists of subscribers, and case studies.

Despite the similarities in the organization of visiting societies, rivalry remained a hallmark of the movement. Religious bigotry, whether real or perceived, was a great incentive to charitable association. The overlapping of competing charitable authorities was staggering in some cities. Agents from rival institutions often visited the same homes each week. In Manchester, visitors from four different institutions distributed tracts to the same households, often leaving the recipients bewildered.[27] In East London some families changed their religion from visitor to visitor, and consequently had to attend different church and chapel services several nights a week in exchange for benefits.[28] Dissembling parents scrubbed their children for the visiting lady in the hope of extracting a few bob. As one East End boy remembered about his father's reactions to the Ragged School Mission: 'They'll be round today . . . now mind, you behave yourself.'[29] An unintended consequence of charitable action was a skin-deep, calculated deference. It was a point of criticism increasingly levelled at religious charities by political economists, who assumed that Christian campaigners were innocent of social science.

To complicate matters further, the visiting societies had to deal with the Poor Law authorities. The New Poor Law of 1834 appears not to have had any marked effect on the growth of subscriptions to the visiting societies, though as a 'charter of the ratepayer' it may have stimulated contributions. Clearly it altered the relationship between poor relief and charitable campaigners. A clarification of the respective spheres of philanthropy and the state emerged, though it was highly artificial. Charity was to assist deserving cases, and the Poor Law would cope with undeserving paupers. This conventional wisdom was ritually espoused in the late nineteenth century, perhaps most notably by the Charity Organisation Society, which worked closely with Poor Law officials. Yet many visitors, preoccupied with spreading the gospel, were oblivious to the new Act. Others disliked its hard-heartedness and worked at cross purposes with Guardians. Still, the economies and severities of the Poor Law, whose overseers shared with district visitors a belief in the need for individual reformation, gave great scope to charitable service. Most poor people, whether deserving or undeserving, preferred the relatively tender mercies of Christian visitors to the Spartan rigours of the workhouse.

The genuinely needy, who far outnumbered the artful mendicants, welcomed the benefits of visiting. These benefits varied with the economy of the community, the nature of the charity, and, not least, the character of the individual visitor. We should not assume in our secular age that the religious message on offer was meaningless to the visited. The many letters from them cited in the charitable records suggest that many humble people, particularly the old and sick, received consolation from the prayers, Bible readings, and long hours spent over their individual souls. The wife of a factory operative wrote to the Shrewsbury teetotal visitor Mrs J. B. Wightman: 'I am thankful to God that ever I had knowledge of you; for, through being induced

to join the pledge, I have been rescued from destruction.'[30] 'I owe my
life to her. If it had not been for her I should have been in my grave',
wrote a miner about Mary Shepherd, a Methodist visitor in
Cheadle.[31] Visitors prone to moralizing were often turned away at the
door. Most visitors, even those whose message was essentially religious, typically delivered the homilies along with a basket of necessities. While many Christian campaigners thought that carrying a
Bible in one hand and a food ticket in the other was undesirable, it was
a compromise that kept many a door from being slammed in the face.

The range of services provided by the visiting societies depended on
each one's aims and resources. They commonly offered food, recipes,
coals, boots, clothing, blankets, tracts, Bibles, a sympathetic ear, and
advice on matters of domestic importance, such as sanitation and
child-care. The distribution of money, which some societies permitted, came increasingly under attack in the nineteenth century as it was
widely thought to encourage pauperism. Collecting money from poor
families for rent payments was more common, especially after the
work of Octavia Hill, a pioneer of housing reform, became widely
known. Visitors also built up and disseminated a wealth of local information, intermixed with gossip, which was often very useful to the
community. Thus they put employers, particularly of domestic servants, in touch with potential employees, and provided a check on
truancy from school, which became more important after the introduction of state education in 1870. Putting their charges in touch
with evening classes, lending libraries, mothers' meetings, and ragged
schools was another feature of their work, as was referring the sick to
local doctors, district nurses, and dispensaries. The crisscrossing of
lives made a neighbourhood more connected and self-governing.

The sheer variety of services offered by visitors suggests that their
motives were various. Humanitarianism, or a simple belief in the
advancement of mankind, should not be discounted, but in the nineteenth century religious motives predominated, particularly among
those of an evangelical persuasion. Hundreds of memoirs and diaries
are illuminating on the issue. Take Mrs Jane Gibson, a Methodist from

Newcastle who visited for the Strangers' Friend Society in London in the early nineteenth century. Her *Memoirs* are full of scripture and citations from Christian authorities. Hannah More is quoted with enthusiasm: 'Charity is the calling of a lady; the care of the poor is her profession.' This calling flowed from 'that cardinal doctrine of the Gospel . . . the vicarious suffering of Christ'.[32] The supreme charity of Jesus in sacrificing His life had the most powerful meaning for evangelicals like Mrs Gibson, for it pardoned their sins and offered them salvation.

Armed with passages of scripture, countless visitors went forth to tread in the steps of the 'Heavenly Visitor'.[33] Their most essential qualification was a love of Christ; and guided by his example, they opened the door of mercy to their fellow sinners. Like Sarah Martin, who felt the 'glorious liberty wherewith Christ had made me free', they loved the poor because Jesus loved the poor.[34] The indirect nature of their love helps to explain its often abstract quality. In *My Apprenticeship*, Beatrice Webb commented on the 'strangely impersonal love' expressed in the charity of her mother's companion Martha Jackson, a 'particular Baptist'.[35] The suffering that women had to witness on their charitable rounds, and that most endured in childbirth, may have contributed to a toughness of mind.

Mrs Margaret Burton, a dressmaker from North Shields, who 'gave herself to God' at a Methodist class meeting in 1802, was another evangelical visitor whose purpose was essentially missionary. When she moved to Darlington she began a diary full of remorseful descriptions of her struggle with Satan. Her heart was like 'a cage of unclean birds'. And, in a much-used metaphor, she asked 'how shall a guilty worm draw nigh to God'?[36] Conscious of her own sin, she became conscious of the sin around her. To conquer it she turned to visiting: 'I furnished myself with some tracts which I distributed, and spoke to them as the Lord enabled me to do. . . . Some received me kindly, one family shut their door against me, but I went again; and one poor old sinner was unkind; however I invited them all to come to my house every Sunday afternoon. If the Lord hath himself set me to this work, I shall have his help and blessing.'[37] Like so many nineteenth-century

women, hers was a life of hard work and religious service, not all of it,
as she related, appreciated. On her deathbed, at the age of 45, she
passed on the duty of good works to her 19-year-old daughter Mary:
'Does my Mary cast all upon Christ?' she asked.[38]

We can answer her question, for a life of Mary, titled *Holy Living*,
exists. As we discover in its pages, Mary was attentive at public worship by the age of 2 and spent much of her time at boarding school trying to save the souls of other pupils.[39] Yet she had setbacks. Her
Devotional Remains (1854) tell a story of guilt, 'heart-burning', and
spiritual vacillation. Marriage to a Methodist missionary, Thomas
Cryer, reinforced her determination 'to be a vessel of His grace, an
instrument for His glory'. It was in her visiting of fellow sufferers that
she found the most 'sin-consuming, self-annihilating, Christ-exalting,
perfect, burning love':

I find the cross in canvassing from door to door for Missions, and perhaps not
succeeding in one case in twenty; I find it still more in begging for a poor
starving fellow-creature, and perhaps now and then meeting with a chilling
repulse . . . but, most of all, I find it in going from door to door on the visiting plan, trying to persuade sinners to attend God's house, and flee from the
wrath to come . . . But O, when I have to make my own way, and meet the
cold looks and even the rude rebuff of those who will not be subdued by
kindness and courtesy, then nature does shrink . . . Yet I dare not give it up:
it is God's work.[40]

The writings of visitors like Jane Gibson, Margaret Burton, and
Mary Cryer confirm that Christian benevolence was not simply the
natural result of conversion, a product of a true acceptance of the
gospel covenant. It was often a product of that anxiety of soul that
asks: 'Am I saved?' The scriptural passage, 'I was sick, and ye visited
me', was, among others, a powerful influence on these women; and
the text that followed, if taken literally, could be unsettling: 'Depart
from me, ye cursed, into the eternal fire which is prepared for the devil
and his angels: for I was an hungred, and ye gave me no meat: I was
thirsty, and ye gave me no drink: I was a stranger, and ye took me not
in; naked, and ye clothed me not; sick, and in prison, and ye visited me

not' (Matthew 25: 41–3). In the mind of an evangelical, eternal fire was not a metaphor but a prospect. Many of those whose 'hearts yearned for sinners' visited the poor or pursued their other charities not only in anticipation of grace but also in fear of damnation.

As the religious diaries make abundantly clear, the Bible offered a principal source of inspiration and consolation, for visitors and visited alike. To evangelicals, it was revealed truth, the fount of justice, and the wellspring of mercy. Just as it served at a charity or Sunday school, so it served in British dwellings, as the first book, and often the only book in evidence. Francis Place recalled that the Bible was the sole book his father owned.[41] There was no shortage of Bibles to go around. The Bible Society alone had produced 20 million copies by the mid-nineteenth century.[42] At every opportunity visitors, canvassers, and colporteurs (agents of societies employed to distribute Bibles) sold them or gave them away, ensuring that they could be found in the homes of the poor. The only British homes where the Bible could not be found were arguably those in which it was not wanted. This was rare, for in popular culture the possession of a Bible was often thought to bring luck.[43] With gains in literacy, more Britons were able to read it than ever before. 'At no other time, either before or since,' observed a historian of English manners, 'has the Bible been so familiar to English-speaking people as it was during the nineteenth century. . . . One consulted this commonplace book throughout life's journey, and sometimes, clasping it in a death grip, carried it to the grave.'[44]

Spreading the word of God provided the most insistent motive for many visitors well into the twentieth century. With few exceptions, the many visiting manuals, handbooks, and hints to visitors corroborate the evidence of the religious diaries and memoirs. The Bible set the scene and tone. 'Let your highest motive be the constraining love of Christ', wrote the author of *Hints to District Visitors* in 1858.[45] In her pamphlet *District Visiting*, published in 1877, Octavia Hill remarked that the task of visiting was 'holy'.[46] 'The foundation of all charity', she noted elsewhere, was the life of Christ.[47] One curious

'Handbook' for Christian visitors, published in 1882, included passages of scripture and suggestive remarks to be used by visitors at timely moments. The dim or uncertain visitor could find inspiration under such headings as 'backsliders', the 'tried and tempted', or the 'dying'.[48] The supreme task of visiting was 'to help others know the love of our Lord Jesus Christ', remarked another manual at the end of the century.[49] The clergyman Arthur Jephson remarked, in *Some Hints for Parish Workers* in 1904, that the chief motive of visiting was 'to turn people from darkness to light . . . from the power of Satan unto God'.[50]

Though religion was a compelling philanthropic motive, we can detect a variety of further motives that were reconcilable with it, from public safety, particularly noticeable during the French Revolution, to the desire of women to escape the confines of domestic routine. The pressures to contribute were not easily ignored in surroundings in which levels of sickness and poverty were so alarming, and many visitors responded in simple humanitarian terms to the temporal needs of their neighbours as well as to the call of Christ. On the other hand, the distractions and delights of visiting poor neighbourhoods made it irresistible to many volunteers, especially the well-to-do, who took pleasure—on occasion erotic pleasure—in 'slumming'. Self-seeking gratification often merged imperceptibly into more serious reform efforts and 'confounded clear-cut distinctions between true and false charity'.[51]

Whether 'slumming' or not, the weekly round among the poor, though often harrowing, could be a source of immense pleasure. To be needed, to be counted upon, to be called 'dear' or 'friend', was a great reward. This was especially so for those with problems at home, who found in charitable work an escape from prying relatives or joyless marriages. As the master of Balliol, Benjamin Jowett, wrote to Florence Nightingale: 'Do you ever observe how persons take refuge from family unhappiness in philanthropy?'[52] For those without families, getting to know their needy neighbours could be a great attraction. One visitor, Anne Clough, who went on to become the first principal of Newnham College, remarked: 'The children know me, and speak my name. This was delicious to me, and worth more than a thousand praises.'[53]

Parish work also provided status in the community. This was particularly important for women, for whom status was in short supply elsewhere in the nineteenth century. For leisured women, visiting provided a widely available, and acceptable, outlet for self expression. The dinner, bazaar, or Sunday school outing that often capped a society's annual work provided entertainment consistent with religious values. Such activities confirm that philanthropic work was not simply a result of religious pressure, though that was usually an important part of it. Visiting, like charity generally, represented basic human impulses: to be useful, to be seen to be useful, to be respectable, to be informed, to be amused, to 'keep up with the Joneses', to gossip, to wield power, to love and be loved. And while middle-class guilt was not an uncommon philanthropic motive, it was perhaps less prominent in an era of accepted social hierarchy.

District visiting marshalled a vast army of volunteers addressing themselves to the administration of relief in Britain. The more they investigated, the more distress they uncovered. Indeed, as the Unitarian writer Lucy Aikin noted, 'a positive *demand* for misery was created by the incessant eagerness manifested to relieve it'.[54] How could the health and happiness of the poorest classes be promoted in those congested and infested slums that blackened the nation's reputation? Social-science techniques grafted onto church organization held out some hope, but the need for experimentation was pressing. Some of the most innovative and important visiting schemes came into view in the mid-Victorian years. Some, like the Salvation Army (1865), had a unique Christian answer to social distress. Others, like the Liverpool Central Relief Society (1863) and the Charity Organisation Society (1869), tempered Christian kindness with social statistics and the investigation of individual cases. Social casework became something of a craze in the mid-Victorian period, heightened by former factual deprivation. But its effect was to encourage visitors to spend more time on temporal concerns and less on proselytizing.

One of the most notable experiments in district visiting (and later district nursing) came from the Ranyard Mission, or the London Bible and Domestic Female Mission as it was called initially. Its history is a telling example of the growing toll that temporal concerns took on religious practice. Founded by Ellen Ranyard in 1857, the mission was a peculiarly Victorian response to the problems of urban distress. It used ingenious methods to penetrate the most dangerous London neighbourhoods, where disease and irreligion were rife and where an overcrowded population threatened to overwhelm the means of subsistence. Mrs Ranyard (1810–75) was born in Nine Elms, the daughter of a cement-maker. Raised as a Nonconformist, she had been a visitor to the poor from childhood. Like other evangelical women, she ransacked the Old and New Testaments to uncover examples of her sex who could be used as models for contemporary conduct. In Phoebe and Dorcas, Ruth and Rebekah, she found women of piety and industry, compassion, and self-sacrifice, just those qualities she most admired.

The female poor aroused her particular concern, and it was during a summer walk through St Giles in 1857 that 'the misery of our sisters there . . . brought forth the idea of the Bible-woman'.[55] The Bible woman was to see herself as a contemporary Phoebe or Rebekah, a concept that had ulterior uses in a charitable world still largely dominated by men. This Bible woman was to be working class, a 'native agent' at home in the courts and alleys, who would not excite the pride or false expectations on the part of the residents. In the early years her job was to sell Bibles and advise on domestic matters under the guidance of lady superintendents. She was, in Mrs Ranyard's words, to be the 'missing link' between the poorest class and their fellow men, the agency by which society's outcasts were to be brought back to morality and religion. In the first ten years the mission recruited 234 Bible women. Careful screening ensured that they were respectable Protestants with few family cares. Given a three-month training in the Poor Law, hygiene, and scripture, the Bible women represented the first corps of paid social workers in England.[56]

Using the postal districts, the Ranyard Mission mapped out London's streets and assigned the Bible women to their own neighbourhoods.

Familiarity with a district was thought essential if the immediacy of parish life was to be re-created in the bowels of London. But selling Bibles was found to be much easier when combined with tips on cooking, cleaning, and other household matters. Before long, the poor subscribed to schemes to pay for clothing, coals, food, and furniture. Inducements to providence were a feature of most visiting societies, and Mrs Ranyard demanded that nothing be provided that was not paid for. Alert to the dangers of indiscriminate relief, she wished to give every encouragement to self-help. Self-help was social gospel to Victorian philanthropists, and the charitable establishment greeted the mission's successes in this sphere with enthusiasm. Soon other institutions, perhaps most notably the Parochial Mission Women's Association, adopted Ranyard's methods.[57] By 1862 there was 'some description of Bible-woman . . . in almost every town in England'.[58] In time they spread across the world, from North America to India, and from Burma to Australia.

Religious instruction and the conversion of London's outcast population were central to Mrs Ranyard's purposes, but over time material concerns, social caseloads, and government initiatives diluted missionary zeal. As Mrs Ranyard's individualist evangelical philosophy had it, the source of social distress was in personal misfortune or moral failing, not the structure of society. But this is not to say that she discounted the environment as an influence on character. On the contrary, because the environment did play a part in shaping the lives of the poor, she was determined to improve their domestic and local circumstances. In her view, the remedy for indigence was to be found in promoting an environment that would transform the poor into accountable, self-respecting members of society. She did not foresee that attentions to the temporal might erode attentions to her clients' souls. But over the decades the missionaries devoted less and less time to face-to-face evangelizing. Consequently, the religious message became diffused, a trend that was taking place in other religious charities across the country.

The Charity Organisation Society (COS), the pre-eminent exponent of social casework, had close ties with the Ranyard Mission, but its ideals were sometimes at odds with the mission's priorities. Deeply

influenced by the writings of the Scottish social theorist Thomas
Chalmers, the COS sought to reduce pauperism and to repress men-
dacity through greater charitable cooperation and social casework. Its
founders sought to create an ethical society in which the deserving
poor were returned to productive labour and citizenship.[59] Selling
Bibles was not an object. Unlike the faith-based charities, the COS
saw religious enthusiasm as an impediment to charitable efficiency. In
the opinion of Charles Loch (1849–1923), the influential secretary of
the COS, charity was not to be the servant of sectarianism but part of
a religion of humanity. Though a committed Christian himself, he
sought 'a nobler, more devoted, more scientific religious charity'.
Social science would produce 'the religion of charity without the sectarianism of religion'.[60] What Loch and his followers failed to
acknowledge was that district visiting owed an enormous debt to sectarian enthusiasm. The rise of social science tempered Christian kindness and placed constraints on missionary impulses. It could only
come at a cost to Christian devotion.

The rise of social casework blurred the boundary between the religious and secular, while fuelling divisions in the charitable sector. The
utilitarian philosophy of the COS, with its impersonal 'scientific charity' and preoccupation with statistical investigation, was at odds with
the revivalism behind traditional visiting practices. The religious reaction to COS philosophy was one of the reasons why the institution's
influence was limited, particularly outside the capital.[61] Many visitors
refused to cooperate with the COS, whose doctrine was widely perceived to be long on red tape and short on Christian charity.[62] This sen-
timent was particularly strong among women visitors, for whom the
personal touch and missionary work were so important. But they were
increasingly on the defensive as clergymen started to criticize religious
partisanship and call for formal training in casework techniques. Not a
few clerics joined the ranks of Christian socialism, which ultimately
proved more hospitable to socialism than to Christianity.

With the years, the visiting societies reconciled their differences with
the Poor Law authorities and took measures to discipline the zeal of

their Christian visitors. Increasingly, visiting handbooks supplemented the spiritual message with information on the Poor Law and public health, education, and emigration. In a guide to visitors published in 1883, Loch declared that 'religious ministration tends to hypocrisy', a view that would have appalled many traditional charitable campaigners.[63] Pushpin not poetry was the mantra of the COS, and it took the lead in producing fact-finding reports on a wide variety of topics of interest to visitors, from treating the blind to providing night refuges for the homeless.[64] In 1896 it instituted a training scheme and later promoted a School of Sociology, which in 1912 amalgamated with the London School of Economics to become the School's Department of Social Science and Administration.[65] To those enrolled in social-work classes at the LSE, the age-old practice of handing out Bibles and tracts looked out of touch, as did time spent over spiritual matters. The training courses that developed before the Second World War in Britain did not show a decisive preference for paid professional work over voluntary work.[66] But clearly professionalization was undermining older Christian traditions.

If the revolution in statistics and social work played its part in the retreat of Christian visiting, it was also part of a wider movement of opinion that would take its toll on Christian practice generally. Just as the advocates of charitable organization were giving district visitors a more professional outlook, assumptions about the causes of poverty were shifting, and the government began to take a greater interest in social matters. The reports from Select Committees and Royal Commissions on subjects such as housing, unemployment, and the aged poor created anxiety and fuelled calls for action. So too did the Boer War, which highlighted the wretched health of many recruits. The growing consciousness of the economic and physical circumstances of the poor and the elderly not only influenced public policy but shifted priorities in many district-visiting societies to material conditions rather than spiritual needs.[67]

Meanwhile, investigations of urban deprivation, including Andrew Mearns's *Bitter Cry of Outcast London* (1883) and the philanthropist Seebohm Rowntree's *Poverty: A Study of Town Life* (1901), made the public increasingly sensitive to the conditions of working-class life. The most influential of the investigations, Charles Booth's *The Life and Labour of the People of London* (1889–1903), was the most elaborate inquiry into urban life in Britain ever undertaken, and it convinced many of its readers that charity could not deliver on its promise of social regeneration. Beatrice Webb, one of Booth's assistants and his cousin by marriage, pictured him as 'perhaps the most perfect embodiment of . . . the Victorian time-spirit—the union of faith in the scientific method with the transference of the emotion of self-sacrificing service from God to man'.[68] It was a sign of the times that Booth, raised a Unitarian, devoted nearly half of his seventeen volumes to 'Religious Influences', a point recalled years later by William Beveridge in his book *Voluntary Action*.[69]

But for all the 'Religious Influences' of the late Victorian years, a growing number of Christians, from Methodist laymen to Anglican bishops, felt that voluntary institutions alone did not have the resources to cope with the problems of health and welfare, issues that were moving up the political agenda as a growing body of social data became available. Increasingly, Nonconformists, though not reducing their voluntary efforts, called on government to intervene on issues of conscience, such as prostitution and drink.[70] Canon Samuel Barnett, the first warden of Toynbee Hall, was among those Anglicans who came to challenge the opposition to government intervention. The author of a book of essays titled *Practicable Socialism* (1888), he encouraged social reformers to forgo their charities in favour of state provision.[71] As he and other Christian socialists were well aware, the money available for church building in the expanding industrial cities was inadequate. Moreover, the Church of England often seemed a forbidding world to the urban poor. The city missions and the Salvation Army were in closer touch with the working classes, who generally accepted religious values but were little interested in the doctrinal concerns of many churchmen.

The shortcomings of the Church of England and the growing body of social data about the physical condition of the poorer classes, to which philanthropists made a major contribution, provided ammunition for those who were coming to different conclusions about the causes of social distress and the most effective way to remedy it. In an industrial economy under strain, people began to take the view that poverty was not simply a product of individual or familial breakdown, but of faults in the economy and the structure of society. As in the debate over state education, the spotlight was increasingly on national efficiency and social reconstruction, not on the poor as a set of individual cases in need of personal reformation. From such a perspective, the efforts of Christian charity seemed not only inadequate but also misconceived. Did rival Christian sects competing for the souls of the poor add to the sum of human happiness or contribute to national efficiency? The voluntary ideal that had been so compelling to respectable Victorians came to be seen as a bankrupt philosophy in the minds of many reformers. Part of the background was a society that was growing at once both more national and more diverse. It was not promising for the future of Christianity that the more culturally diverse parts of the country were the least congenial to religious observance, and consequently charitable activity.[72]

Charity flourished in the provinces and in the parishes, and especially in prosperous parts of the country with homogeneous populations and a strong religious presence. Its critics, often seated in the capital, sought to create a greater sense of national community out of diversity. Consequently, many of them looked to government to provide it through more uniform and comprehensive social services. As one authority remarked: 'When the focus shifted from "the Poor" and what could be done to relieve their distress, to poverty and what could be done to abolish it, then it became inevitable that the State should intervene more decisively and that the scope of private charity should be correspondingly altered.'[73] Those who took the collectivist line, among them churchmen like Canon Barnett, believed that their more 'scientific' appreciation of the causes of poverty would lead to its elimination. In time, this impersonal approach to welfare, the belief in the efficacy of legislation and state intervention, became as compelling to its advocates as Christian service had been to the Victorians. The expectations thus aroused would place an enormous burden on later governments and form an ineradicable part of the prevailing climate of opinion in Britain in the second half of the twentieth century.

Central government had been drawn into the social arena in the Victorian years by its financial assistance to charitable societies, by its commissions and inquiries, and by its consequent intervention in such important matters as sanitation, factory life, and education. The promotion of religion was not a government priority. How could it be, in a society with so many religious divisions? By the Edwardian years government measures in health, education, and welfare helped to trigger an assumption that further state involvement was inevitable, if not desirable. It was against this background that the Liberal government passed its pioneering, albeit piecemeal, social legislation in the early years of the century, which included school meals (1906), old-age pensions (1908), and compulsory insurance for certain categories of employee against illness and unemployment (1911). Such legislation had a direct bearing on the day-to-day work of many household visitors, who felt obliged to spend time on their rounds discussing pensions and other entitlements.

The ad hoc legislation did not portend an inevitable progress towards the 'Welfare State', but it sent out the signal that government posed a serious challenge to charity's pre-eminence. Importantly, it encouraged the public to look to government rather than charity for relief, just as they now looked to government for education. The fact that Poor Law authorities did not administer state pensions and other benefits made them all the more acceptable to working-class beneficiaries. But for the visiting societies and other charitable agencies that had developed a working relationship with Poor Law officials, it was a further challenge. State benefits free from the stigma of the Poor Law narrowed the scope for charity. The longstanding, if often artificial, division of responsibility between voluntary and public provision was breaking down as government entitlements eroded distinctions between deserving and undeserving cases. The philosophy of personal service and neighbourliness was increasingly under attack from those, like Sidney and Beatrice Webb, who sought a national minimum of civilized life paid for by the taxpayer. Sidney Webb, who anticipated a progressive takeover of charitable provision by the state, spoke for many of advanced views in calling collectivism 'the mother of freedom'.[74]

Politicians, fearful of raising taxes, often argued that government benefits were not a substitute for charity. Lloyd George, for his part, recognized that 'if the voluntary system were to collapse, the State would necessarily have to step in. The flow of voluntary contributions would be checked. Endowments would be lost. The cost would fall upon the heavily burdened taxpayer or ratepayer.'[75] Despite the political reassurances, many philanthropists felt obliged to reappraise their role. Some of them feared for their jobs, others for subscriptions. Others still worried that the growth of government responsibility for welfare would lead to the devitalization of Christianity. Those motivated principally by religion worried about the potential decline in moral activism if people turned to the state for salvation. The fiercely individualistic COS, which remained hostile to state intervention, believed that government benefits would divorce poverty from morality and happiness from duty. Charles Loch thought an electorate clamouring for rights and entitlements from government would soon deride the duties of citizenship. And he added: 'To shift the responsibility of maintenance from the individual to the state is to sterilize the productive power of the community as a whole, and also to impose on the State . . . so heavy a liability . . . as may greatly hamper, if not also ruin, it.'[76]

As a result of the growth of government responsibility for social provision, district visiting societies, like philanthropic bodies generally, were on the defensive. On the economic front, market forces were undermining the viability of local communities and their charitable agencies. The doubling of population over the reign of Queen Victoria and the intermittent periods of economic depression after the 1870s had put additional pressure on voluntary services, exposing their lack of coordination. In a culture growing more urban and diverse, they had difficulty rebutting criticisms that charity was patchy and inadequate. As the Victorian historian J. R. Green complained, there were 'hundreds of agencies at work over the same ground without concert or co-operation or the slightest information as to each other's exertions'.[77] Overlapping provision led not only to patchiness and inefficiency, but was an invitation to hypocrisy and improvidence. Against the mounting criticism, the argument that charitable associations were expressions of local democracy carried less and less weight.

Fragmented by sectarian rivalries, traditional campaigners were at a disadvantage. In an age of social science, mass politics, and national priorities, they looked increasingly parochial. They often assumed that distinctions between rich and poor were God-given and likely to persist. Conditioned by the Christian view that humanity was corrupt and poverty ineradicable, they found it difficult to compete with secular philosophies that offered visions of mankind perfected. Meanwhile, political economists complained of sentimental philanthropists more interested in saving souls than in attacking the causes of poverty. Philanthropists could be their own worst enemies, and in an era notorious for indiscriminate almsgiving, exploitation of their good offices thrived. As a Yorkshire beggar told a district visitor when asked if he could read or write: 'No Ma'am, I can't. . . . and if I'd known as much when I was a child as I do now, I'd never have learnt to walk or talk.'[78]

Increasingly, Christian campaigners laid themselves open to attack from intellectuals and reformers by their piety and lack of social theory. In an age besotted by casework and social statistics, visitors themselves became more and more conscious of their lack of training. One is reminded of the Mrs Ramsay in Virginia Woolf's *To The Lighthouse* (1927), who 'ruminated' the problem of rich and poor on her visiting rounds in the years before the First World War. Armed with 'a notebook and pencil . . . she wrote down in columns carefully ruled for the purpose wages and spending, employment and unemployment, in the hope that thus she would cease to be a private woman whose charity was half a sop to her own indignation, half a relief to her own curiosity, and become what with her untrained mind she greatly admired, an investigator, elucidating the social problem.'[79]

In the early twentieth century charitable activists, however professional, looked increasingly old-fashioned to social reformers in the

Liberal and Labour parties. Household visiting became an easy target. In the Royal Commission on the Poor Laws (1905–9), one witness said that it was necessary 'to abolish district visitors and to educate the clergy'. The commission noted that the number of people who take the trouble to give wisely to charity remained small compared with the number of givers, and that 'the wisdom required is so great that perhaps the numbers will always remain small'. Such criticism was meat and drink to those who sought a radical overhaul of the social services and a more comprehensive system of relief. Such reformers often equated charity workers with sectarian busybodies, so many Mrs Pardiggles and Drusilla Clacks, people of privilege who propped up an outmoded social order. The fact that the vast majority of visitors were women, in a society in which men often dismissed the work of women, did not bode well for philanthropists in the battle of ideas.[80]

Since women were the backbone of the visiting movement and other charitable campaigns, it is worth asking whether the growing authority of women in charity predisposed male planners to favour political programmes that were relatively free from female interference or control. Arguably, the evolution of the state welfare services, created and dominated by men, was not unaffected by the feminization of philanthropy that took place in the nineteenth century. The philanthropist Josephine Butler argued in 1869 that large legislative welfare systems were 'masculine' in character, while the parochial system of personal ministration, with its corollary of re-creating domestic life in institutions, was essentially 'feminine'.[81] The fact that Beatrice Webb (who rejected her Christian upbringing) was a leading advocate of a system of state-based welfare illustrates the limitations of such a generalization, but the distinction pervades the literature.

As both Butler and Webb recognized, Poor Law and Home Office officials were often unsympathetic to women volunteers, who wished to minister to individuals; and they had no wish to pay for the amenities that women often wanted to improve workhouse and prison conditions. As Louisa Twining, the secretary of the Workhouse Visiting Society, discovered, women visitors to public institutions were frequently accused of uninformed meddling, which their reputation for compassion compounded.[82] Mr Lydgate, the provincial doctor in George Eliot's *Middlemarch*, expressed a common male prejudice about women on first meeting the charitable Dorothea Brooke: 'She is a good creature—that fine girl—but a little too earnest. . . . It is troublesome to talk to such women. They are always wanting reasons, yet they are too ignorant to understand the merits of any question, and usually fall back on their moral sense to settle things after their own taste.'[83]

When the Home Office took over responsibility for the prison service in 1877 and centralized the system under a Prison Commission, the notion of treating prisoners as part of an extended family—a goal of Elizabeth Fry—was seen as both alien and unmanly. Under the government inspectorate a 'secret world' developed in which there was little scope for women visitors. But government officials were not the only ones to criticize female philanthropists. Political economists often complained of their amateurish and sentimental activities.[84] In turn, female philanthropists, who found the 'dismal science' lacking in humanity, often resented 'masculine officialism' and criticized government bureaucracy as inflexible.[85] Women stood to lose power in a politicized system of relief, yet entering the world of government service offered potential opportunities to extend female influence.

The charitable experience of women was not straightforward, nor easy to categorize. Benevolent women found themselves torn between a desire to express their compassion, which pushed them towards politics and the wider world, and their desire to be modest and unassuming, which kept them back. For some, charity was little more than a consolation, or a break from domestic routine. But for many others it was a liberating influence, which served to promote female emancipation. Despite its conservative associations, charitable activity was a lever that women used to open the doors closed to them in other spheres, not least politics.[86] Typically, the women who grew up in Victorian and Edwardian Britain to become prominent in public life had a religious upbringing and district-visiting experience. Think of Octavia Hill (1838–1912), a founder of the COS, who was celebrated for her work in housing reform and the Open Space movement. Take Dame Millicent Fawcett (1847–1929), the leader of the women's suffrage movement, who was in and out of charitable campaigns all her life. Or take Eleanor Rathbone (1872–1946), the MP and advocate of family allowances, whose extensive philanthropic work, dating to her religious childhood, was a formative influence in the development of her social policy.[87]

As such careers illustrate, charitable work was applicable to just about every profession in Britain. Through their extensive contacts with charitable organizations women increased their interest in government, administration, and the law. In particular, district visiting propelled women into working with Poor Law and school boards and increased their interest in the problems of poverty, welfare reform, and ultimately politics. Gradually they were mastering skills suited to Poor Law administration and local government as well as social work. As a religion of action, visiting, like charity generally, slowly challenged the complaisancy of women, gave them practical responsibility, and heightened their self-confidence. Whether visiting disciplined the poor is questionable, but it certainly disciplined generations of women visitors. 'The practice of . . . superintending the poor', wrote Lucy Aikin in 1841, 'has become so general, that I know no one circumstance by which the manners, studies and occupations of Englishwomen have been so extensively modified, or so strikingly contradistinguished from those of a former generation.'[88]

In the nineteenth century there were few opportunities for the employment of middle-class women beyond philanthropy, but as other work became available they often turned their attention to fields for which philanthropy was a preparation. Women with backgrounds in charitable work were elected to the new school boards as early as 1870. Five years later the voters of Kensington elected the first woman, Martha Merrington, as a Poor Law guardian. By 1898 there were 950 women guardians.[89] In 1894 the Local Government Act established the right of women to be elected as urban or rural district councillors and parish councillors.[90] In 1920 Clement Attlee, who had lectured at the LSE and whose mother had been a district visitor for her church, listed fifteen careers open to women with experience in voluntary social service, from inspectors under the Midwives Act to managers of labour exchanges.[91] As the prejudice against women in local government, medicine, and the law eroded, recruitment to the visiting societies suffered, especially among women of advanced views.

The Church of England presented the most enduring 'wall of prejudice' to women. This was deeply ironic, for arguably it was in the service of religion that women had made their most notable contribution to society. While the church warmed to government intervention, it failed to do much to improve the status of women in its ministry. The Revd R. W. Harris, addressing a Church Congress in 1902, took the familiar line on women taking up formal positions in the church: 'your real influence does not lie in public life and never will. It lies in the power you exert over men, individually and personally.'[92] In 1920 a report presented to the Lambeth Conference on the position of women conceded that the church had 'failed to treat women workers with generosity or even with justice', but reminded the bishops of 'the elementary facts of human nature', and quoted the scriptures: 'She shall be saved through her child-bearing.'[93]

The Church of England's opposition to the ordination of women and its failure to reward their pastoral work in the early decades of the twentieth century had effects that should not be overlooked. Women were well aware of the extraordinary contribution made by their sex to the work of the churches in the nineteenth century. (They collected their own statistics on such issues.)[94] Meanwhile, the extension of the suffrage to women heightened their expectations of church reform. The lack of recognition—and salaries—for their pastoral service came as a bitter blow to many women, particularly church feminists, who saw feminism advancing on other fronts. Frustrated, some of them drifted away from parochial and charitable work into the careers opening up for women, which helps to account for the drop in the number of district visitors in the Church of England after the First World War.[95]

The war itself sent out mixed signals to charitable campaigners. It offered them fresh opportunities but tested their resolve and their finances. Wartime drives took away erstwhile subscribers, while operating costs escalated. Yet institutions old and new were zealous in support of the British cause. Though rarely keeping up with demand, the public generously supported societies and funds set up for servicemen and their families. The Red Cross alone raised £21 million through wartime appeals.[96] During the conflict 10,000 new societies were founded, from King George's Fund for Sailors to Miss Gladys Story's Fund for Bovril.[97] The royal family, led by the formidable charitable campaigner Queen Mary, took the lead in various relief schemes. Among the most significant was the National Relief Fund, popularly known as 'the Prince of Wales's Fund'. It worked closely with government departments and eventually channelled nearly £7 million into military, naval, and civil relief through existing charities before it was wound up in 1921.[98]

Among the more interesting institutions created during the war were the Women's Institutes, founded in 1915 to assist in food production, improve housewifery, and generally represent the interests of rural women. From early on they received support from the Board of Agriculture, which was happy to assist voluntary organizations that could help address the immediate problem of food shortages. In a period when voluntary bodies found it increasingly difficult to be self-supporting, the Women's Institutes joined the growing number of charities happy to accept state funding.[99] Unlike more traditional women's organizations, such as the Mothers' Union, it sought to bring women together across class and religious lines. In keeping with shifting attitudes towards religious instruction elsewhere, its constitution prohibited discussion of denominational issues.[100]

As the National Relief Fund and the Women's Institutes suggest, the First World War allied charity to national purpose—and the priorities of government—to a degree unknown since the Napoleonic wars. But as issues of health and welfare shot upwards on the political agenda, the war exposed the shortcomings of charity and pointed to the need for greater state assistance. The war effort drew heavily on church and charitable institutions for recruits, and as the years passed and the casualties mounted, it fractured parish life and dealt a blow to religious observance. As men went to the front, the women who took over their jobs had less time to give to those institutions that might otherwise have filled their idle hours. In a conflict of such dimensions few charities were unaffected, from parish visiting societies to the COS, which felt the effects of a general reassessment of voluntary policy taking place at the time. As early as 1915 the *Charity Organisation Review* reported that the conflict was reducing the number of volunteers turning up for work at charitable agencies.[101] With ever more distractions and rival centres of loyalty, charities had to adapt or decline.

Christian visiting struggled but was far from exhausted in the inter-war years. In the Church of England alone there were 74,647 district visitors at work in 1918, and still 59,292 of them in 1939.[102] But in a world in which religious zeal was in decline and government planning on the rise, charitable institutions found themselves increasingly stretched. As the government took over greater and greater responsibility in the inter-war years for housing, health, education, and welfare, the visiting societies, like other voluntary institutions, felt increasingly uneasy about their capacity to cope. Government expenditure on the social services, which was £2.4 per head of population in 1918, rose to £12.5 by 1938.[103] Meanwhile, the number of established civil servants, most of them men, had risen to 387,000, 10 per cent of the working population.[104] The expansion was to a large extent accounted for by the growth in the welfare services, activities once monopolized by the charitable sector.

A shifting boundary in the delivery of services between the state and voluntary organizations was a feature of the early decades of the twentieth century.[105] But for all the growth in government welfare spending and the number of established civil servants, successive inter-war governments failed to tackle social issues head on, which gave impetus to charitable work. Between the wars many of the advances in policy continued to depend on charitable service.[106] The poor themselves, as ever, carried out a great deal of both charity and mutual aid. Meanwhile, women's organizations blossomed, not least to promote birth control and children's health, areas of long-standing interest to district visitors. But for those who thought more deeply about social policy, there was a growing assumption that the state was better equipped to provide uniform provision across the country, and that only the state had the financial wherewithal to address the level of need. A growing number concluded that the voluntary sector was better suited to identifying new areas of social concern and successfully lobbying to meet particular needs.

Whether they wished to or not, many charitable campaigners spent more and more of their time with the statutory services, or serving on care committees, pensions' committees, and trade boards. Recognizing their financial constraints, charitable campaigners were now more amenable to partnerships, willing, as Loch put it, to take shelter with the state 'like creatures in a storm'.[107] Like other COS leaders, Loch, who resigned as secretary in 1914, had become increasingly out of touch with the rising currents in British life. The society's insistence that the self-reliant individual was the solution to social ills, which had its basis in the Christian conception of personality, had lost much of its attraction, while its dislike of government intervention blinded it to the implications of Liberal social legislation. The belief that government intervention was by its very nature corrupt and demoralizing found more fertile soil in America, where Loch had visited in 1896. After the First World War the COS was steadily losing ground to less ideological organizations such as the Guilds of Help and the Councils of Social Service, which were committed to greater cooperation with government.[108]

Despite the lingering antagonism between voluntarists and state officials, which was particularly marked in discussions of the future of the voluntary hospitals, where valuable properties were at stake, the inter-war years witnessed growing collaboration between voluntary and public bodies. By the mid-1930s it was estimated that 37 per cent of the total income of the charities of England came from payments for services from public authorities.[109] The calls for a more professional relationship were partly a result of the inability of charity to cope on its own with the daunting social problems created by unemployment, and partly a result of the shift in attitudes towards the nature of poverty. The momentum was on the side of those who favoured greater state intervention. In the charitable sector a significant minority, represented by the National Council of Social Service, which received two-thirds of its income from central and local government sources, spearheaded the campaign to forge a more professional and effective partnership with government.[110]

The ideal of state partnership was sometimes called 'the new philanthropy', the title of a book by the eminent social worker Elizabeth Macadam (1934). Though its claim to originality has been overstated, 'the new philanthropy' encouraged a more predominant role for the state in the social services. In accepting bureaucratic regulation, it had an underlying materialistic ethos that further narrowed discussion of voluntary activity to the relief of poverty. For many charities, state partnership meant that they would have to relinquish some of their independence, and set aside their religious concerns in favour of secular social work.[111] Those institutions sensitive about their independence, or their religious principles, simply shifted their functions into areas where partnership with the state was unnecessary. Many of the small, inter-war visiting societies carried on pretty much as in the past, showing little interest in calls to work more closely with the statutory services. For them, and other parish charities, the Second World War was a calamity.

The impact of the Second World War on state social policy has attracted such attention that its impact on the churches and the voluntary sector has been obscured. As in 1914, the crisis posed both a threat and a challenge. Churches and charities responded to the emergency with improvisation and dedication, from looking after evacuated mothers to knitting socks for the Soviet army.[112] But the continual calling up of their personnel for the forces put them under enormous strain. Thousands of clerics became chaplains to the forces. Meanwhile, many women left their parish institutions to join the Women's Voluntary Service (WVS), which was set up in 1938 to carry out a range of social services at the behest of government.[113] The shift to a war footing led to smaller congregations and dramatic changes in visiting practices. A familiar pattern emerged in churches and chapels across British cities. As Donald Soper, the Christian socialist superintendent of the West London Mission, lamented: 'congregations evaporated, coffers depleted, subscriptions halved.'[114] Church membership in his own congregation at Hinde Street dropped from 180 in 1939 to 107 in 1947. During the Blitz, the Mission turned its buildings into bomb shelters and designated its hall as a Rest and Feeding Centre. It was fortunate to escape with only modest bomb damage.[115]

The Second World War took a much heavier toll of the infrastructure of Britain than the First. Nothing in history so unsettled traditional visiting practices. Nearly 4 million houses—almost one-third of the total housing stock—were damaged or destroyed in the bombing raids.[116] London was particularly hard hit, though other cities, including Plymouth, Hull, and Coventry, also suffered disproportionate losses. The effect on district visitors was little less than catastrophic, as those who still turned up for work often found nothing but ruins, or families broken up by the evacuation of children. In the first three days of the war one-and-a-half million people, including 827,000 schoolchildren, retreated to the countryside.[117] The most destructive phase of the aerial bombardment that ended in June 1941 left about 2,225,000 people homeless. It also damaged or destroyed up to 4,000 schools, many of them religious establishments, which represented about 20 per cent of all primary and secondary schools in England and Wales.[118] Meanwhile, the large number of voluntary hospitals and dispensaries damaged or destroyed by German aerial attacks across the country placed an enormous burden on charitable finances and undermined morale in the voluntary hospital sector, weakening its negotiating position with government.[119]

Importantly for the history of visiting—and Christianity—the Blitz devastated a large number of churches and chapels, city missions, and other religious institutions. By 1942 over 1,000 Anglican places of worship, from parish churches to Lambeth Palace and Coventry Cathedral, had been destroyed or badly damaged, a number that rose in 1944 with the onset of flying bombs.[120] Tellingly, the Church of

England stopped providing statistics on the number of district visitors early in the war. The devastation was so significant that it destabilized traditional parish life in the church and required a new system of parochial organization to be created.[121] The Methodists had, if anything, more to endure, for the Blitz destroyed or badly damaged 2,600 of their churches out of a total of 9,000 in Britain. Across the denominations, it was estimated that 15,000 ecclesiastical buildings, including churches, convents, and mission halls, suffered damage.[122] The number represented one building damaged or destroyed for every parish in England and Wales. The loss of spiritual and social capital, built up over the centuries, was immeasurable.

Whatever the effect of aerial bombardment on religious belief, it dealt a serious blow to religious observance and charitable practice in Britain. It was not surprising that church attendance and visiting numbers fell during the war. For a start, there were fewer clergymen available to perform services and oversee parish charities, as many of them died or had commitments elsewhere. Many a churchman, having lost both his church and congregation through air raids, 'found his life's work brought to a calamitous end'.[123] In the industrial cities, where the bombing was most acute, the supply of ordinands and curates in the Church of England dried up. In Birmingham, for example the number of curates fell from 178 in 1939 to thirty eight in 1948.[124] Even in the south of England, the number of curates after the war was only 60 per cent of pre-war levels. In 1914 there had been 20,000 Anglican clergy at work in England and Wales. By 1950 there were only 15,000, which meant only one parish priest for every 5,000 people in London, Liverpool, and Manchester.[125] Social dislocation, lack of funds, and cultural change contributed to the decline in religious commitment and denominational discipline, but there were also fewer churches to fill. Many of those destroyed were never reconstructed.[126]

As A. J. P. Taylor put it, 'the *Luftwaffe* was a powerful missionary for the welfare state'.[127] As religious and charitable institutions collapsed into rubble, state planning blossomed. During the war, partnerships between charities and government departments increasingly enmeshed volunteers in bureaucratic regulation. The Emergency Medical Service, a centralized state agency empowered by the Ministry of Health, provided treatment for air-raid victims and transformed the hospital services. The war also saw the beginnings of the transference of voluntary social service to the local authorities.[128] Meanwhile, William Beveridge hammered home the persuasive thesis that unemployment was a problem of industry, not of personal character. His report, *Social Insurance and Allied Services*, published in 1942, called for a comprehensive social policy to tackle the evils of Want, Disease, Ignorance, Squalor, and Idleness. It provided a blueprint for post-war reconstruction through government planning. Few now praised charitable agencies as a democratic safeguard, or as Stanley Baldwin put it in the 1930s, 'a means of rescuing the citizen from the standardizing pressure of the state's mechanism'.[129]

A return to the pre-war compromise between state and voluntary social provision was not an option. As Beveridge put it, 'a people's war' required 'a people's peace'.[130] Reconstruction arrived under the post-war Labour government, which took key industries into public ownership and nationalized the health and social services under central control. The universal social-security system promised to protect every citizen from destitution and want. Meanwhile, the creation of the National Health Service pushed charitable campaigners to the periphery of the debate on health. The vast expansion of state-directed health and welfare services created widespread disarray in the voluntary sector. It was an especial blow to the visiting societies, which were still reeling from the afflictions of war. The 1948 National Assistance Act, which marked the end of the Poor Law, dealt a further blow, for it provided a safety-net for those who fell through the insurance system. What was the point of organized visiting and other forms of charity that provided material benefits in the post-war world of cradle-to-the-grave social provision from the state?

As the government's activity in the social sphere tended to divorce material from spiritual welfare, philanthropy became more a question of personal choice for Christians. Many of them, caught up in the post-war enthusiasm for state planning, felt that compulsory taxation was a more efficient way of promoting social justice than voluntary donations. State spending on the social services now dwarfed the funds available to charities. In 1951 government expenditure on the social services had risen to £44.4 per head of population, up from £12.5 in 1938.[131] Greater government spending was all the more necessary because of the erosion of charitable tithes and contributions. As Christian funds and enthusiasm declined, the individualist argument against state intervention largely disappeared from public view. The evangelical conscience, which had been the engine of so much social change in the past, was largely exhausted. Where it still flourished, it had, as often as not, been transformed into Christian socialism, as in the case of the irrepressible Donald Soper, who called on government to remedy social abuse from his soapbox in Hyde Park.[132]

Most people welcomed the expanding government services, not least leading churchmen, who had become highly sensitive to the issues of poverty and unemployment in the inter-war years.[133] In 1941 William Temple, appointed archbishop of Canterbury the following year, argued that the 'welfare state', a term then coming into favour, was an expression of national benevolence. 'The State', he declared, '. . . is a servant and instrument of God for the preservation of Justice and for the promotion of human welfare.'[134] The wartime experience of religious leaders was further proof, if proof were needed, that the churches and the voluntary services could not cope without massive assistance from government. A report presented to the Lambeth Conference in 1948 titled 'The Church and the Modern World' neatly summarized the Anglican hierarchy's view of the government takeover of responsibility for education and welfare, a transformation that Archbishop Temple called 'epoch-making in its consequences'.[135]

For this development the quickening of the social conscience, modern techniques, and the changing economic pattern are almost equally responsible. Certainly the motive, as Christians should gladly acknowledge, has been social justice and humanity as well as nationalism and industrial efficiency. The process has been accelerated as governments become sensitive to the views and needs of great industrial populations. Wars instead of delaying the process have hastened it by accustoming peoples to the mobilization of a nation's resources and manpower. . . . The process is inevitable; it is not likely to be reversed. None the less, it is presenting voluntary and free associations with new problems, and in particular is altering the boundaries of the respective spheres of Church and State.[136]

The report noted the 'delicate problem' presented by the 'omnicompetent' state to the Christian community. It warned of 'the natural bias of the state towards totalitarianism' and the need to promote local government and voluntary associations as a safeguard. 'Democracy', it declared, 'cannot work without the Christian qualities of self-restraint and discipline, and the training provided by Christian fellowship.'[137] But anxious to keep pace with social realities, the bishops passed a resolution at the Lambeth Conference in 1948 that echoed Archbishop Temple's wartime views: 'We believe that the State is under the moral law of God, and is intended by Him to be an instrument for human welfare. We therefore welcome the growing concern and care of the modern State for its citizens, and call upon Church members to accept their own political responsibility and to cooperate with the State and its officers in their work.'[138] In keeping with official opinion in the Church of England, the archbishop of York, Cyril Garbett, declared that the welfare state embodied 'the law of Christ'.[139] Such opinions, unexceptional at the time, were, to use Temple's words, 'epoch making' in the history of the church.

The shift of opinion in the church hierarchy was understandable given the level of social deprivation and a demoralized charitable sector. The bishops continued to see a need for voluntary agencies, working with the state services. But the Lambeth Conference resolution endorsing the welfare state dealt a crushing blow to parish charity. For reasons of doctrine and limited resources, regular parochial visiting was consciously 'abandoned' in the Church of England. The loss to the community did not go unnoticed. Archbishop Garbett witnessed the process: 'It is almost impossible to exaggerate the greatness of the loss when there is no regular pastoral visitation.'[140] But swept up in the tide of nationalization, churchmen discarded the parochial idealism that had motivated their Victorian forebears. They consoled themselves with the argument that the state had a 'moral and spiritual function' and was essentially Christian.[141] They did not make an issue of the connection between the rise of state social provision and the decline of Christian observance, if only because they continued to believe that the state was acting on Christian principles. But as government took over primary responsibility for social welfare, the church was 'in practice disestablished'.[142]

The Church of England's shifting views on social policy in the first half of the twentieth century, capped by its post-war approbation of the welfare state, played a more significant part in the decline of religious observance than might be imagined, if only because parish societies so often connected the citizenry, particularly women, to religious institutions. The decision to bow to the state was fashionable, perhaps irresistible, at the time; but it was to have unintended consequences. After all, it was the welfare role of religion that made it relevant to society. As long as the churches had an obvious social purpose, they retained an appeal to those with a sense of civic responsibility. In relegating Christianity's historic charitable role to the sidelines, they estranged many traditional parishioners.[143] What was the point of worshipping in Westminster Abbey when Jesus, now a socialist, had departed for Whitehall?

Contemporaries noted a falling off in church attendance at the end of the war. It was 'indisputable', observed a report on religion in England issued by the Anglican Church in 1945, 'that only a small percentage of the nation to-day joins regularly in public worship of any kind'.[144] In the late 1940s and early 1950s a desire to return to traditional values encouraged increased church membership and Sunday school enrolment, but the trend was short-lived.[145] Given the reduced status of charity, a return to 'practical Christianity' was an uphill struggle. With the cultural revolution of the 1960s, a return to Christian piety could not be sustained. Children, as noted earlier, fled their Sunday schools and reshaped their lives in secular recreations. Women, once the backbone of church membership and parish charity, reshaped theirs 'within work, sexual relations and new recreational opportunities'.[146] Christianity and feminism, highly compatible to nineteenth-century women campaigners, had diverged.

District visiting societies, with their age-old links to women and religion, suffered more than most charities in the post-war years. Visiting society after society collapsed for want of money, volunteers, and purpose. (Against the tide of closures, the Church of Scotland engaged thousands of visitors in a campaign called 'Visitation Evangelism' between 1947 and 1956.)[147] Many visitors gave up and moved on, their enthusiasm for social engagement exhausted. Others stayed on in an altered role. Others still found employment in the state services. Among the casualties in the shift to secular social work was the Ranyard Mission. During the First World War the 'Bible woman' had turned into a diocesan social worker and her title was changed to 'Mission worker'. The charity's faith and money finally ran out in 1953, when the mission abandoned the social-work side of its operations. Its old ally, the once mighty COS, which had placed the methods of social science above the virtues of Christian service, was more resilient. In 1946 it changed its name to the Family Welfare Association and narrowed its remit.

The transition 'from charity to social work' had been decisive. In 1960 there were nearly 40,000 employees in the state welfare services.[148] By this time the number of district visitors, once perhaps numbering as many as 200,000, had been so dramatically reduced that official records no longer recorded their existence. Before long organized visiting was so uncommon that many social workers did not realize that their forerunners were missionaries. Some institutions, among them the Salvation Army and various city missions, continued household visits to those who fell through the government's safety-net, but they had to adapt their practices to suit the purposes of social workers.[149] Jesus, the 'Heavenly Visitor', would have been found unfit for modern social work. The religion of visiting, of neighbourliness, and personal ministration had been shattered by social science, war, church policy, and collective provision.

4

Mothering

A child left to himself bringeth his mother to shame.

(Proverbs 29: 15)

Only God can create a mother. But Society needs a great deal of mothering, much more than it gets.

(Gen. William Booth, *In Darkest England and the Way Out*, 1890)

'The nation comes from the nursery,' declared Samuel Smiles '. . . and the best philanthropy comes from the fireside.'[1] No other institution better expressed that most powerful and compelling image of philanthropy than the mothers' meeting, which centred on the nursery and the fireside. The image of a mother with a child in her arms—the symbol of charity in art—served as a badge for innumerable charities dedicated to the health and happiness of the British family, but in the mothers' meeting it was life itself. The assembled women, surrounded by their children in needlework and prayer, merged the maternal and familial ideal with the religious. To Victorians, who deified the domestic, they were Christian charity incarnate.

For nearly a century mothers' meetings were a crucial agency in British social service. They are now little remembered except by members of societies that carry on the tradition in an altered form. (Mothers' meetings were socially distinct from ladies' sewing parties, which made goods for sale to charity.) Sometimes called mothers' classes or maternal associations, they were so widespread by the late nineteenth century that perhaps as many as a million women and children attended them regularly. Most married women from the poorer classes either turned up at a meeting or were invited to do so. Most middle-class women with religious enthusiasm either ran one or were under pressure to do so. They may be seen as part of the great Christian crusade to convert the nation and in so doing create a common culture. To sustain that crusade, it was imperative to promote the spiritual and material welfare of working-class mothers and their young, who were often strangers to religious institutions. Like the Sunday school, the mothers' meeting became vital to the transmission of the faith. The assembled mothers were to ensure that the habits of Christian authority and benevolence passed from generation to generation.

As with so many unostentatious charitable institutions, it is impossible to put a precise date on the first mothers' meeting. But it has been argued that Elizabeth Twining, the sister of the workhouse reformer Louisa Twining, set up the earliest one in about 1850, which she attached to a ragged school in Clare Market, the site of the present LSE.[2] Several ladies connected to the London City Mission (1835) formed another one in Davies Street, Berkeley Square, in July 1852. It expanded, divided, and established the formula of needlework and religious instruction typical of the mission's many other meetings over the next hundred years.[3] Mary Bayly, the author of *Ragged Homes and How to Mend Them*, established another class in the potteries area of Kensington in 1853. The poor women who turned up looked on her, in her words, 'as they would have done at the entrance of the white bear at the Zoological Gardens'.[4] The Ragged School Union adopted Bayly's experiment and eventually ran about 200 weekly meetings from its schools and mission rooms.[5] For her part, Ellen Ranyard met her first group of wives and mothers in London in 1857, and ten years later her charity was renting 230 mission rooms in London alone to provide accommodation for its weekly classes.[6]

Established by virtually every religious denomination, mothers' meetings sprang up around the country in the mid-Victorian years, in remote rural areas and city slums. In Bradford, the Town Mission sought to promote churchgoing among 'careless wives' through fortnightly meetings.[7] In Lambeth, a London borough not noted for a high level of religious observance, Anglicans and Nonconformists eventually ran fifty-seven meetings.[8] The mothers' meeting was in the ascendant when Mary Sumner, wife of a leading churchman and mother of three, founded the Mothers' Union in 1876. As she saw it, the mission of the society was to 'reinstate the home into its true position as the primal training place for children', and thus mothers' meetings became central to her purposes.[9] The Mothers' Union soon became one of the most formidable societies in the Church of England, with a membership that rose to over 400,000 women on the eve of the First World War.[10] Such institutional support turned the humble mothers' meeting into the most pervasive female agency for bringing women together on a regular basis outside the home in British history. Not even the expanding female trade unions could match the membership figures for mothers' meetings.

Successful at home, mothers' meetings spread abroad, wherever British women were found as missionaries, wives of missionaries, or simply in residence.[11] No other charitable agency took up the specific issue of working-class mothers and their children with greater enthusiasm. Geared to the perceived needs of underprivileged women, mothers' meetings became, as one philanthropist put it, 'part of the work of every organization seeking to help the poor'.[12] No other agency, save district visiting, worked more assiduously to bring domestic order to the lives of poor families, and it did so without having to knock on their doors. One male witness remarked that, along with district nursing, the mothers' meeting represented 'the most practical and successful' philanthropic work of women.[13] After dropping in on the class in Davies Street, Berkeley Square, Lord Shaftesbury hailed the mothers' meeting as 'one of the most remarkable inventions of modern times'.[14]

What brought the mothers' meeting into existence? In the broadest sense it was a peculiarly female response to the problems and opportunities associated with economic and religious change. In other words, it was an aspect of what may be described as a maternal culture that began to take institutional form in a century of religious activism. In keeping with the social attitudes of Victorian Christians, privileged women shared many of the assumptions that commonly are labelled paternalistic. Like paternalists they believed that society should be organic and pluralistic, led by people of property with a sense of social responsibility. But as they saw themselves as different from men, with different sources of information and inspiration, they translated these assumptions into something distinctively female in their parish work. In their domestic routine they displayed those qualities that were habitually described as feminine and motherly, among them compassion, tenderness, and self-sacrifice. As commercial expansion gave them the leisure to join or to run their own charities, female campaigners redirected these maternal qualities to the world outside their homes. By definition, the meetings were an exclusive organization and their expansion an expression of a vital maternal culture with financial resources.

Christianity, it was argued, gave enormous scope to women as wives and mothers and, by extension, enormous benefits to society. From their domestic citadel women could make forays to spread that tenderness and compassion, thought to personify the female character, through society. Insofar as the family was seen as the foundation of education, it honoured women, whose educational role in the family was rarely challenged. Insofar as religion was seen as the foundation of family life, it flattered women, who were reputed for their piety. Naturally enough, women turned their attention to causes in tune with their own experience and their own values, most notably those connected with women and children. That the government was unwilling or unable to contribute much to these causes was a considerable stimulus. So too was the hesitancy of many philanthropic men, who were poorly equipped to pursue charitable practices which were assumed to be decidedly female in character. But it was said that the so-called female traits were simply a reflection of woman's dependence, the by-products of lives narrowly confined to home and family.

Like medieval churchmen who fell back on morality to increase their power in a society dominated by an armed aristocracy, women cleverly exploited the belief in their superior morality to increase their power in a society dominated by men. They could only give up a belief in the distinctions between the sexes at some peril.

The charitable activity most common among women who established mothers' meetings was district visiting, which, as noted in the previous chapter, was widespread by the 1830s. Female visitors pointed out the desirability of bringing poor women together on a regular basis, free from the isolation of their homes. As one writer remarked in the 1870s: 'almost every district visitor has a mothers' meeting.'[15] Yet many meetings were unconnected with any formal society and began simply out of religious zeal and social conscience. For clergymen's wives, running a meeting became virtually obligatory. They and other women with a strong parochial sense cleverly took advantage of the opportunities afforded by the informality in church or chapel life, which was most notable in evangelical communities. But whatever the origins of the meetings, they may be seen as a form of female religious and community life carried on with the blessing of church or chapel, but little subject to clerical restrictions. The mothers' meeting gave women the freedom to preach without offending churchmen, and an opportunity to convert and to assist poor wives independent of their husbands.

As part of maternal culture, the mothers' meeting was justified and ennobled by scripture. As in their other charitable activities, philanthropic women scoured the Bible for references that would testify to their claims for a wider role in missionary work and social reform. Dorcas, a woman who made garments for the poor (Acts 11: 36), gave her name to countless Dorcas meetings in the nineteenth century, which supplied clothing to missionary stations. Phoebe, called 'deaconess' in the original Greek Version (Romans 16: 1), was invariably cited as a justification for the deaconess movement in the Church of England. Could churchmen oppose a mothers' meeting, when a virtuous woman 'spreadeth out her hand to the poor; yea, she reacheth forth her hands to the needy' (Proverbs 31: 20)? Could a husband oppose a meeting, when 'a child left to himself bringeth his mother to shame' (Proverbs 29: 15)? 'Suffer the little children to come unto me', said Jesus (Mark 10: 14), and so the Victorians sought to follow his example, not least through the agency of benevolent mothers.

At the heart of mothers' meetings, for many of those who ran them, was the example of Jesus. There had been 'a halo . . . above the head of every true mother since Jesus was born of Mary', remarked an Edwardian missioner to an annual diocesan service.[16] Christ's respect for motherhood and concern for children was ritually celebrated by Christian women. So inspired, they let flow that maternal missionary zeal, which they called love, and broke out of their own domestic routine to extend those domestic Christian influences to less privileged women. No other institution was in greater accord with middle-class Victorian attitudes towards family life and the place of women than the mothers' meeting. Whether conscious of it or not, the women who ran the meetings exploited that public respect for the family as a means of emancipation from their homes. Catherine Booth, a pioneer of women's work in the Salvation Army, had her husband William Booth just where she wanted him when he wrote: 'Only God can create a mother. But Society needs a great deal of mothering, much more than it gets'.[17]

Mothers' meetings would not have expanded so rapidly nor have been counted such a success if the poorer classes had stayed at home. Attendance at the meetings ranged from six or eight to hundreds, the average size being fifty or sixty.[18] One of the largest meetings was in Kilburn, London, in the 1890s, where 426 names were listed on the register, with an average weekly attendance of 310.[19] Some organizers frowned upon large meetings because there was little opportunity to get to know the members personally. All women were welcome, and a fair share of older girls and women without children attended. But the recruitment of working-class or cottage mothers, who were invited to bring their infants with them, was the priority. In an era when the industrialization of women's work outside the home had eroded traditional home-making skills, the organizers assumed that poor women were in desperate need of a domestic education.

As elsewhere in the charitable world, mothers' meetings were also an opportunity to pick up and hone administrative and social skills. Through running meetings and dealing with local traders, Poor Law guardians, and other societies, women developed habits of citizenship and association. Such habits did not accrue only to the many middle-class women involved. Just as working-class women played a part in the Sunday school movement, so they played a part in running mothers' meetings. Whether setting out on their own or working in concert with women of a higher social station, they had a particular knowledge of local conditions, which gave shape to many of the welfare schemes attached to the meetings. Moreover, they cast votes on rules and procedures, a privilege denied them elsewhere. The phrase 'nursery school of democracy' has especial meaning for the mothers' meeting.

The meetings ran weekly, sometimes fortnightly, and met for two hours or so during those times of the day when women were relatively free from domestic duties or the demands of husbands. (After 1870 more of their children would have been in school.) The organizers favoured weekday afternoons, or evenings in those communities where many women worked during the day. Churches, chapels, schoolrooms, libraries, and drawing-rooms were common venues. Mission halls, which were often built specifically for working-class religious purposes, were ideal settings for meetings. Attendance tended to be higher in the winter, when a fire was provided and Christmas promised a season of special events and entertainments. In the summer the poor were more often away from home and the heat made sitting in crowded rooms for long periods uncomfortable. Despite a high turnover of members, many meetings ran for decades and boasted dedicated women who continued to turn up in old age.

Why did so many women from the humbler classes join a mothers' meeting? The answer was obvious to the institution's promoters: all mothers had an instinctive desire to protect and to provide for their children.[20] Humble mothers, particularly those with absent, jobless, or drunken husbands, needed a strategy for the survival of their children; the mother's meeting offered a reliable source of material support and solidarity. To this end the meetings dwelled on those concerns common to women, such as needlework, childbirth, and the moral education of the young. Such matters brought women together who had little in common otherwise. The mothers' meetings suggested that sex was an important determinant in Victorian England, perhaps as important as class. In a world in which women were thought to have distinctive characteristics, in which women of all ranks could find themselves excluded and mistreated because of their sex, class differences and antagonisms between women could be set aside in the interests of female solidarity. This is not to say that meetings were free of class tension or that they all ran smoothly. Many a member left a mothers' meeting because she felt patronized or was not offered an opportunity to make her views heard.[21]

Most of the women who sponsored meetings were highly sensitive to the class distinctions that divided themselves from those they wished to benefit, and they sought to play them down by treating the poor with courtesy and respect. Comparing the privileged lives of educated women to the lot of the poor, Mrs Sumner remarked, 'I doubt if we could face their difficulties or live their lives as bravely and contentedly as they do'.[22] This remark displayed some self-knowledge, for Mrs Sumner, according to her granddaughter, never in her life had to put on her own stockings.[23] As a bastion of hierarchical, conservative values, the Mothers' Union was not among the more successful charities in breaking down class barriers, a fact the society frequently lamented.[24] It came to be seen, nonetheless, as 'the most important volunteer organization within the Church of England in the late Victorian and Edwardian period'.[25]

In setting up a mothers' meeting the priority was to create a happy working environment, an atmosphere in which the members felt comfortable. In most meetings one or two women supervised, though in the larger groups more assistance was required. Some women, of course, were better at putting members at their ease than others, but all wished to achieve it. Many of them, if we are to believe the charitable reports, also managed to form close and lasting friendships among their charges.[26] Mrs Henrietta Barnett, who with her husband Canon Barnett set up three mothers' meetings in the parish of St Jude's in the

East End in the 1870s, was in no doubt that the classes promoted friendships between organizers and humble mothers. Over twenty years after leaving the parish, she continued to receive numerous Christmas blessings from former members of her classes.[27]

In urban meetings it became common for working-class Bible women or missioners to help out, an idea pioneered by Mrs Ranyard. Often recruited from the meetings themselves, they spoke the language of the poor and came from the local neighbourhood. They were thus very useful in easing tensions and getting proceedings under way. The organizers insisted on setting a high moral tone, a spirit of mutual respect and reverence. Complaints about neighbours or other members were out of order. Sensitive to criticism that the members did not contribute enough themselves to the meetings, the wiser supervisors brought them into discussions and made sure that they voted on the rules governing their gatherings.[28] These and other means kept personal feuds and social differences from disrupting proceedings. There was often disruption enough coming from outside, especially in the slums. Reports were common of fights on the doorstep of mission halls, stones thrown through windows, and eggs pelted at the members. In Spitalfields, on one occasion, a black man barged into a meeting and danced in the midst of the assembled mothers.[29]

Mothers' meetings were an expression of a holistic view of human life. They were divided into two complementary parts, religious and secular, both of which were designed to promote family life among women who were often unruly and despairing. Many meetings, regardless of their particular faith, offered short stories or readings from poetry. Tennyson was a favourite. Catholic classes used the penny publications of the Catholic Truth Society, stories, or extracts from improving books. Evangelical meetings invariably opened and closed with a prayer, and usually contained a hymn. Typically, there was also a religious address, often in the form of a commentary on a tract or passage from scripture. This form of address was much favoured by women who might have liked to take holy orders. Many meetings resembled Bible classes, with extensive readings from the Old and New Testaments, especially those passages that touched on the role of women. The prayers and addresses were chosen with the needs of individual members in mind, so that, for example, a woman who had just lost a child would be singled out for sympathetic attention. Whatever form the address took, it usually lasted for twenty or thirty minutes and was defended on the grounds that poor mothers enjoyed listening to the educated reading aloud.

Though clerics or male missioners sometimes participated, the meetings were a distinctively female form of Christian worship that often served as a substitute for church or chapel attendance. Historians of religion have made little of it, but many meetings reached those levels of working-class life untouched by formal religion, especially in urban centres that were poorly served by the churches. As Mrs Barnett remarked, 'to be a member of a meeting may be very far from being a member of a church . . . but such membership may be preparation for the highest of all memberships in the body of Christ'.[30] The results of the 1851 religious census, which revealed the habitual neglect of public worship in many poor neighbourhoods, were a humiliation to Christian campaigners. In the London slums the Ranyard Mission assiduously recruited those women who considered themselves unfit for church or chapel services. So too did the London City Mission, which used specialist, paid male missioners and their wives to work among foreigners, gypsies, dockers, cabmen, and others who were little seen at Sunday worship.

For many women who had a vague sense of religion but who failed to attend church or chapel because of the distance, a husband's objection, or the want of a suitable dress, the local mothers' meeting provided a welcome alternative. Their letters attest to their gratitude, as well as to their religion. The poor 'Mothers of Millwall' wrote to Mrs Ranyard: 'It is now 6 years ago that through your kindness Mrs . . . opened our Mothers' Meeting in A Small Back Room. There was fifteen of us then but God has prospered us tenfold and the Meeting has been a Blessing to us our Homes and our Husbands but above all to our souls which were dead in trespasses and sins and are now alive unto God and His kingdom.'[31] One poor woman who wrote to Mrs Bayly spoke for many others when she said that her meeting had given her the sympathy of other women, a training for her children, the consolation of religion, and, not least, 'rest' from her arduous labours.[32]

Religion was crucial to a mothers' meeting, but the secular side of the programme proved very popular. Here the common denominator was needlework. Throughout a meeting the members were busy with their needles, which usually they were asked to supply. Both organizers and members agreed that sewing was invaluable in the domestic economy. Even in the late nineteenth century, most of the clothing of women and children was made at home, or in working parties or mothers' meetings. But to the organizers sewing had other advantages, which merged with female piety. Deeply ingrained in women's culture, needlework signified those feminine ideals of home, family, respectability, the suggestion of love for others.[33] During a meeting, it also provided an automatic distraction for the hands, which freed the mind to imbibe the religious message. With heads bowed over their needles, as if in prayer, members got on with domestic work that would otherwise have been done at home. As a historian of embroidery has argued, 'sewing allowed women to sit together without feeling they were neglecting their families, wasting time or betraying their husbands'.[34] Mrs Bayly discovered that husbands, even those hostile to religion, were reconciled to their wives joining a mothers' meeting because it provided clothing for the family without inconvenience to themselves.[35]

When the women arrived, usually wearing something black, they rummaged through a stock of prints, calicoes, and flannels piled on a table. The organizers took pride in the fact that the material provided was superior to the 'rubbish' found on local barrows, and they recognized that this was an attraction of the meetings. After the opening prayer and the taking of attendance, the supervisor organized the sale of the material and noted the purchases in a book set aside for this purpose. Apart from patterns, which were usually supplied free, little was provided that was not paid for. This was holy writ for most of the women who sponsored the meetings, for they were anxious to promote self-help and thrift and hoped that such attitudes would spill over into family life. Some meetings offered prizes for sewing competitions, but rarely were 'bribes' or other inducements permitted. Louisa Twining, who ran one of the more than a hundred weekly classes in connection with the Parochial Mission Women's Association in the 1870s, argued that cloth bought in bulk by the organizers and sold at cost to members offered sufficient inducement to mothers.[36] Few went away empty handed. As an institution providing necessities, the mothers' meeting, like the charity bazaar, may have checked the development of local retail shops.

As initially conceived, the mothers' meeting provided a form of discount fabric shopping in a convivial religious atmosphere, an opportunity to carry on sewing while listening to readings or picking up tips on domestic management. The interests and activities taking place in the meetings expanded considerably with the years, though religion and needlework remained constants. The beneficiaries could accept the religious indoctrination or simply feign respect for it. As suggested, the promoters knew that mothers, whatever their station or outlook, were not indifferent to their children's prospects. Most were grateful for the support and camaraderie that the meetings provided, and we should not assume that they were alienated by the homilies, which encouraged acceptable social behaviour in their children. Respectability, after all, was not the preserve of the rich, and the mothers' meeting was designed to bring respectability to the many women down the social scale who wanted it for themselves and their families.

It was always thought to be an advantage of mothers' meetings that they provided a refuge from domestic drudgery. The social investigator Charles Booth believed that they filled 'a real want', for they gave 'to tired and worried women a peaceful hour enlivened by conversation or reading aloud'.[37] It became painfully clear to not a few organizers that many poor women attended in order to escape from men. Their weekly fellowship with other women was the one 'bright spot' in the otherwise dreary routine, refreshment for 'the wounded spirit', to use the language of the day.[38] 'In one thing they were all agreed,' Mrs Ranyard observed after her first meeting, 'they all had bad husbands.'[39] Drink and familial violence were persistent problems in the slums and rural areas, and thus temperance and moral reform were high on the list of subjects discussed at mothers' meetings. The implications of mothers' meetings for the mental health of women should not be underestimated. Insofar as they kept families intact and out of pauperism, they were bound to have social benefits as well. But there was always the worry that by providing the necessities of family life, the mothers' meetings fostered intemperance among husbands.[40]

For the many women and children who were brutalized by drunken men in the past, the need for the reform of behaviour was no laughing matter. Social investigations are full of the most horrendous scenes of violent husbands undone by drink. The number of offences determined summarily for drunken and disorderly behaviour in England and Wales rose threefold between 1857 and 1876.[41] General Booth, no stranger to exaggeration, argued that 'nine-tenths of our poverty, squalor, vice, and crime spring from this poisonous tap root'.[42] Mothers' meetings, which provided solidarity and consolation to many long-suffering women, may be seen as one of the principal agencies to promote temperance. They were part of the long-standing female campaign to reform the nation's manners and morals. 'Reform the mothers', it was argued, 'and you begin at the root of our social evils.'[43] Out of such beliefs came ideas that were to have quite fascinating, unexpected repercussions, not least for men.

'Get at the mothers, and you'll get at the men of the nation.'[44] And so it turned out, though perhaps not quite as this mother intended. For, not satisfied with organizing women, the promoters of mothers' meetings organized men in what were called 'fathers' meetings' or 'men's classes'. The object was to round off the work of the maternal meeting, which was thought incomplete as long as husbands and fathers were neglected. Combined meetings in which working-class husbands and wives joined in prayer or Bible instruction were common enough in nineteenth-century charities. Mrs Pennefather, for example, ran one in her North London Training Home in the 1860s.[45] But one of the earliest meetings set up exclusively for fathers was operating in 1864 under the auspices of the Greenwich and Deptford Auxiliary of the London City Mission.[46] By 1872 the Ranyard Mission sponsored a fathers' class, with an attendance rising to 200 working men. Run along the lines of a mothers' meeting, it had a strong religious message tempered by practical instruction.[47] Needlework was not included, for it was thought inappropriate for grown men.

Though never ubiquitous, like the mothers' meetings, fathers' classes became increasingly common in the 1880s, perhaps because they offered popular activities such as hymn-singing and lectures on practical subjects. They were numerous in the Ragged School Union, for example, where along with parents' meetings and mothers' meetings they formed an integral part of that charity's temperance and missionary work.[48] The West London Mission, a Methodist society established in 1887, also ran men's classes alongside its mothers' meetings.[49] Whether run by the sisters as an adjunct to their maternal meetings, or by male missionaries, an essential purpose of such classes was to combat drink and promote male respect for Christian family life and motherhood. These were purposes in tune with those of the many other agencies of moral reform, such as the White Cross Army, which recruited large numbers of working-men in the 1880s.[50] The transformation of the relations between the sexes seemed all the more urgent to female reformers in a society in which so many men frequented those institutional expressions of working-class culture, the pub and the working-men's club.

Obviously, the campaign for the reformation of manners and morals was not altogether successful. Large numbers of working-men were reluctant to turn up at church or chapel, nor were they freed from their addiction to one-another as drinking companions. The fathers' meeting, like the mothers' meeting, now appears a historical curiosity. It could be argued that mothers' meetings and other forms of female philanthropy contributed to the popularity of pubs and other male working-class preserves, for in bringing women together outside the home, they left men to their own devices. Certainly, conflicts must have arisen between sober and pious wives and their less-than-temperate husbands, which raised tensions in working-class neighbourhoods. This, along with the antagonism between the rough and the respectable poor, helps to explain the eggs and stones that were hurled at women attending mothers' meetings.

Some of the ideas discussed in fathers' classes must also have alarmed many working-men (and may come as a surprise to us). In one piece of fathers'-meeting literature it was argued that when men marry they place their women on a level of 'complete equality', free 'to do as they please', and that wives had 'as much right' to a man's earnings as he had himself.[51] Women's rights were implicit in much mothers'-meeting literature as well. For many women, who interpreted scripture liberally, the inequalities between the sexes would disappear as Christianity advanced. One woman's reading of the Bible led her to the conclusion that Christianity supported equal pay for women and their right to sit on all public bodies on equal terms with men.[52] Most Victorian female reformers hailed religion as an emancipating influence.

The fathers' meeting suggests the dynamism of those familial ideals at the heart of maternal culture, but it was only one of many institutions with an essentially religious purpose that developed out of the ethos of the mothers' meeting. As we have seen, parish life was wonderfully rich in interrelated and mutually supporting voluntary societies. Indeed, the ideal of parochial service was predicated on the strength of these institutions. Many of them involved needlework in some way. At the heart of female culture in the nineteenth century, needlework was crucial to women's philanthropy at home and abroad. Middle-class working parties and Dorcas meetings supplied clothing to be sold or recycled in mothers' meetings. Mothers' meetings, in turn, not only produced garments for the use of members, but frequently contained their own Dorcas societies, which sent clothing to foreign mission stations to be distributed by the wives of missionaries.[53]

As it reached young mothers and infants, the mothers' meeting was seen as a crucial training ground of religious experience. And while it sought to promote church or chapel attendance, it promoted a host of closely related institutions which, like itself, often served as a substitute for church or chapel; among these were prayer meetings, maternity societies for pregnant women, Bible classes, temperance societies, juven-ile missionary associations, and Bands of Hope, which provided respectable recreation for children. Invariably, mothers and their young were encouraged to join one or more of these gatherings, which carried on the work of evangelizing in another form. Ideally, as the younger generation of girls became wives themselves, they would return to the mothers' meeting, which had initiated their religious edu-cation. So the Christian cycle turned.

Class, regional, and religious differences ensured that mothers' meetings were richly various. A gathering of the Mothers' Union among cottage wives in a lady's drawing-room in rural Devon would seem a strange world to the women who attended a class in a mission hall in a Liverpool slum. But whatever their setting or character, the meetings sought to promote schemes relevant to local needs. Across the country, one major problem was the irregular management of domestic finance, usually blamed on husbands, which compelled many wives to have recourse to pawnshops.[54] Fathers' classes were eventually part of the campaign to regulate household expenditure. But from the early years, savings banks or provident societies became associated with mothers' meetings and spread widely. Thrift, it should be remembered, was a sign of respectability among the labouring classes; it did not have to be imposed from above.[55] In the first ten years of its operations, Mrs Ranyard's Mission collected £44,000 for clothing and furniture through provident schemes.[56] It was assumed that people with property were respecters of property.

By the end of the century the range of social schemes, activities, and entertainments was phenomenal. Clothing, boot, blanket, and coal clubs were commonly attached to mothers' meetings and augmented the savings banks and thrift societies. In addition to its penny banks and clothing clubs, the West London Mission provided 'numerous small pensions' for needy senior members of its meetings. Here was a clever application of the bazaar to social purposes, for they were financed from sales of work.[57] The meeting in Kilburn, though unusually large, was not untypical of urban gatherings. In the 1890s it boasted a blanket club, a medical club, a doctor's fund, a sick benefit society, a lending library with 320 volumes, and a crèche in an adjoining room.[58] Other meetings lent saucepans, sold recipes, or offered lantern lectures, reading classes, singing classes, and country holidays. Most hosted annual parties and outings and provided the ubiquitous teas. All in all they could be marvellously adaptable institutions, wrapped in Godliness, which saturated the poor with an ingenious mix of benevolence and self-help. It is not surprising that they were so popular with the labouring classes, though not, presumably, with the pawnbrokers. It was common for charities to 'sift' through their members to get rid of 'travellers', who went from meeting to meeting taking advantage of the benefits.[59]

With the years, more and more attention was given over to an expansion of the mothers' meeting as a clearing-house of information on family welfare. From the early days talks on cookery, diet, and health, and the management of babies were common. The pioneers of the movement recognized that it was easier to give hints on cleanliness and sanitation to poor women in meetings rather than in their own homes, where they were more inclined to be affronted.[60] The Ladies Sanitary Association (1857), which produced millions of tracts on public health and related matters, paid tribute to the growing importance of the meetings when it declared that they were 'just the opportunities for imparting sanitary knowledge to poor mothers'.[61] With the assistance of institutions such as the Ladies Sanitary Association and the Charity Organisation Society, the meetings gradually became more informative and less amateurish. As Henrietta Barnett put it, readings from 'goody-goody books' were dropped in favour of talks on more relevant matters. In her own meetings she and her husband introduced illustrated newspapers to help explain public events.[62]

Any issue with domestic implications became suitable for discussion at a mothers' meeting, from infant welfare to the state of the housing market, from venereal disease to votes for women.[63] Such issues led female philanthropists into little-known territory, not least the male preserve of government. In their view, stable family life would render state activity in social policy unnecessary. Yet those who promoted mothers' meetings called for government action on specific issues. As early as the 1850s, Mrs Bayly asked for greater state involvement in sanitation and housing.[64] Whether shy of the state or not, female philanthropists kept in close touch with government proposals affecting family life. The Mothers' Union, for example, sought to influence legislation on issues such as education and housing.[65] In 1910 it gave evidence to a Royal Commission on marriage and divorce. Thus the tendrils of the humble mothers' meeting reached the corridors of power in the state.

As practical, temporal activities came to the fore, a subtle shift in tone and emphasis can be detected in mothers' meetings. The many references to parties, outings, and teas suggest the growing importance of the meetings in the recreational lives of members and their families, especially in the country and in those communities where entertainments were in short supply. In many meetings the religious emphasis gradually diminished, perhaps because of pressure from a membership more interested in diversions and physical well-being than in the rigours of religious instruction. As the religious content of the meetings eroded, so too did denominational doctrines and traditional Christian taboos. What was happening to Sunday schools and other religious institutions was also happening to mothers' meetings—a gradual process of secularization. Such a process could only be worrisome to those who believed that it was imperative for the future of Christianity that religion be instilled in the young.

The decline of religion in mothers' meetings, however, should not be overstated. Well into the twentieth century all of them contained a religious element, and many remained centred on Bible readings and prayer. For its part, the Ranyard Mission was slow to introduce entertainments and thereby relax the religious format of its meetings. But then it worked with the poorest class of women, whose need for spiritual consolation was thought paramount. As noted elsewhere, attentions to the soul took precedence in an age in which the body was at such risk. But as education and the standard of living improved for many families—a trend not unconnected with mothers' meetings—more was required than the Christian prescription that the poor should put up with their conditions in the hope of better things to come. The mothers' meeting had to move with the times.

Nowhere is the versatility of the mothers' meeting better illustrated than in its connection with children's health. The welfare of children was, of course, a central issue for women; and it had stimulated the creation of myriad charities, many of them run by females, for over a century. The organizers of mothers' meetings, like philanthropists before them, were painfully aware of the high rate of child mortality, and they compiled their own rudimentary statistics that showed the dimensions of the problem in their neighbourhoods. Having practical experience of dead and dying children themselves, they had a heightened sense of the terrible toll of infant mortality, which government statisticians only corroborated. Mrs Bayly, for example, discovered in the 1850s that there were almost two infant deaths per mother among women in the Kensington potteries.[66]

It was not surprising, therefore, that talks on infant health became increasingly common. Louisa Twining invited Dr Pope of the National Health Society to give a series of lectures to her London mothers' meeting in the 1870s.[67] The Barnetts provided talks by an expert on 'Bodies and Babies' in 1881.[68] The Ranyard Mission showed its sensitivity to the issue through its extensive district-nursing programme, initiated in 1868. With a growing interest in maternity and antenatal care, its Bible nurses visited women in confinement and inspected the babies and toddlers at mothers' meetings, often referring cases to hospitals and dispensaries. By 1908 the mission also received assistance from the London County Council, in the form of a lady who did the rounds of mothers' meetings giving lectures on child-care.[69] The time spent listening to lectures on such topics could only diminish the time spent on religious conversion. Like the district visiting societies, mothers' meetings were under pressure to keep pace with social reform at the expense of traditional religious priorities.

Despite the long-standing interest of historians in child welfare, the subject has been treated with virtually no reference to mothers' meetings.[70] The local institutions that receive attention are the infant welfare centres and the schools for mothers, which emerged in the Edwardian years, partly in response to the growing government concern over child mortality and the needs of national efficiency after the Boer War. Some of them qualified for and took up government subsidies before the First World War and received assistance from the medical profession; thus they came into the state's purview and consequently the records of government in a way that mothers' meetings rarely did. This helps to explain their prominence in the histories of child welfare. So does the tendency, which became widespread in the heyday of the welfare state, to dismiss charity as amateurish and class-ridden, of interest chiefly because it encouraged state intervention.

The neglect of mothers' meetings would astonish Edwardian women. For many of them, infant welfare centres and schools for mothers were institutions that carried forward their own traditional concerns. As one writer put it, the centres were 'descendant[s] of the mothers' meeting'.[71] The majority of them, like mothers' meetings, were agencies run by women, with little or no support from government authorities. Religious charities, including the Ragged School Union, ran many of them alongside more traditional mothers' meetings.[72] Looking back on her own maternal classes in the 1870s and 1880s, with their emphasis on children's health, Henrietta Barnett remarked that they were 'an anticipation of the Schools for Mothers now subsidized by government'.[73] It is hard to avoid the conclusion that had women like Barnett, Bayly or Ranyard been medical men or employees of the state, the mothers' meeting would have been more widely celebrated.

Seeing the subject of infant welfare primarily from a male or a collectivist perspective, historians of social policy have concentrated on government and the medical establishment.[74] Indeed, studies of the infant welfare movement are essentially coterminous with the history of state intervention. The way the questions have been formulated emphasizes the role of the state and relegates the charitable sector, and therefore women, to the periphery. We should not conclude that the mothers' meeting was simply a forerunner of the state services for children, rapidly vanishing with increased state intervention in the early twentieth century. A woman writing of the Salvation Army's social work, a charity deeply involved in the welfare of children, remarked in 1906: 'The real work of social reform . . . appears to be so far beneath the notice of Parliament, municipal authorities, and Poor Law guardians.'[75]

The reasons for the decline of the mothers' meeting, like the decline of visiting societies and Sunday schools, are complicated, and should not be seen as simply a result of waning religious enthusiasm, though that had much to do with it. In the broadest sense, anything that threatened the self-sufficiency and status of the family threatened the mothers' meeting, from the increasing availability of cheap manufactured clothing to widening employment opportunities for women. The drop in the birth rate, which began in the 1860s, was perhaps the most obvious threat. Six live children were born to married couples on average in the mid-Victorian years, a figure that was down to just over two per couple by 1940.[76] The dramatic decline in fertility not only diminished the number of potential recruits to mothers' meetings, it shortened the span of years during which mothers might find them useful. In reducing the burden of domestic responsibility, it also freed women to take up paid employment outside the home, which improved the living standards of many families.

An essential reason for the existence of the mothers' meeting was the widespread poverty in the Victorian years. As living standards improved, some organizers noted that their meetings had lost their sense of purpose and had become little more than gatherings for gossip and recreation. The Ranyard Mission, which carried out a survey of the conditions of trade in London's slums, noted a 'vast' improvement in the condition of mothers in the 1880s.[77] By the early twentieth century it lamented its failure to adjust to the needs of better-off and better-educated wives and mothers, who were beginning to drift into other organizations. In more and more meetings singing classes, lantern lectures, and other entertainments filled the hours formerly devoted to Bible reading, needlework, and prayer. As with Sunday schools, the emergence of more tantalizing distractions was to take a toll.

During the First World War the Ranyard Mission reported that its mothers' meetings were falling into disrepute with respectable women, who regarded them as occasions for 'gossip and cadging'.[78] Thus it introduced fresh ideas and invented new names for the meetings, such as women's fellowships and mothers' clubs. But the results were not altogether encouraging. The Mothers' Union also worried about its meetings becoming 'stagnant', and during the war many of its working-class members moved on to other institutions, such as schools for mothers and women's institutes.[79] Many working-women, it would seem, moved on to the Women's Co-operative Guild (1883), much celebrated as a fountain of socialist feminism. But in this case, as in others, mothers'-meeting traditions persisted. As Beatrice and Sidney Webb remarked, 'the Guild started as a sort of Co-operative "mothers' meeting" with co-operative literature being read to assembled wives bowed over their needles'.[80]

In accelerating social change, the First World War had an unsettling effect on mothers' meetings. Charities like the Mothers' Union, the Girls' Friendly Society, and the Ranyard Mission were zealous in their support of the British cause and demonstrated their patriotism by promoting the sale of war bonds, making articles for men at the front, and assisting recruitment drives. The Mothers' Union also assisted the Board of Trade in registering women willing to do war work.[81] Their close contacts with the missionary movement and their other links overseas strengthened their loyalty to an empire that they had adopted as part of the mother's domain.[82] At first, they little realized that the war would undermine the ideological basis of the British Empire, and would have implications for maternal culture and the lives of women. Nor did they fully understand how damaging the war would be in the long term for their communities.

As we have seen elsewhere, the world of parish charity suffered a serious blow in the First World War. The opportunities provided by the war to work and travel far from home put the small world of the mothers' meeting into perspective. One witness put it neatly: women and girls were 'cast from the service of the home and of the class amid the whirl of wheels'.[83] It was thus not surprising that working-women often moved on to institutions which they believed to be more relevant to their lives. Meanwhile, there was the growing difficulty of recruiting younger members to mothers' meetings, which often meant that a rump of older women had to carry on as best they could for as long as they could. When mothers died off without being replaced by their daughters, that generational cycle, so important in the transmission of Christianity and other cultural norms, was broken. To many Christians, the religious certainties that once shaped British culture were irrecoverable.

For all the difficulties and uncertainties, the mothers' meeting showed remarkable resilience in the inter-war years. The institution had problems keeping pace with cultural change, but it continued to be far and away the most pervasive grass-roots agency dealing with issues of maternal and child welfare in Britain. At the end of the First World War there were 1,525 infant welfare centres in Britain, most of them voluntary societies without state subsidies.[84] In 1918 the Mothers' Union alone was running regular meetings in each of its 8,273 branches in Britain.[85] By 1938 the society reached a peak of over 600,000 members in 14,000 branches at home and abroad, making it one of the largest voluntary agencies in British history.[86] Its objects, headlined in the *Mothers' Union Journal*, were 'to uphold the sanctity of marriage', 'to awaken in mothers of all classes a sense of their great responsibility as mothers in the training of their boys and girls', and 'to organize in every place a band of mothers who will unite in prayer, and seek by their own example to lead their families in purity and holiness of life'.[87] Its motto was the familiar verse from Proverbs: 'Train up a child in the way he should go, and when he is old he will not depart from it.'

As it turned out, the Second World War had a greater impact than the First World War on mothers' meetings and maternal culture. Total war not only reduced those social distinctions which were bound up with mothers' meetings, but the aerial bombing often disrupted or put an end to proceedings. The destruction of homes and schools, churches and chapels, has been mentioned in regard to the decline of Sunday schools and district visiting. Mothers' meetings suffered likewise. In the late 1930s the Ragged School Union ran just under 200 of them, the highest figure ever reported by that society.[88] But when bombs destroyed thirty-eight of its missions, the institution reported a dramatic decline in classes for mothers.[89] Meanwhile, all the charities that sponsored mothers' meetings had to cope with the continual calling up of their volunteers for the forces. The evacuation of children further dislocated families and neighbourhoods. Before long, the emergency resulted in many missions and other religious buildings being requisitioned by the authorities. Rooms in which mothers' meetings had been held became recreation centres for servicemen or wards for casualties of the Blitz.

To grieving mothers, disillusioned servicemen, and troubled clergy, the settled world of Victorian and Edwardian Britain seemed a distant memory. Many charities that ran mothers' meetings found it impossible to recover lost ground in 1945, especially as the war had changed the public's expectations in regard to the social services. The post-war evolution of the welfare state in Britain reduced the demand for charitable services, especially among those institutions that provided medical or material benefits. Those savings banks and provident schemes, for example, which were still a feature of mothers' meetings in the interwar years, became outmoded with increased state benefits and a rising standard of living. Would women who had moved far from home during the war, who had taken up new employments and seen fresh opportunities, wish to do voluntary work for disrupted charities? Once having worked alongside men in the services, industry, and agriculture, could those age-old beliefs in the differences between the sexes, which underpinned maternal culture, any longer satisfy or persuade? The growing state culture, secular and materialist, and traditional female culture, Christian and parochial, were increasingly at odds.

The waning of religious enthusiasm took a heavy toll on those expressions of maternalism that mixed so well in the mothers' meeting, compassion and needlework. That religious precept stimulated compassion is obvious, but there was also an element of religion in needlework. Before the mass marketing of manufactured clothing,

sewing took up so much of a woman's existence that it was part of her
femininity. Sewing and religion merged in the church-stitch-church
routine of women's lives, a tendency strengthened by the biblical prescription that women should sew for the benefit of others. But just as
there were signs that British women were losing their piety, reports
appeared that they were also losing touch with their needles and consequently their meetings, a trend accelerated by the availability of the
sewing machine. In a society growing more prosperous, many women
who would once have joined a mothers' meeting now owned their
own sewing machines, or could afford ready-made clothes. Such
changes would have alarmed those god-fearing pioneers who created
the mothers' meeting in the nineteenth century. For they never
doubted that their dear cause floated on a sea of faith and flannel. It
could only sink when the praying and the sewing stopped.

To the faithful, Christianity was the fountain of family and community values and, by implication, national purpose. The Girls'
Friendly Society put its finger on the dangers to religion when it
reported on a society in which people were no longer buried in the
same churchyard as their parents and grandparents.[90] In the increasingly mobile post-war society, the Christian mothers' meeting, like
charitable culture generally, could not survive intact. As women
entered the labour force it left them with less time for charitable work
but with more money to enjoy new distractions elsewhere. As the welfare state and secular culture took hold, the churches and the city missions lost their sense of direction and their associated charities suffered
accordingly. Like the visiting society and the Sunday school, the
mothers' meeting was another institutional victim of cultural change
and Christian decline. In some institutions the meetings transformed
into women's fellowships and mother-and-toddler groups, which
illustrated a degree of charitable adaptability to post-war circumstances.[91] Still, the churches paid a price for the collapse of the mothers'
meeting, for it was, like the Sunday school, a 'nursery' of religion. Its
demise was a further blow to Christian observance. In the general
enthusiasm for state entitlements and widening opportunities, few
noticed the loss of self-government and spiritual capital.

5

Nursing

Be a man, sir—a Christian. Have faith in the immortality of the soul, which no pain, no mortal disease, can assail or touch!

(Elizabeth Gaskell, *North and South*, 1855)

I believe it is repugnant to a civilized community for hospitals to have to rely upon private charity. . . . I have always felt a shudder of repulsion when I have seen nurses and sisters who ought to be at their work . . . going about the streets collecting money for the hospitals.

(Aneurin Bevan, *Parliamentary Debates*, 30 April 1946)

There is some truth in the view that the belief in God's goodness is inversely proportional to the evidence for it. When God is good, there is less reason for him to be invoked. Faith follows pain and personal suffering. Christianity, born with a death, feeds on the dying. Around countless sickbeds it gave an answer, however melancholy, to the problem of evil, of suffering, and of death itself. To Victorians life was capricious and physically painful. Medical relief was, by our standards, inaccessible and unsophisticated. In a world in which life was hazardous and the hereafter a potential torment, religion was compelling. It provided both an explanation for calamity and a treasury of consolation. God, in a well-worn nineteenth-century phrase, was the 'great practitioner', Jesus the 'physician of the soul' and the 'great deliverer'.[1] The dying sinner-cum-sufferer, at home surrounded by family and friends, is one of the more enduring images of Victorian life and literature. To the Christian mind these ritual visitors at the bedside were reminiscent of that most famous scene at the foot of the Cross. They bore witness to deliverance.

Body and soul, medicine and religion, were usually united in the nineteenth century. As in ancient cultures, a holistic view of human life was commonly held. Victorian medical practitioners often accepted a moral responsibility towards patients. The churches, for their part, accepted a medical responsibility towards parishioners, and much medicine was practised with their support and under their authority.[2] This unity of interest flowed from a central doctrine of Christianity: that sin leads to suffering. Healing and preaching were linked in the gospels. Thus, medicine in the hands of Christians passed naturally into ethics. Ethics in religious hands found expression in, among other causes, medical philanthropy. To consecrate medicine to the service of Christ, to provide the everlasting remedy, the 'double cure', was the challenge of missionary medicine.[3]

It was a challenge all the greater at a time when the medical profession dealt largely with prognosis and therapy of symptoms and could take little direct credit for any reduction in mortality rates. The inability of medicine to restore patients' bodies or to offer an explanation for death gave strength to religion. Exposed to sickness and death, remarked a fellow of the Royal College of Surgeons, doctors must have a 'solid ground of hope in the prospect of leaving this world'.[4] Evangelicals were not simply inured to suffering, but saw pain in a positive light, as facilitating conversion. The belief that the soul survived the body was profoundly reassuring. Immortality made death immaterial. As Dr Donaldson told the grieving Mr Hale, who sat by the deathbed of his wife in Elizabeth Gaskell's *North and South* (1854–5): 'We cannot touch the disease. ... We can only delay its progress—alleviate the pain it causes. Be a man, sir—a Christian. Have faith in the immortality of the soul, which no pain, no mortal disease, can assail or touch!'[5]

For all the Christian concern, there was a desperate need for medical care in nineteenth-century Britain, especially in the poorest neighbourhoods.

In the slums, little relief was on offer beyond making the sick and dying more comfortable, and praying for their souls. What was to be done when medicine was both unsophisticated and in short supply? Countless people died in the most miserable circumstances, often alone and unattended. General Booth recorded various scenes of desolation in *In Darkest England and The Way Out*:

A poor woman in Drury Lane was paralyzed. She had no one to attend to her; she lay on the floor, on a stuffed sack, and an old piece of cloth to cover her. Although it was winter, she very seldom had any fire. She had no garments to wear, and but very little to eat.[6]

Found a man lying on a straw mattress in a very bad condition. The room was filthy; the smell made the Officer feel ill. The man had been lying for days without having anything done for him. A cup of water was by his side. The Officers vomited from the terrible smells of this place.[7]

In such cases, it was highly unlikely that a doctor would ever turn up. The sick could only pray that a relative or neighbour would help them, or a district visitor, or, at best, a nurse. The above-mentioned cases were among the fortunate, for Salvation Army officers provided what modest assistance they could muster: a wash, clean clothes, food, blankets, and a Bible. Conversion would have been their next priority.

To the sick treated in one of the nation's hospitals, vigilance at the bedside was phenomenal. The voluntary hospitals were typically Anglican and had a strong clerical presence on their governing bodies. Bibles, provided by the Bible Society, could be found at the head of each bed, and the authorities dispensed large doses of scripture as a matter of routine.[8] They also required those discharged to attend their parish church to give thanks for recovery.[9] Those who did not live to give thanks received spiritual guidance from those who gathered round their deathbeds. The London Hospital, during the cholera epidemic of 1866, gives a fascinating glimpse of the concern for the religious welfare of patients. Doctors, nurses, the hospital chaplain, local clergy, members of the Hospital Committee, scripture readers, and women visitors moved through the wards as the disease gathered up its victims.[10] The profusion of religious practitioners revealed expectations for the patients.

When medical treatment failed, they simply read the scriptures: 'Believe on the Lord Jesus Christ and thou shalt be saved' (Acts 16: 31); 'Behold the lamb of God which taketh away the sin of the world' (John 1: 29). Christianity may have made it more difficult to live, but if we are to believe the many nineteenth-century witnesses to the faith, it made it easier to die.

In a time of cholera, hospitals concentrated the mind on salvation. But the zeal to save souls was ever present. To god-fearing Victorians, the preoccupation with death and dying deeply influenced their work across the philanthropic world, from refuges for the destitute to sanatoria for gentlefolk. Even under normal conditions, the fixation with sin and suffering pervaded institutional life in Britain. In workhouses and prisons, as in hospitals and dispensaries, carefully chosen texts opened compulsory meetings for prayer. 'Give ye rest to him that is weary' (Isaiah 28: 12) and 'Blessed are the dead, which die in the Lord' (Revelation 14: 13). Such texts were meant to inspire the living and comfort the dying. In the wards and waiting-rooms special emphasis was given to that cardinal doctrine of evangelicalism, Christ's atonement. 'For God so loved the world, that he gave his only begotten son, that whosoever believeth on him should not perish, but have eternal life' (John 3: 16).

But the zeal to save souls was not confined to the institutional sick-room, as the work of the visiting societies confirm. To the Victorian mind, the home was the principal 'moral universe'.[11] It was, as a female poet wrote, ideally suited 'to heal the wounds that sin has given, to point the Christian's path to Heaven'.[12] Evangelical piety was never more conspicuous than during visits to those dying at home. Take the case in Brighton visited by the philanthropist Sarah Robinson in 1858, who, like so many others, suffered without hope of a medical cure: 'My then minister requested me to accompany him on a visit to a case of particular interest,—that of a young girl of seventeen, blind, deaf, and dumb; often suffering much pain, and, with the exception of her right hand, entirely paralysed . . . the only method of communicating with her is to pass the fingers of her right hand over the letters of a raised Alphabet, and so spell out word after word.'[13] Robinson's solicitude increased as she watched the girl approach the world to come. She wrote up the case in *Light in Darkness* (1859) and in the sequel, *The Darkness Past* (1861). From her testimony, such bitter-sweet cases ought to pave the way for conversion and salvation, so as 'to abolish death, and to realize for man a perfect and endless life'.[14]

The communion of medicine and religion was especially prominent where women worked. In an era of evangelical revival, the female con-tribution to medicine flowed naturally from missionary impulses. And in the battle with sin and suffering waged around the nation's sickbeds, nursing played a growing role. As elsewhere in Europe, nurs-ing in Britain was traditionally women's work. As Florence Nightingale observed, 'every woman is a nurse'.[15] While treating the sick was as old as life itself, religious foundations were among the first institutions to encourage nursing as a vocation. The poet and man of letters Robert Southey was among those who sought to promote nurs-ing among Protestant women, modelled on what Catholic orders had achieved in Europe. He had been impressed by what Elizabeth Fry had achieved in prisons through religious piety, and he wanted to see nurs-ing extended. 'A school of medicine ought also to be a school of Christian humanity', he wrote in the *Colloquies* (1824). 'It is not to the hospitals alone that this blessed spirit of charity might be directed; while it reformed those establishments by its presence, it would lessen the pressure upon them by seeking out the sick, and attending them in their own habitations.'[16]

Historians have tended to play down the religious element in nineteenth-century British nursing, for it fits ill with the rise of nurs-ing as a profession. But when a host of nursing institutions came into existence in the Victorian years, they were widely seen as an extension of mission work. As befitting a movement that developed out of ancient forms of Christian life, nursing had less to do with preventing disease than with assuaging it through religious ministration. Mrs Fry's Institute for Nursing in Devonshire Square (1840) was very much in this tradition. Originally called the Protestant Sisters of Charity, it was among the first purely nursing orders in Britain. Another was the

Anglican community of St John's House (1848) attached to King's College Hospital, which provided many of the nurses in the Crimea. The eminent parties who launched the society endorsed the following proposal: 'It is absolutely necessary to the success of the design and the real amelioration of the class of person for whose benefit it is intended, that the proposed establishment should be a religious one, and that all connected to it should regard the work in which they are embarked as a religious work.'[17]

Home nursing, like nursing generally, had been carried out for centuries by ancient religious orders, by deaconesses and sisters of charity. The well-to-do could afford to employ a nurse in their own homes, but the care provided could be primitive. In *Martin Chuzzlewit*, Dickens caricatured the 'monthly nurse' in the figure of Sarah Gamp, whose love of drink made it possible for her to attend 'a lying-in or a laying-out with equal zest and relish'.[18] In the early nineteenth century much of the nursing of the poor in their homes was carried out informally by district visitors, who, as we have seen, ministered to maternity cases and the sick as best they could, given the limits of their training and the facilities available. In Britain, district nursing as a distinct occupation largely grew out of the medical needs discovered by missionary-minded household visitors. Caring for patients at home was all the more urgent because the poor, like the better-off, were reluctant to enter hospital. When Southey called for a school of medicine enveloped in Christian humanity to train nurses to treat the poor in their homes, he was preaching to the converted, an audience of underemployed women eager to pursue a religious vocation.

The first organized district-nursing scheme is difficult to date, but in the 1860s there were several institutions in the field, including Mrs Fry's Institute and St John's House, which promoted household visiting as well as hospital nursing.[19] In the latter institution much time was spent on religious instruction in the training of the sisters and probationers, including lessons on the Parables of our Lord and the Book of Common Prayer.[20] In the provinces, the Liverpool Training School and Home for Nurses took the lead. Established in 1859 by the Unitarian philanthropist William Rathbone, it too had an underlying spiritual purpose. As Rathbone said in his last message to his nurses in 1901: 'We hope that you will always bear in mind that, in all nursing work—but especially in the work of nursing the sick poor—intelligence and skill alone are not enough, but that you are Christian ministers, *ministering* to the comfort and character of your fellow-creatures.'[21] As the founders of nursing associations were aware, it was unrealistic to expect middle-class women to take up nursing without a strong religious motivation, for it was essentially manual work, which implied a loss of status.[22]

One of the most remarkable district nursing societies—the Bible nurses—emerged in mid-Victorian London, and it sheds considerable light on the role of Christianity in nineteenth-century medicine. The institution's decline in the twentieth century may be seen as a case study in the transformation of nursing as it became secularized, professional, and subject to government regulation. The scheme was the creation of Ellen Ranyard, whose London Bible and Domestic Female Mission, discussed earlier, had been such an innovator in household visiting. Mrs Ranyard was intimately acquainted with the level of disease hidden from view in London's rookeries and alleys. And she was painfully aware that her Bible women, even with the best intentions, were unfit to provide anything but the most primitive medical assistance on their visiting rounds. But as they discovered, the problems of the sick poor, unattended by formal medicine, were too profound to be ignored. Fearful of the dangers to religion of mixing temporal and medical relief, she turned her mind to another specialist scheme: Bible nursing.

The gospels strengthened her opinion that opportunities must be found in disease, so that good might be plucked from evil. Experience had taught her that the promise of medical relief opened doors to Christian teaching that might otherwise be closed. With a long-standing interest in health and sanitation, she was in touch with several nursing pioneers, including Pastor Fliedner at Kaiserwerth, and Agnes Jones, who would go on to become head of nursing at the Liverpool Infirmary. After some early trials with untrained nurses in several

London districts, Mrs Ranyard suggested that Miss Jones should train a corps of Christian nurses in London to complement the corps of Bible women. But lack of funds and the untimely departure of Miss Jones because of a family emergency put an end to this particular idea.[23]

Mrs Ranyard's medical scheme had to wait until 1868, when sufficient funds became available to provide a nursing centre. In that year she signed up her first Bible nurses, who were incorporated into the existing mission. (The institution's name was changed in 1900 to the London Biblewomen and Nurses' Mission and changed again in 1917 to simply the Ranyard Mission.) With an income of roughly £4,000 a year by 1875, most of it from women, Mrs Ranyard's nurses were to be the first trained district nurses in London.[24] (The East London Nursing Society was also founded in 1868 but employed far fewer nurses.)[25] The mission constituted the most formidable association nursing the sick poor in their own homes in Victorian London. And among the many district-nursing societies active in the metropolis in later decades, it remained significant.

Mrs Ranyard's nurses, like her Bible women, were drawn from the respectable working class. She was not insensitive to the call to open up nursing as a profession for females from the middle classes, but she did not assume that ladies would have a greater influence over patients than working-class women. She was little concerned with the fashionable view that nurses of a higher social position would raise the status of nursing in the public mind. Her essential purpose was to minister to the urban poor. In her opinion, a nurse recruited from and living in the district she served was the most likely person to promote this aim. As she said in regard to her Bible women, 'we found we could go deeper down into the hearts of our own sex' than ladies.[26] In the relative isolation of working-class homes, Bible nurses were far less circumscribed than nurses who worked in hospital wards under the gaze of matrons and male authorities. Not without a hint of pride, she observed that her nurses were unrefined, yet their salaries, £39 a year in the 1870s, were roughly in line with the pay of trained staff nurses in hospitals, who often came from a higher social class.[27] How unusual for working-class women to find themselves in employment where they might wield more power and work fewer hours than others in the same field who were their social superiors!

The first Bible nurses were drawn from the ranks of the Bible women. But the most fertile recruiting ground soon became the mothers' meetings, which were so closely associated with the mission's work in the slums. Mrs Ranyard's volunteers were, ideally, single women aged between 25 and 35, or women with one child in school, or women who had lost children. Physical and mental stamina were essential. The best nurse, it was argued, was not one with book knowledge, but one who could adapt her knowledge to circumstances. That she be deeply Christian was critical. Mrs Ranyard had strong Anglican ties, but she instructed her staff to work with Christians outside the Established Church as well. Her tolerance did not extend to Catholics, whose influence in London's slums alarmed her. Despite the competition with Catholics for souls, the Ranyard nurses were not to be of the 'preaching' sort. The mission was sensitive to remarks of would-be critics, such as the doctor who asked about the name 'Bible nurse': 'pray tell me is she to be always preaching?'[28] The effective nurse was to be quiet, kind, and capable, with an abundance of mother wit, a woman who could unite practical and spiritual qualities. The mission was known to sack nurses for 'moral faults'.[29]

The training of the Bible nurses was makeshift and rather perfunctory in the early years. Florence Nightingale had pointed out a difficulty of district nursing when she wrote: 'one of the chief uses of an hospital, though almost entirely neglected up to the present time, is to train nurses for nursing the sick at home.'[30] Mrs Ranyard arranged openings for trainee nurses at several London hospitals. In the first seven years, 1868–74, Guy's Hospital trained seventy-eight nurses, while the Westminster Hospital and the London Hospital also provided facilities.[31] In an uncharacteristic compromise Florence Nightingale contributed £20 to the Ranyard scheme for specific supplies, but her training school at St Thomas's refused to cooperate because it required a two-year nursing training.[32] Initially, Ranyard trainees spent three months as a Bible woman, then three months in the hospital wards, and then three months on probation in a district. The hospital course was not such a long one as that required for a hospital nurse at the time, but, as Mrs Ranyard argued, it was long enough 'for our purpose'.[33] Her medical purpose was to get the poor to nurse one another, which was in keeping with her motto: 'to help the poor to help themselves.'

This aim required considerable thought and baggage. In the early years the Bible nurses did not wear a distinctive costume, for it was believed that the poor disliked uniforms. But the mission recommended that the nurses wear a dark gown and carry a flannel apron and a tin basin around their waists. In the 1890s a grey-blue dress with a dark cloak and bonnet, with a badge bearing the insignia LNR (Ranyard's pen-name) became required dress. Perhaps this change was in response to the nurses affiliated to the Queen's Institute (1887), who wore distinctive uniforms. From the earliest years the Ranyard Mission provided a divided handbag for flat articles, including Bibles, scripture portions, and the gospel of holistic nursing, Florence Nightingale's *Notes on Nursing*. Also added were items not always found among the poor themselves: scissors, knives, pins, needles, and thread.[34] Another bag supplied by the mission contained sheets, towels, medicine, carbolic lotion, and soap. Evangelicals, who took cleanliness to be an outward sign of respectability, endowed soap with a seemingly miraculous power. Perhaps the German historian Heinrich von Treitschke had a point when he told his students that 'the English think soap is civilization'.[35]

Supplies were collected weekly from the 'Mother House' (a usage borrowed from Pastor Fliedner) at 2 Regent Square. Each nurse possessed a printed card to record her list of supplies. In keeping with district-visiting practices, coals, blankets, clothing, toys, and money were available when needed. The provisions distributed drew upon the diets recommended by the London hospitals. The emphasis was on food that was both nutritious and easily digested and conformed to what was thought especially appropriate for fever patients.[36] Provisions included tea, sugar, rice, cocoa, cornflour, sago, arrowroot, tapioca, and oatmeal.[37] Beyond these items, the case studies suggest a penchant for mutton chops and wine. Mrs Ranyard's nurses were ardent opponents of drink, but they were not above a belief in the restorative power of the grape. Fully equipped, the Bible nurses were a formidable and recognizable presence as they plunged into the unsanitary recesses of London.

Like their colleagues the Bible women, the Bible nurses worked with middle-class superintendents wherever possible. This separation of function was a reflection of the class divisions that Mrs Ranyard, like other nursing reformers, accepted as God-given and likely to persist. (We should not assume that in accepting social divisions philanthropists approved of them.) The superintendents referred and oversaw cases and kept their nurses in touch with hospitals, dispensaries, and parish churches. They also distributed supplies, inspected the nurses, and paid their salaries, which rose to £90 a year by the First World War.[38] Many of them drew on their own hospital-visiting experience. A doctor's wife was thought to be the ideal person for the job. Wives of clerics, it was found, were usually too busy elsewhere. Doctors themselves sometimes helped the mission by making home visits to the sick poor and by providing supplies and advice. Discreet overtures were made to women doctors through the Female Medical College, Fitzroy Square, but little assistance was forthcoming as women doctors had little time to spare.

Despite assistance from several sympathetic physicians, most of the cases attended by the Bible nurses were far removed from any doctor's oversight. This was not a question of fees so much as the shortage of doctors available in slum neighbourhoods. The national ratio of doctors to population in 1871 was 1 : 547.[39] But in the poorer parts of London it was much higher. In Bethnal Green at the turn of the century there was only one doctor for every 3,000 residents. In Kensington it was one for every 480 of the population.[40] Sick clubs and out-patient clinics run by the charitable existed in many districts to promote medical self-help among the poor. Sir Frederick Treves, surgeon to the London Hospital, congratulated the Bible nurses on their invaluable work in the slums, and remarked that hospitals and the medical profession knew very little about the sick from the poorest classes.[41] Treves failed to mention an important reason for this. The sick poor often told charitable visitors that they 'would rather stay and suffer, and die in the midst of all the filth and squalor that surrounds them than go to the big house, which, to them, looks very like a prison'.[42]

As Mrs Ranyard and her colleagues were aware, there was a tremendous demand for district nursing in London, a demand that could never be met by her charity's resources. In the early years, a Bible nurse typically visited eight to ten cases during her seven-hour work day. Fifteen to twenty patients would be recorded in her books in a given week, many of them requiring daily attention. Weekend work was often required, but night duty was uncommon, for neighbours could usually be found to assist in emergencies. By the end of 1868, their first year of employment, fourteen Bible nurses had made 5,000 visits to ninety-nine patients. The figures rose to 111,601 visits to 4,392 patients in 1874.[43] By this time forty-five districts had been mapped out for the fifty-seven nurses in service. A few districts, including Islington, Wandsworth, and Notting Hill, had two nurses, but most had only one. In 1894 the mission employed eighty-two nurses who made 215,000 visits to just under 10,000 patients.[44]

These and other statistics show that as time passed the Bible nurses had more patients on their books but made fewer visits per patient. In 1868 they made, on average, fifty visits to each case. By 1894 they visited only twenty-one times per patient. In 1874 each nurse treated, on average, seventy-seven patients a year; in 1894, 122 patients. What do these statistics suggest? Perhaps the health needs of London were so great that the mission decided to spread its services over a larger number of patients. Perhaps there was a decline in chronic illness, or more effective nursing, or a dramatic increase in the number of cases referred to hospitals and dispensaries. There is evidence that the Bible nurses increasingly concentrated their energies on maternity and terminal cases, which did not so often require prolonged treatment. Mrs Ranyard's essential aim may also help to explain why fewer visits were being made per patient. Under the influence of her nurses, the poor may have become more self-reliant, thereby reducing the need for repeated nursing visits.

Many of the cases that the Bible nurses visited would, of course, be treated in hospital today. The most depressing case studies of diseased and dying patients abound in the publications of the mission. But in the early years it released little statistical information that would give us a reliable breakdown of cases. This was perhaps because the body was a less compelling subject to Mrs Ranyard than the soul. In the nineteenth century the Bible nurses did little about infectious diseases because they worried about spreading them. Thus measles, smallpox, and scarlet fever were beyond them, except insofar as they could disinfect, advise, and offer supplies. Non-contagious diseases were more susceptible to nursing: cancers, tumours, dropsy, ulcers, abscesses, tuberculosis, skin disease, epilepsy, rheumatic fever, fractures, accidents, burns, bruises, and sores, and what were called 'sloughs of despond' all came under their care. A printed card, which all nurses carried with them to record cases, is a rough guide to what they most commonly confronted in the 1870s. Patients were then classified under four headings: surgical, helpless, consumptive, and confinement.[45] Of the just under 10,000 cases treated in 1894, the most frequent came under the following classifications: confinement, general medical, fever, surgical, and bronchitis. With relatively few cases, consumption appears to have taken up less nursing time than twenty years earlier.[46]

The home nursing practised by the Bible nurses was a mixture of patching up and preventive work, with an emphasis on poor families looking after themselves as much as possible. Mrs Ranyard knew that the charity of the poor to the poor was essential to survival in the slums, and she wanted to extend it to include effective medical attention and help with matters of personal hygiene. Apart from teaching the poor to treat themselves, the nurses applied lotions, poultices, fomentations, water dressings, and leeches. They bandaged limbs, and cleansed sores and wounds. In the early years they frequently had to wash a patient before treatment could begin. Aware that disease spread from impure air and a lack of breathing space, Mrs Ranyard recognized a need for well-ventilated rooms at cheap rents.[47] Cleanliness and sanitation were high on the mission's list of priorities, along with general assistance around the home. The nurses bathed and managed the helpless, cooked, dusted, and made beds. Bible quilts were a distinctive feature of the mission, 'silent comforters' as they were called, complete with scripture portions sewn into the patchwork.[48] Presumably the poor read the Beatitudes as they crawled in and out of bed.

In commenting on the numerous charitable experiments addressed to the bodies and the souls of the poor in the nineteenth century, the writer Lucy Aikin observed that there was 'much quackery in both departments'.[49] Some of the practices of the Bible nurses may seem faintly ridiculous to our minds, but they should not lead us to dismiss their work. It is impossible to measure with any precision the gains in health they achieved. If effective medical treatment is narrowed to successful drug therapy, they did very little. But their labours take on some significance if we include preventive medicine, or treatment that enabled families to combat attacks from more serious diseases, or which made possible an early return to employment. Keeping families intact and out of pauperism were fundamental aims of district nursing, as in district visiting.

Medical historians who concentrate on drug therapy and hospital care are often unimpressed by the role formal medicine played in reducing mortality rates in the nineteenth century. A more sanguine view of medicine's contribution to health is taken by those who define therapy more broadly, and who consider the part played by unregistered practitioners in spreading an awareness of public health and personal hygiene. If they are right, some small credit should be given to the Ranyard nurses and their colleagues the Bible women, who, along with the army of district visitors from other societies, advised poor families on matters of health and sanitation. Mrs Ranyard had imbibed the message, so fashionable in the mid-Victorian years, that air purity and sanitary reform were essential to combat the high levels of mortality widely associated with overcrowding in the slums.[50] Perhaps the drop in crude death rates, which became marked from about 1870 onwards, owed much to the poor looking after themselves more effectively. Charles Booth, who was familiar with the district-nursing schemes around the country, believed them to be the most 'directly successful' form of philanthropy.[51]

The district-nursing programme pioneered by Mrs Ranyard was a striking example of medical treatment provided for a specific section of the community, working-class families who needed assistance in coping with their medical needs. Her nurses did not need to study surveys by Booth or Rowntree or departmental reports on physical deterioration to illuminate the need for community health. Along with other medical charities, they had been providing it for years, albeit on a limited scale, before government became aware of its significance. The provision of personal health care at the neighbourhood level by the district-visiting societies was in contrast to the government's interest in national measures to improve public health in the same years. The state's efforts often foundered on the inadequacy of local-government administration, but as in education and the social services, health was emerging as an important political issue. The politicians, unlike missionary nurses, did not see the well-being of the poor in holistic terms, or subject to religion.

The Ranyard Mission published case studies regularly, to inform the public and to lift the spirits of the staff. They are invaluable records of missionary nursing practices, slum conditions, and diseases. Here is a case which may be seen as typical of what the Bible nurses thought important and why:

We first went to see a young man who had been crippled and totally helpless for thirteen years from spinal complaint. He lies upon a water bed; every part of him is so paralysed, excepting his right hand and arm, that he has no power to move a limb. Nurse helps his mother to move him off his bed twice a week to change the water, and make it fresh for him, but his whole body is so stiffened that it is like lifting a corpse and any attempt to bend the muscles causes him the greatest agony.

Entirely dependent on a little parish relief and the kindness of friends (for his poor old mother can do nothing but attend to his wants), he yet seems 'to have all things and to abound.' He is one who has searched the Scriptures from beginning to end, and his memory is so good that he is never at a loss when speaking about them. . . .

His pain is very great at all times, but no one would think it to see his heavenly and peaceful countenance, and his far-seeing eye, which seems to be looking into eternity.[52]

It would seem that there was little that could be done physically for this particular patient, except to make him more comfortable. The nurse was first and foremost anxious to prepare his soul, and perhaps her own, for eternity. This was in keeping with Mrs Ranyard's instructions that her nurses do what they can for the body, but the soul may be saved. Reading some of the case studies one wonders whether the emphasis on the soul flowed from a contempt for the body, a fear that the flesh was prone to depravity. Be that as it may, attendance at the deathbed was a routine occurrence for the Bible nurses, for roughly 5 to 10 per cent of their patients died within a fortnight.[53] Nothing, however, moved them more quickly than the news of an impending death. The case studies are weighted toward terminal patients, who were most vulnerable to religious conversion. There is ample evidence in the records of the Ranyard Mission that patients often received considerable relief from the spiritual message provided. We might keep in mind that the Bible nurses provided a highly personal service, often spending long hours with patients. It is interesting to note that in the early twentieth century the Ranyard nurses devoted most of their attention to the aged poor. This was not simply because the old were in need of medical treatment, but because they were relatively more susceptible to religious conversion.

It would be misleading to give the impression that the Bible nurses were so preoccupied with their religious mission that the medical care they provided was of little importance to them. With the years their medical training was revised and improved.[54] In the 1880s the London Hospital offered the Ranyard Mission a more thorough training than had previously been available. By 1893 the nurses had one year at a general hospital and then attended a special hospital to gain a certificate. A probationary training in the districts followed. There they received systematic courses in anatomy, physiology, and general nursing, on which the mission examined them at the end of their first and second years. St Bartholomew's, Charing Cross, and St Thomas's hospitals asked them to care for all their external maternity cases, which was a tribute to their growing reputation. To keep the training and equipment up-to-date, the mission set up a medical council in

1896, headed by a panel of leading physicians. Five years later the hospital training was raised to a two-year minimum. By 1907 nursing was so well established as a profession that the mission ceased to train nurses in hospital at its own expense and drew on fully trained nurses who were religiously committed. Thus a three-year training became the norm in 1908, by which time the mission had moved its headquarters to 25 Russell Square. Mrs Ranyard, who died of bronchitis in 1879, did not live to see these changes

As time passed the mission came into contact with public authorities while retaining its ties with other charitable agencies. From the earliest years the nurses received lectures on the Poor Law and the principles of relief and sanitation; and the Charity Organisation Society began to provide lectures on pauperism and related topics in the 1870s. Other charities in close cooperation with the Ranyard Mission were the East End Relief Society and the Mothers' Union. The Bible Society was a long-standing ally and continued to provide grants to the mission until 1916.[55] The growth of government also led to expansion, a refinement of duties, and greater attention to statistics. In 1899, when nursing care for schoolchildren came to public notice, the Ranyard nurses provided assistance. When the London County Council set up Minor Ailments Centres in 1912, the mission supplied nurses. It also worked with the Central Council for District Nursing in London, which developed out of a Local Government Board conference in 1913.[56] These and other initiatives illustrate that the Bible nurses were gradually being transformed into a more professional body. They became increasingly sophisticated through more extensive medical training and the grafting of social-science methods onto religious precept. In this they reflect the history of district visiting and nursing generally.

As the tension between religion and medicine increased, the Ranyard Mission struggled to sustain the evangelical zeal that had been its hallmark. The mix of scientific discourse and spiritual argument became more difficult to justify in a more 'specialized, impersonal, and bureaucratic society'.[57] Other nursing institutions by this time were making a clear-cut philosophical distinction between treating the body and attentions to the soul. An unwillingness to accept such a distinction made it impossible for the Bible nurses to affiliate to the Queen's Institute, which prohibited proselytizing. Ranyard nurses continued to be selected on the grounds of religious conviction. In 1919 the Diocesan Board required them to pass examinations in theology.[58] But the mission's records show an increasing interest in drains and inoculations, state assistance and nursing technique. Their professional nursing training was now in a different language from that of Mrs Ranyard's day. Talk of 'sin-sick souls' and the 'double cure' seemed more and more dated and inappropriate. Healing and preaching were linked in the gospels, but in South London, where the Bible nurses came to focus their attention, reading the scriptures was beginning to look a poor substitute for treatment.

With the years, the mission's religious message became diffused and could no longer be worn on the uniform. In the early twentieth century the title 'Bible nurse' was dropped in favour of 'Ranyard nurse'. By then, unpaid 'lady' superintendents were more difficult to recruit, and it became common for nurses to be promoted to supervisory positions. These changes were in keeping with shifting social conditions and the altered character of the mission as the staff took on more diocesan social work and less face-to-face evangelizing. For their part, the nurses became involved with the Girl Guides and recreation centres for the elderly. It is noteworthy that after the Second World War a Ranyard nurse visited sixteen to eighteen cases a day on average.[59] In the 1870s the figures were eight to ten a day. This increased caseload can be explained in various ways, but certainly many hours were saved, if not souls, by the reduction in time spent on Bible reading and religious conversion. It would be interesting to know whether patients preferred a quick, concentrated medical service to the greater degree of personal contact that they got when the nurses spent more time being missionaries. To government officials, who worked side by side with the Ranyard nurses, a heavy caseload had an agreeable look of utility.

From their urban experience the Ranyard nurses knew better than most that changes in family life, including changes in medical treatment, would have repercussions for religion. Improved prospects for patients' bodies undermined attentions to the soul. In the nineteenth century, for example, dying children concentrated the minds of parents on salvation, their own as well as their children's. The Ranyard nurses were very familiar with the distressing level of infant mortality through their maternity work. But it gave them opportunities for proselytism. The marked decline in infant mortality after 1900, and the expansion of hospital confinements removed some of the physical suffering and mental anguish but reduced opportunities to evangelize. Meanwhile, improvements in diagnosis reduced the belief in miraculous cures in the minds of patients and their families. The separation of the living from the dying, which became more common as sick and terminal patients were removed from their homes into expanding hospitals and nursing homes, also broke the cycle of domestic Christianity. Religion lost some of its poignancy and power as those ritual visits of family and neighbours around the domestic sickbed declined. As religion faded so too did traditions of bereavement. By the mid-twentieth century the British public had largely lost touch with the age-old religious practices that made it easier to mourn their departed loved ones.[60]

The introduction of new drugs and painkillers meant that death itself, so important in stimulating and renewing Christian piety, lost some of its transforming power. With relatively few expectations of medicine or of a scientific cure, the Victorian mind turned more readily than we do now to spiritual matters, to the need for a summing up. For their part, nineteenth-century Bible nurses did not delude their patients with false hopes of prolonged life. After all, the *Book of Common Prayer* intoned: 'In the midst of life we are in death.' If anything, they anticipated death and took hope from a patient's reconciliation with it. But as their medical training became more professional and more effective, patients' souls slipped away from them. With higher hopes of sustaining life, they, like their patients, were distracted from thoughts of an afterlife. The history of declining Christian belief in the twentieth century is a complicated one, but more attention might be paid to changes in medical practice, to falling mortality rates, to the growth of institutional care, to mourning rituals and painkillers.[61] Few people are reasoned out of their religion. Arguably, chloroform did as much to imperil faith as Darwin.

The First World War had serious consequences for nursing, as for medical care generally. On the administrative front it triggered the passage of a Bill, long under discussion, which established a system of state registration of nurses. This was seen as a victory for those who wished to give nursing greater status as a profession. On the medical front the war 'forced the new science to organize its material for mass application'.[62] As a result Britain became a healthier country to live in, which heightened expectations of further developments.[63] Notable advances in surgery and the treatment of wounds and shock contributed to greater public approval of hospital and convalescent care, which highlighted the importance of nursing, both in hospitals and in homes. New medical devices, fracture clinics, and radiology departments pushed up costs and increased the pressure on nurses, who were expected to take on more elaborate skills. Meanwhile, the emergency stepped up the need for around-the-clock nursing, which had been made possible by the electrification of hospitals. District nursing felt particular pressure from the million-and-a-half men who returned from the front permanently disabled by wounds or the effects of gas.[64]

As the war pointed to health as a national asset, it created and exposed deficiencies in health provision and its organization. Medical costs mounted, but capital expenditure in a hospital or a nursing order, unlike a business, did not increase its earning-power, but simply its spending capacity. One result of the war that had consequences for nursing charities, and philanthropy generally, was a vast increase in levels of taxation on higher incomes. Families living on earned income of £10,000 a year, for example, paid over 500 per cent more in tax in 1918–19 than in 1913–14.[65] As post-war taxation helped pay for the expansion of government services, the voluntary sector struggled to make ends meet. In the depressed economic climate, legacies and large donations were harder to come by and charities had to turn to borrowing, to more elaborate appeals, and to government assistance.

In the straitened circumstances of the inter-war years, an era of ever-greater patient demand, the voluntary hospitals and related institutions were under enormous financial strain, which intensified calls for government action.[66]

Despite the introduction of state registration for nurses and calls for greater coordination between the voluntary and public hospitals, little was done in the inter-war years to encourage greater rationalization of nursing services. In the medical world, calls for state partnership, which were having an effect elsewhere in the voluntary sector, fell on deaf ears, partly because of the power of the charitable hospitals and partly because of the government's lack of interest. With the return to normalcy in the 1920s, the many local nursing charities, like the hospitals, retained their separate identities. For its part, the Ranyard Mission had its hands full in South London, not least with casualties of the war. In the nursing world generally, dissatisfaction over pay and conditions persisted, but few interested parties saw much scope for improvements, given the vested interests at stake. As a result, nursing recruitment suffered. The Athlone Committee, which reported on nursing services in 1939, discovered that many potential recruits preferred to take humble white-collar jobs.[67] It was not until the Second World War that the state of the nation's nursing services commanded attention and there was general agreement that a return to pre-war health provision was impracticable.

The Second World War had more serious consequences for medical administration and the future of nursing than the First because aerial bombardment damaged or destroyed so many of the nation's hospitals, dispensaries, nursing facilities, and appeal offices. Scores of nurses were found dead or injured amidst the rubble. In the London region alone, 326 hospitals and kindred institutions, many of them charities, had suffered bomb damage by July 1941, with thousands of beds permanently lost.[68] St Thomas's, one of Britain's oldest Christian charities, lost 508 of its beds out of a total complement of 682.[69] The renewal of German aerial attacks in 1944 damaged a further seventy-six London hospitals, both voluntary and municipal.[70] Clearly the Blitz softened up the hospitals for post-war reorganization. As a consequence of the destruction to hospital property, the Ministry of Health had difficult decisions to face. As early as 31 October 1940, a departmental minute questioned whether the hospitals would survive without ministerial action.[71]

The projected cost of rebuilding war-torn hospitals not only undermined the morale of charitable campaigners but absolutely required government action, an important issue that historians have largely ignored in their accounts of the creation of the National Health Service. It is worth remembering that the capital assets of Britain's voluntary hospitals were worth about £300 million before the war.[72] Even after the bombing, the hospitals were worth a sum large enough to put a gleam in the eye of the minister of health and worth fighting over by the charitable campaigners who had raised the money to pay for them. To the more ardent hospital voluntarists, including not a few working-class supporters, the nationalization of their independent 'local' hospitals would be an act of vandalism comparable to the dissolution of the monasteries. Sir Bernard Docker, chairman of the British Hospitals Association, compared it to 'mass murder'.[73]

The Second World War turned nursing, like the hospitals, into a national issue. It was estimated that the country needed between 37,000 and 67,000 trained nurses to cope with air-raid casualties and to keep the hospitals running, but shortages were endemic and wastage rates high.[74] In the emergency, the public looked to government to provide assistance. It became imperative for the various nursing organizations to forge closer links with the military authorities and government departments. Training, registration, and status were problems that required immediate attention, for many unqualified women had turned to nursing for adventure or simply to avoid munitions work. Increasingly, the Ministry of Health took on an advisory role and nurses became subject to its influence over pay and conditions. As elsewhere in the social services, greater professionalism and government regulation went hand in hand.

In the post-war reconstruction, the future of nursing was uncertain. The nursing charities, which had struggled to retain their autonomy during the war, were so unsettled that a return to pre-war levels of fund-raising seemed impossible. Would the public respond with its traditional enthusiasm to future appeals to self-help after all the sacrifice the war itself demanded? Where were the contributions to come from? While the wealthy became poorer through taxation, the poorer classes expected to be richer in terms of free welfare services provided by government, albeit at subsistence levels.[75] The 'planning wing' in the Labour movement was decidedly unsympathetic to a charitable revival. To leading politicians in the post-war Labour government, the traditions of Christian nursing, with their bazaars and flag days, were demeaning. To the minister of health, Aneurin Bevan, it was 'repugnant to a civilized community for hospitals to have to rely upon private charity. . . . I have always felt a shudder of repulsion when I have seen nurses and sisters who ought to be at their work . . . going about the streets collecting money for the hospitals'.[76]

The year 1948, which saw the creation of the National Health Service, was a momentous one for nursing. It was now necessary for this traditionally conservative, fragmented profession to embrace a future in the context of a comprehensive health service. The talk was no longer of 'selective provision' for the 'sick poor', which had been a guiding principle of voluntary medicine, but of universal care in a national system. In the NHS, the perennial nursing issues—planning, grading, and superannuation—seemed light years away from the religious priorities of Victorian nursing. Nurses had less to lose than the doctors in the New Jerusalem, for they were not dependent on fees for their services. But just where nursing institutions and sisterhoods fitted into the new arrangements was unclear, for incorporating religious charities into the NHS was not a priority in the Ministry of Health. When the Labour government nationalized the voluntary hospitals, over 1,000 of them, it also decided that 200 or so other 'disclaimed' hospitals, homes, and religious societies, including the Ranyard Mission, would retain their independence but cooperate with the health service wherever practical.[77]

In district nursing, voluntary associations continued to play a significant role until the 1950s.[78] It was a sign of the times that the

Ranyard Mission relinquished the mission workers, the former Bible women, in 1953, on financial grounds, though some of the employees found work in their respective dioceses.[79] By then, home nursing had become a statutory responsibility of the local authorities, but carried out with the help of voluntary societies. Eventually, over 140 Ranyard nurses worked for the London County Council.[80] But in 1965, three years before their centenary, the NHS incorporated them into its district-nursing programme.[81] This occasion must have touched off mixed emotions for those in the mission who remained loyal to Mrs Ranyard's ideals. She had always been chary of the state, which she saw as a potential threat to voluntary effort, self-help, and Christian teaching. Nor would she have approved of a standard text on community nursing published in 1970, which admitted that nurses visiting the sick at home were 'sadly lacking in their appreciation of their role in the care of the dying'.[82]

In the post-war world the nurses of Mrs Ranyard's day, with their Bible learning and missionary zeal, would have seemed bizarre. In a secular medical culture, nurses no longer prayed at the bedside of the dying. They no longer had to attend church every Sunday and sit in the nurse's seat.[83] They no longer had to pass tests in theology or recite the parables. They no longer had to wear uniforms that resembled the habit of a religious order. (After the Second World War nurses' uniforms took on a military cast, which is suggestive for the history of nursing.)[84] As it turned out, Christian charity was simply unable to keep pace with the greater expectations of health, with scientific medicine or egalitarian principles. The Ranyard Mission held out longer than most nursing institutions, but it could not sustain its independence under the weight of wartime and post-war government pressures. In a democracy that offered comprehensive health care free at point of use, a self-governing agency with religious leanings looked increasingly obsolescent. It was a fate repeated across the voluntary sector, as institutions collapsed or changed their priorities to suit a government agenda. In less than a century district nursing, like nursing generally, had been transformed in ideological, professional, and administrative terms.

Loyalty to religion became an impediment in the brave new secular world of the twentieth century. Nurses, like social workers and teachers, had their origins in religious vocation, and their meager pay and onerous work reflected the public's willingness to take advantage of altruistic motives. With the years, the very Christian piety and voluntary culture that had inspired nursing came to be seen as a brake on its progress in a society in which most people expected their health care to be delivered by the state. But there was a price to be paid for progress. It was paid by Christianity, by charity, and perhaps even a little by the sick. But it was a price worth paying by patients, who now expected medicine to cure their infirmities; and by nurses, whose status no longer turned on the expression of Christian devotion. The body had bested the soul, and there was no going back to Victorian missionary medicine and its obsession with sin and the hereafter. In a culture that rejoiced in earthly gratification, heaven had lost its allure.

6

Foreground

> The making of a good society depends not on the State but on the citizens, acting individually or in free association with one another, acting on motives of various kinds—some selfish, others unselfish, some narrow and material, others inspired by love of man and love of God.
>
> (William Beveridge, *Voluntary Action*, 1948)

> We are still living on our capital of Christian inheritance. Today, there remain in our national attitudes, traditions and standards which are part of our Christian inheritance, but the capital is running out. The next generation will inherit less than we did in the way of Christian values.
>
> (Eric Treacy, bishop of Wakefield, *C. of E. Newspaper*, 1974)

The relationship between government and the people changed so dramatically in the twentieth century that we may, like G. M. Young, see late Victorian Britain as an *ancien régime*.[1] While central government was little noticed in the 1850s, the tendrils of the state were everywhere to be seen a century later, from the local surgery to the unemployment office on the high street. Translated into quantitative terms, government spent less than 8 per cent of gross national product in the 1900s and over 50 per cent in the 1960s.[2] Victorians held government in esteem, but expected little from it on social issues. In a national culture dominated by Christianity, they commonly believed that poverty was ineradicable, yet they sought its amelioration through voluntary service. A century later, most Britons believed poverty could be abolished, but that responsibility for welfare provision resided in the political process. An opinion poll in 1948 found that over 90 per cent of people no longer thought there was a role for charity in Britain.[3] With collectivism in the ascendant, the payment of taxes had become the primary civic duty.

Individuals could take satisfaction from paying their taxes, but they were in many ways more impotent in an age of universal suffrage and parliamentary democracy than their disenfranchised ancestors had been under an oligarchic system.[4] Paradoxically, there was more social connectedness in the age of Queen Victoria, with all its class distinctions and fear of representative democracy, than in post-war Britain, with its New Jerusalem egalitarianism. Those very distinctions and fears made social contact between the classes essential. Self-governing local institutions, from lowly mothers' meetings to the mighty voluntary hospitals, had connected citizens to their communities and gave them a measure of direct control over their own affairs. In an era of religious commitment, limited government, and strong local allegiances, social responsibility was not simply a corollary of privilege but a corollary of citizenship. But by mid-twentieth-century Britain, participatory citizenship, for all its virtues, no longer looked a plausible remedy for the ills of a nation so damaged by war and intent on social reconstruction.

The expansion of government had been in train for a century or more, but the creation of the welfare state signalled that there was a decisive winner in the debate over social policy. The extraordinary circumstances of 'total war' had boosted Labour's planning mentality, and its leadership paid scant heed to the democratic impulses and good offices of charitable associations with their ethic of personal service. After all the strains and suffering of the 1930s and 1940s, fairness was a powerful argument on the side of widening government provision in the health and social services. Voluntary institutions, with their limited resources and attachment to selective provision, were not able to answer it. Nor did rival local charities, with their ad hoc remedies and seemingly inefficient muddle, offer a compelling alternative to the rationale of planning with a capital P.

In what may be seen as the welfare equivalent of urban renewal, comprehensive reconstruction ravaged much of the historic fabric of the voluntary social services. In a representative democracy, social policy had shifted from the local to the national, from the religious to the secular, and the parish and the congregation bowed to the constituency. Indirect, representative democracy, expressed through Cabinet government, now reigned supreme in educational and social policy over the spontaneous form of democracy that was immanent in voluntary institutions. To put it another way, the ministerial, civil-service state had dislodged civic pluralism, whose foundations lay in Christian notions of individual responsibility. In a world in which political and social thought had turned on its axis, voluntary agencies were now open to the criticism that they were intrinsically undemocratic in nature.

The shift from voluntary to state social provision was significant, not only for the history of politics and social policy but also for religion. Christian institutions were conducive to the growth of grass-roots democracy, but democracy in its representative form proved less conducive to Christianity. As we have seen in the cases of schools and welfare charities, representative democracy and vital religion proved less than companionable. The 1870 Education Act that followed the extension of the franchise in 1867 diluted religious schooling and undermined denominational renewal. Later social legislation contributed to the collapse of nursing associations, visiting societies, and other parish charities. It was not a coincidence that the expansion of government and the contraction of religion happened over the same period, for the modern British state was constructed against religious interests and customs of associational citizenship. The reform of the suffrage that prompted welfare legislation may be seen as an underlying cause of Christian decline. Indeed, the expansion of government into education and the social services was both cause and effect of Christian decline. It is notable that high levels of welfare and low levels of religious adherence go together across much of Europe.[5]

In their enthusiasm for state intervention, the British churches themselves contributed to their own difficulties. Once religious leaders set aside the parable of the Good Samaritan and began to see government intervention as a solution to the crisis of urban poverty, the effect on Christian charity was predictable. In moving away from nineteenth-century liberal conventions, they had departed from tradition. But, unable to think of themselves as less than Christian in doing so, they did not foresee the threat to religion inherent in government expansion. For a time, the hybrid doctrine of Christian socialism papered over the cracks. It was more a sign of exhaustion than of faith when the Church of England, battered by war and financially troubled, resolved in 1948 'that the State is under the moral law of God, and is intended by Him to be an instrument for human welfare'.[6] Obeisance to the 'omnicompetent' state was an abdication of a historic responsibility, and it reflected a social and cultural transformation that had repercussions for Christianity that were arguably as great as any since the eighteenth-century religious revival.

In the belief that the state was fulfilling 'the law of Christ', Christian leaders failed to appreciate the consequences of endorsing a collectivist, secular world without redemptive purpose. Salvation, after all, was not among the benefits at the social-security office. With associational Christianity on the slide, it would have been fair to ask, like one historian of religion: 'How many drunkards have the Darwinians reclaimed?'[7] Collective provision eroded community religious life, partly because charities linked so many families to churches and congregations. In their appeal to altruism and piety, visiting societies and mothers' meetings, Sunday schools and Bible classes made denominational membership meaningful. The attractions of state benefits in a culture growing more materialist and national made such institutions seem increasingly dated and irrelevant. With their disappearance, religious observance was bound to suffer. In the shifting post-war culture, Christianity was increasingly a private matter of individual conscience.

Rendering unto Caesar the things that traditionally were beyond Caesar's domain was particularly risky for the Church of England, for it bonded Anglicans to Whitehall, not to Lambeth Palace. By the mid-1960s a book on social work in the Church of England described Britain as 'a post-Christian society'.[8] One is again reminded of Tocqueville, who saw 'inevitable dangers' to religious faith 'whenever the clergy take part in public affairs'. (Have American church leaders forgotten his warning?) He concluded that if state religions were 'sometimes of momentary service to the interests of political power, they always sooner or later become fatal to the church'.[9] The great currents of the twentieth century were largely beyond the control of the Church of England. The collapse of parish charities, those points of light into the twilight zone of ignorance and squalor, was perhaps unavoidable given the effects of war and reconstruction. But rarely has a British institution so willingly participated in its own undoing. The bishops blew out the candles to see better in the dark.

Few post-war commentators questioned whether the welfare state was capable of replacing the once dominant Christian idea of common purpose in social thought, much less whether the idea of purpose itself could survive in a secular society driven by materialist objectives. Clearly, the bishops were in tune with prevailing opinion that only government action could transform society and end the miserable poverty of the past. At mid-century, support for the welfare state reflected the political consensus of the day. Out went selective social provision, replaced by the universal benefits that only the state could provide. Beveridge had called his plan for social reconstruction a 'British Revolution', by which he meant it was 'a natural development from the past'.[10] But the welfare state departed from tradition more than its proponents conceded, not least from the tradition of Christian social service. It introduced for the first time in British history the sense that there were political solutions to virtually all human ills. In a secular age given to egalitarian rhetoric and redistributive justice, there seemed less need for personal service or participatory citizenship. If by the push of a ministerial button a programme of social progress could be set in train, was there any need to look after thy neighbour?

In the immediate post-war years the once proud tradition of voluntarism looked increasingly provincial and amateurish. In the negotiations over the NHS, for example, there had been little predisposition to compromise with the 'local' charitable hospitals, which to Bevan were 'a complete anachronism'.[11] After the damage the hospitals suffered during the war, it was widely assumed that only nationalization and government funding could save them. But to many charitable campaigners, the issue of local democracy remained. The outgoing governors of the Worcester Royal Infirmary put it directly at the time when their institution was taken over by the state: 'We may not have the wealth of Government, nor the power to command a big staff, nor the funds to build all we require, but we have a priceless asset, that as a people we want to maintain our democracy not only in a parliamentary way, but in our social service.'[12] But in a political culture that now placed less value on the intermediary institutions of civic life, they and individuals like them faced an uncertain future.

In the heyday of the welfare state, charities were widely seen as ineffectual remnants of Victorianism, associated with fruitless pieties and middle-class busybodies. Richard Crossman, appointed secretary of state for Health and Social Security in 1968, observed that to radical socialists philanthropy was 'an odious expression of social oligarchy and churchy bourgeois attitudes' and 'do-gooding a word as dirty as philanthropy'.[13] The use of 'do-gooder' as a term of abuse was revealing, for it encapsulated the transformation of values that had taken place. In the health services, according to the King's Fund, the distinguished London hospital charity, 'the very use of the word voluntary' was anathema to large sections of hospital management.[14] Trade unionists and many civil servants shared Bevan's aversion to hospital charity, which the fledgling NHS sidelined. The Ministry of Health forbade the new hospital boards from taking part in the activities of Leagues of Friends and even had hospital collection boxes removed from post offices.[15] Volunteers were widely thought to be irrelevant, at best peripheral figures providing auxiliary labour, typified by the Red Cross lady running a trolley shop.

Clearly, something fundamental had happened to British culture, once so Christian and voluntarist, in which the burden of care shifted so radically to government, in which charitable service became characterized as an 'amenity' or a 'frill'. The traditional liberal ideal of balancing rights and duties had been supplanted, as a leading social critic observes, 'by a politics of dutiless right'.[16] 'The impression was given', as Crossman conceded, 'that socialism was an affair for the Cabinet, acting through the existing Civil Service.'[17] It was perhaps not surprising that collectivists did not encourage popular participation in their reforms. Social laws offered a blueprint for the reconstruction of society that did not require the participation of volunteers or summonses to self-help. If the interests of the state and society were identical, intermediary institutions were superfluous. In effect, the post-war political environment disinherited the Christian spirit of the Victorians, and with it a great swathe of associational culture. Ironically, the inheritance that politicians and civil-servant mandarins welcomed—and polished—was a paternalism that exceeded that of the voluntarists they often disavowed.

Douglas Jay, financial secretary to the Treasury in the Attlee government, famously expressed a view of the state that was characteristic of mid-twentieth-century state paternalism: 'In the case of nutrition and health, just as in the case of education, the gentlemen in Whitehall really do know better what is good for the people than the people know themselves.'[18] Such attitudes were not universal among Labour leaders, who in their public statements were known to temper their enthusiasm for planning with a measure of pragmatism. Herbert Morrison, though a zealous advocate of statutory provision, did not wish the state to destroy voluntary effort, which was 'fundamental to the health of a democratic society'.[19] Attlee, speaking as president of Toynbee Hall, a charity traditionally favoured by Labour, recognized that philanthropy was 'not confined to any one class of the community', and argued that 'we shall always have alongside the great range of public services, the voluntary services which humanize our national life and bring it down from the general to the particular'.[20]

Despite the occasional puffs to philanthropy by Labour leaders, self-governing charities were politically out of favour, treated as reserves in the provision of services. Many commentators assumed that the days of the independent charitable society, free from government assistance, were, as an authority on the social services put it in the 1950s, 'at an end'.[21] Ironically, the Labour party had grown out of a voluntary culture. Many of its early leaders owed a debt to church and chapel for their subsequent careers. But the post-war Labour party, perhaps forgetting that Christianity fostered the doctrine of human equality, had little time for religious charities. Nor did it favour societies for mutual aid, which along with Nonconformity had given socialism its democratic infrastructure and moral centre.[22] Local government fared little better, for the loss of its principal service, the municipal hospitals, was a blow to morale and recruitment. Having subdued its rivals, central government was on its way to perfecting what may be described as executive democracy, illiberal in character, in which citizens became 'consumers' of government rather than its 'producers'.[23]

As Max Weber pointed out, 'bureaucracy inevitably accompanies modern mass democracy in contrast to the democratic self-government of small homogeneous units'.[24] In compensation for the decline of rival sources of democracy, politicians and social commentators sought to replace the sense of community, which people had built up in the past out of family life and self-governing local institutions, with a sense of national community, built out of central bureaucratic structures and party politics. In passing social legislation, government acted in the name of freedom, progress, and social justice. The beauty of such abstractions perhaps blinded the public to the dangers of overburdening the state. Despite the warnings of the liberal economist Frederick Hayek and others, there was relatively little public debate over the insensitivity of central government to the periphery. It was not a strong current in political discourse to argue that effective social reform might come from below, from local institutions that derived their energy and legitimacy from openness to the immediate needs of individuals and communities. The more the government expanded its role into areas that were formerly the responsibility of families and voluntary institutions, the more it reduced the scope for individual service and social interaction.

With the years, the notion that a representative government had tutelary power over the citizenry took hold, and with it the concept of ministerial responsibility for social provision from the cradle to the grave. The Treasury may have been an odd ministry to create the 'Heavenly City' of socialism, in which bureaucracy would disappear. But government benefits, reliable and universal, made central government control virtually irresistible. Few wanted a return to inter-war conditions, or opposed advances in health care, least of all the middle classes who were the principal beneficiaries of the National Health Service.[25] The vast expansion of government services created a hybrid form of social imperialism, in this case turned inwards on little England. Indeed, the collapse of the empire and the need to employ overseas civil servants and retired servicemen may have helped the cause of administering what, to many Whitehall mandarins, was a world of underlings at home. The health service, in particular, was heavily dependent on such people to fill its many management positions. When the King's Fund set up its Staff College to train senior administrators for the NHS in 1949, its warden was a former brigadier and its atmosphere resembled an officer's mess.[26]

In the late 1940s and 1950s British citizens showed little uneasiness with the greater ministerial control over their lives, for they widely identified with the achievements of the welfare state, not unlike the way in which the Victorians identified with Christian charity. Few feared 'that the extension of state services might be threatening to subvert the traditional roots and moral sinews of British society'.[27] There was, however, a measure of opposition to the effects on the individual of an impersonal state weakening traditional allegiances and local institutions. The philosopher Michael Oakeshott, harking back to Tocqueville, saw the decline of free associations and a concentration of state power leading to a loss of liberty.[28] The journalist and professional misfit Malcolm Muggeridge, who eventually became a Catholic convert, complained that an unwitting public was swimming 'into the Great Leviathan's mouth'. He had a 'recurring nightmare' in the 1950s: 'In our inimitable English way we are allowing a Servile State to come to pass of itself without our noticing it . . . In the nightmare it seems clear that all the faceless men, the men without opinions, have been posted in key positions for a bloodless take-over, and that no one is prepared to join a Resistance Movement in defence of freedom because no one remembers what freedom means.'[29]

Muggeridge had probably been reading *The Servile State* (1912), written by the Catholic man of letters Hilaire Belloc. Belloc, who saw servility on the rise with the retreat of Catholicism, had argued that 'Socialist doctrine' led to a hybrid form of 'slavery', in which the proletariat exchanged their freedom for 'security and sufficiency'.[30] Muggeridge may also have been reading G. K. Chesterton, another Catholic social critic, with whom he was sometimes compared in later life. In *What's Wrong with the World* (1910) Chesterton had argued 'that if some form of collectivism is imposed upon England it will be imposed . . . by an instructed political class upon a people partly apathetic and partly hypnotised. . . . But the world will be like a broken-hearted woman who makes a humdrum marriage because she may not make a happy one. Socialism may be the world's deliverance, but it is not the world's desire.'[31]

In the writings of Oakeshott, Muggeridge, Belloc, and Chesterton there was much that was reminiscent of Tocqueville's critique of state power, in which Christianity figured prominently. As Tocqueville observed, a democratically elected government works for the happiness of the citizenry, but it wants to be the only agent and final arbiter of that happiness. In an age of egalitarianism, Tocqueville argued, the citizenry is attracted by 'uniformity of legislation' passed by a single, central power. Through social legislation, the state serves the physical needs and regulates the affairs of its citizens but turns them into dependent clients and fixes them 'irrevocably in childhood'. As a safeguard, democracy must be tempered by Christianity, which has a crucial role to play in shaping social organization. Self-respect, in his view, required a high degree of self-government in an egalitarian society. Without it, citizens unwittingly became their own oppressors. And Tocqueville concluded:

Among democratic nations it is only by association that the resistance of the people to the government can ever display itself: hence the latter always looks with ill favour on those associations which are not in its own power; and it is well worthy of remark that among democratic nations the people themselves often entertain against these very associations a secret feeling of fear and jealousy, which prevents the citizens from defending the institutions of which they stand so much in need.[32]

In 1949 echoes of Tocqueville could be heard in the House of Lords, in a debate on the voluntary sector. Several peers, unsettled by the genie of big government that had been let out of the bottle, worried about 'the natural bias of the welfare state towards totalitarianism'. Voluntary action, as the bishop of Sheffield argued, was one way of keeping it in check. The Labour peer Lord Nathan, formerly a Liberal, joined in the paean of praise to philanthropy, describing charities as 'schools in the practice of democracy'.[33] Lord Pakenham, another Labour peer and prominent Catholic layman, was ideally suited to soften Labour's statist image. As an aide to Beveridge he had helped prepare the ground for the post-war social services, but as an irrepressible philanthropist he reminded his contemporaries of Lord Shaftesbury. 'The voluntary spirit is the very lifeblood of democracy', he concluded: 'We consider that the individual volunteer, the man who is prepared to serve the community for nothing, is he whose personal sense of mission inspires and elevates the whole democratic process of official governmental effort.'[34]

Lord Beveridge also seemed to be having second thoughts about the impersonal bureaucracy that had come into existence after the war. Since his days at Toynbee Hall, he had believed in the complementary nature of charitable work and state action. In the inter-war years he had been an enthusiastic member of the King's Fund propaganda committee, which defended the voluntary hospitals from ministerial interference.[35] By the time of the publication of his book *Voluntary Action* (1948), he had become sensitive to the state's capacity to destroy 'the freedom and spirit . . . of social conscience' without which the assertion of rights was meaningless:

The making of a good society depends not on the State but on the citizens, acting individually or in free association with one another, acting on motives of various kinds—some selfish, others unselfish, some narrow and material, others inspired by love of man and love of God. The happiness or unhappiness of the society in which we live depends upon ourselves as citizens, not only the instruments of political power which we call the State.[36]

In the House of Lords, he observed that 'Beveridge . . . has never been enough for Beveridge'. Like Mill, he worried about state control over the nation's affairs. Some things 'should in no circumstances be left to the state', he concluded, 'or we should be well on the way to totalitarian conditions'.[37] Yet Beveridge, unlike a nineteenth-century liberal, did not imagine voluntarism working outside the auspices of government, what he called a 'Minister-Guardian of Voluntary Action'.[38]

In *Voluntary Action*, Beveridge pointed to the diminished role of the churches in post-war Britain and bemoaned the loss of religious faith that inspired philanthropy in the past: 'That there has been loss of religious influence is certain. That this means a weakening of one of the springs of voluntary action for social advance is equally certain.'[39] Looking back on the Victorian pioneers of social reform, whose strength and conscience flowed from Christian purpose, he observed that 'there had been a great alternative to pursuit of gain, as the guiding force in society; there was force for good inspired by religious belief and based on membership of a Christian community. . . . When and how shall we replace the lost power of widespread religious belief, the material resources which must support the Philanthropic Motive as the body clothes the soul, and the sense of brotherhood in the human race?'[40] As Beveridge saw it, Christian charity provided not only a buffer between the citizen and the state but between the citizen and the market too. Such idealism, couched in religious language, was beginning to sound old-fashioned even in 1948.[41]

As Beveridge recognized, the fate of British philanthropy largely mirrored that of Christianity in the first half of the twentieth century. But the impact on charities of broadened government services, though profound, proved erratic in the post-war years. The nationalization of the voluntary hospitals killed off a number of their associated societies, including the League of Mercy, the British Hospitals Association, and agencies that provided crutches and surgical appliances. Other institutions, including the King's Fund, the Saturday Fund, and the Nuffield Provincial Hospitals Trust, shifted their priorities as necessary. So did the Charity Organisation Society, which, as mentioned, changed its name to the Family Welfare Association. Some institutions, like the Women's Institutes, became less political and gave greater emphasis to the social side of their activities.[42] Societies with a long-standing role in social service, such as the Salvation Army and the London City Mission, must have wondered about the efficacy of legislation, since so many people continued to require their attentions. The fact that lighthouses were run by civil servants and lifeboats by philanthropists suggested a degree of muddle in British social administration.

Though charity survived, and in places thrived, long gone were the days when campaigners could make claims about the pre-eminence of voluntarism in British life. As religion lost its fervour and the welfare state emerged, surviving charities were relegated to the margins of social reform and the national debate on social policy. As state provision was egalitarian and materialistic, it tended further to erode religious associations. For those of a philanthropic disposition who lost their faith, allegiances often shifted from religious charities to other bodies that were thought to be more relevant to social needs. Those who retained their faith often found new causes overseas in such institutions as Christian Aid, which began life in 1945 as Christian Reconciliation in Europe, or the Catholic Fund for Overseas Development (CAFOD) founded in 1962. Mutable and restless, charity was well placed to pioneer ahead of government or to work in areas in which the state had little interest. Putting a brave face on the diminished status of voluntary activity, some concluded that the welfare state was a blessing in disguise, for in freeing charitable workers from former thankless tasks it offered fresh opportunities.

The welfare state proved less than monopolistic, and there were plentiful opportunities to work with it or alongside it. Charity, though battered and diminished, settled into a constructive anonymity in the 1950s and 1960s. As ever, there was a chronic need for informal benevolence, which was met by neighbours and extended families. 'The extent of neighbourliness, especially in times of adversity, cannot be overstressed', remarked a student of one working-class district in Liverpool in the 1950s.[43] In Bradford in the 1960s, voluntary workers were much in evidence in the social-service departments, but for every one of them there were four others providing informal, but regular, neighbourly help.[44] When the Nathan Committee investigated charitable practices in the 1950s, it uncovered such a rich seam of unpublicized neighbourliness and familial kindness in poor communities that it concluded that such actions made 'satisfactory relationships possible'.[45] If some social reformers had their way, more public money would have been spent propping up these traditions.[46]

Apart from casual charity, older institutions carried on, while new ones emerged partly as a reaction to the very sense of powerlessness that individuals felt in the face of an imperfect democracy and the standardizing tendencies of central government. The nationalization of the health and social services thus sharpened as it narrowed charitable campaigns. The limitations of the welfare state, which became more apparent with the passing years, also held out the prospect of charities and government departments working more closely together. Partnership precipitated changes within charitable societies themselves, bringing them into line with modern practices. But it posed dangers to the independence of voluntary bodies and further isolated those institutions that wished to maintain a Christian outlook. Where charity carried on or pioneered new campaigns, it had less and less to do with religious purpose.

The strategic planning in welfare provision that characterized the post-war decades ended in doubts, reassessment, and recrimination. After the oil crisis in the mid-1970s, the spending limits of state social services propelled a revival of interest in the charitable sector. Diversity, innovation, and cost-effectiveness were thought to be among the principal virtues of charity, and these became increasingly apparent against the background of government economies and the spiralling costs and bureaucratic inefficiencies of the welfare state. By the time Margaret Thatcher came to power in 1979, social engineering was out of fashion. Under her leadership, central government became a reluctant patron of the welfare state, and the emphasis in health and social services shifted to the pursuit of efficiency, private-sector expansion, and pluralism. The New Right, with its reversion to the language of the minimal state and the need for voluntary endeavour, echoed sentiments that had been little commended since the heyday of Victorian liberalism.[47] But such sentiments were being voiced in a world that had lost its Christian underpinnings. Thatcher's millionaires, unlike the Colmans, Rathbones, or Cadburys of the past, had other things to spend their money on than their fellow citizens.

As an admirer of Victorian values, Mrs Thatcher often spoke in glowing terms of voluntarism. In an address to the Women's Royal Voluntary Service in 1981, she saw 'the voluntary movement . . . at the heart of all our social welfare provision', and told her audience that 'we politicians and administrators must not forget that the state has a limited role' and that 'the willingness of men and women to give service is one of freedom's greatest safeguards. It ensures that caring remains free from political control.'[48] In the event, state funding for charities increased in the 1980s, but became more selective, while the cuts imposed on local government reduced the money available for local institutions.[49] Meanwhile, Section 5 of the 1980 Health Services Act permitted NHS hospitals to organize their own appeals. In giving what amounted to charitable status to statutory bodies it alienated many in the charitable sector.[50] In the ambiguous welfare world of the 1980s, it became necessary to use the word 'independent' before the name of a non-governmental charity, for it was no longer obvious that a charitable institution was not a government body.

Given Mrs Thatcher's tributes to the voluntary sector for promoting freedom and benevolence, one might have expected her administrations to offer rather more inducements to giving. Many charitable campaigners looked forward to changes in the tax system to encourage contributions. It was not until 1987 that the Conservative government introduced a 'give as you earn' scheme. But with tax relief set at a ceiling of £240 on donations, it was far too modest to make much of a difference. For all the upbeat talk about a return to charitable giving, Mrs Thatcher's support for reducing the tax burden on the sector had strict limits. While pressure to provide relief grew year by year, the Treasury worried lest leakage of the tax base threaten government spending. 'Widespread tax deductibility for charitable donations would be a voyage into the fiscal unknown.'[51] The grocer's daughter, ever watchful over the purse-strings, was not inclined to make the voyage.

The Victorian values of Mrs Thatcher were highly selective. The idea of the enabling state and the 'mixed economy of care', which coloured Conservative thinking, appealed to many charitable campaigners. But voluntarists found government a volatile partner under Mrs Thatcher. She not only expected more from the charitable sector than many in it felt able to perform, but as it transpired, she had a need for political control that expressed itself in greater centralization, not less. The prime minister failed to recall that the Victorians saw little virtue in the centralization of power or in blurring the boundaries between the state and voluntary sector. To Victorians, for whom the essence of voluntary institutions lay in self-government, Mrs Thatcher would seem officious and overbearing. This was the view of many of her contemporaries. The commission appointed in 1983 by the archbishop of Canterbury to examine urban poverty thought her policies crude and divisive.[52] The historian Raphael Samuel argued that Mrs Thatcher's appeals to Victorian values were often invoked for purely symbolic purposes. Their introduction enabled her to cast the welfare state in the guise of 'old corruption' and vilify Labour as ossified, while diverting attention from the greater centralization of power that was taking place during the 1980s.[53]

Mrs Thatcher was another example of the tendency of post-war prime ministers, sometimes consciously, sometimes not, to undermine the independence of voluntary institutions. While British governments of both right and left enlist the citizen volunteer when it suits them, they have rarely had much regard for the charitable independence, in part because voluntary campaigners openly criticize government policy. As the journalist Simon Jenkins puts it: 'Of all the paradoxes of Thatcherism, none is greater than this: that more open government should have been used, not to enable the public to participate more fully in democracy, but as a tool of state centralism in its quest for national efficiency.'[54] Whatever her intent, under the guise of Victorian liberalism Mrs Thatcher carried forward the very collectivist agenda that she disavowed. For all the Tory rhetoric summoning up Victorian values, the public showed little wish to return to them. In 1988 a survey of British opinion noted: 'after nine years of Thatcherism the public remained wedded to the collectivist, welfare ethic of social democracy.'[55]

The collapse of the Soviet Empire in 1989 had more positive repercussions for voluntary institutions than Mrs Thatcher and the New Right. The decline of world socialism led to a swing in the pendulum of social perceptions, perhaps as great as at the end of the nineteenth century, when views about the causes of poverty began to move in a direction unfavourable to voluntary service. For a century the Labour left had had an antipathy to charities, but now that 'real existing socialism' was found wanting around the globe, those 'bourgeois freedoms' offered by voluntary agencies had more to recommend them. No one doubted that economic dislocation created severe social problems, yet much less was heard after the events of 1989 about the links between distress and the structural faults of capitalism. Instead, there was a return to those mid-Victorian concerns about urban poverty, the collapse of the family, and the relevance of parish solutions. In promoting the virtues of democratic pluralism, 1989 effectively changed the language of politics, reshaping the context in which charity was understood. In the 1990s charity came to be elided with notions of civil society or community service, which made it more palatable to erstwhile critics.

In the 1990s the leaders of the Labour party, reeling from Thatcherism at home and the collapse of socialism abroad, felt obliged to distance themselves from their collectivist past. The public had grown chary of calls to socialist ardour, and notions of community and civil society offered Labour an opportunity to build a new constituency. 'It is by casting aside the rigid dogmas of the past', said Tony Blair in 1994, 'that we begin to see a new and exciting role for the voluntary sector—not an optional extra but a vital part of our economy.'[56] In 1998, as prime minister, Blair pronounced that it was 'the grievous 20th century error of the fundamentalist left' to suppose that the state could replace civil society and advance freedom.[57] Having abandoned Clause 4 socialism, New Labour was promoting an agenda that sounded reminiscent of the 'new liberalism' of the Edwardian era with its heady mix of Lib/Lab traditions. In practice, however, there was not much difference between Blair's enthusiasm for voluntary-sector expansion, couched in the rhetoric of renewal and contributory citizenship, and Mrs Thatcher's support for voluntary endeavour on the grounds of liberty and enterprise.

In 1988, the year before the collapse of the socialist states of central and eastern Europe, Gordon Brown had decried charity as 'a sad and seedy competition for public pity'.[58] But in 2001, as chancellor of the Exchequer, he launched a campaign, backed by government funds, to reinvigorate charitable service and civic spirit: 'Politicians once thought the man in Whitehall knew best. Now we understand that the . . . mother from the playgroup . . . might know better.'[59] The pronouncement, which calls to mind Josephine Butler's perception that legislative systems are 'masculine' and parochial service 'feminine', should not be taken at face value. New Labour praises local democracy, but is it talking about a democracy in which independent institutions outside ministerial control are encouraged to criticize government policy? Should parliament pass the current Charities Bill, which seeks both to enliven and further to regulate the voluntary sector, it will be interesting to note its consequences.[60]

The use of charities to do the government's bidding may be seen as the elusive 'Third Way', a devolved form of government control that turns the intermediary institutions of civil society into agencies of the state through contracts and financial control.[61] Should the percentage of charitable revenue from government sources continue to rise and individual donations continue to decline, more and more societies will become servants of the state. Since the 1980s a few social critics and a smattering of politicians have argued that government funding and the voluntary ethos are incompatible. To Timothy Raison, Home

Office minister responsible for the Voluntary Services Unit under Mrs Thatcher, financial independence was 'the cornerstone of the voluntary movement'.[62] Digby Anderson, a former director of the Social Affairs Unit, put the case for 'stopping the hidden expansion of the welfare state through the permanent subsidy of "voluntary" bodies by the central and local state'.[63] As some in the voluntary sector see it, Britain is witnessing a further stage in the perfection of the state monolith under the guise of partnership, a process that one charitable director calls a 'cultural takeover by stealth'.[64]

Successive governments have increased the grants available to voluntary bodies in recent decades. In the mid-1980s about 10 per cent of overall charitable revenue came from government sources.[65] Ten years later, despite Conservative reservations, the figure stood at 45 per cent, while donations from individuals declined.[66] State funding is a principal reason why the voluntary sector retains a substantial presence in the health and social services. But there is a price to pay in autonomy and independence when charities become little more than agencies of central or local government. The partnership between voluntary bodies and government, which began in earnest after the First World War, is in marked contrast with the nineteenth century, when relatively few institutions accepted government funding.

In the scramble for scarce resources, many contemporary charities eagerly accept government support. The National Lottery, introduced in 1994, carried the process of state intervention into a new realm. Sucking in money that might otherwise have gone to good causes, the Lottery then allocates some of it to charities, making them dependent on handouts from agencies subject to government guidelines. 'Everyone is a winner', proclaims the Lottery website.[67] But as it has been said, 'Lottery funding of charities is about as voluntary, from the point of view of the punter, as VAT.'[68] Greed, it would seem, is overtaking altruism as an inspiration for raising money. The appetite for state funding, whatever the source, has grown to the point where the question now being asked is whether charitable institutions are any longer voluntary? The Charity Organisation Society had addressed this issue as early as 1920: 'The state-aided voluntary society, to some of us a contradiction in terms, and to some a counsel of despair, is not, we hope, the only alternative to the extinction of voluntaryism.'[69]

In mass democracies, politicians and government bureaucrats wish to regulate and co-opt rival centres of authority. This process has occurred under both Labour and Conservative governments, and it applies to local government as well as voluntary institutions. With the decline of Christianity, an alternative view of the way in which poverty might be addressed largely faded. As charities are brought into the orbit of government, they take on board a view of welfare introduced by the state. In contemporary Britain, charitable officials often come from a background in government service and wish to distance themselves from Victorian traditions. As they often point out, partnerships with government enable charities to stay in the mainstream of policy and to improve their services and facilities.[70] Nor does the acceptance of government funding necessarily compromise charitable independence. But there is a cost to civic democracy as the two sectors merge. As charitable agencies become increasingly accountable to government, they are prone to forfeit their role as critics of government policy. A charitable official put it neatly years ago: 'no one is rude to his rich uncle.'[71]

The disparity in the scale of their respective operations exacerbates the problems charities face in forging close ties with government departments or local authorities. The voluntary society is invariably the 'junior partner in the welfare firm', which makes criticism of government policy more difficult.[72] An example from the hospital sector illustrates the point. In 1952 the government set up a committee, chaired by the economist Claude Guillebaud, to investigate the costs of the NHS. The King's Fund asked the head of its Economy Department, Captain J. E. Stone, arguably the leading expert on hospital administration in Britain, to write a detailed report on the state of the NHS. He produced an outspoken, devastating critique of the service and its financial management, which singled out 'its rushed introduction; impersonal character; emphasis on control; uncertainty; division of responsibility; lack of any systematic provision for cooperation; apparent lack of funds; and lack of an informative accounting system'. Given these failings, the patient, according to Stone, was 'being lost in the intricate working of a vast administrative machine'.[73]

On seeing the report, a member of the Fund's Management Committee took Stone aside and told him that his criticisms were 'inappropriate' and would not be submitted to the Guillebaud inquiry. Instead, the charity presented a brief, anodyne report, with an appendix on hospital toilets, in which it declined to comment on NHS finances.[74] The Fund's reluctance to rock the boat when it was beginning to forge partnerships with the Ministry of Health was typical of the timidity that had overtaken the voluntary sector. But it was unfortunate for the hospital service, which might have benefited from Stone's informed criticism. Like Guillebaud, Charles Webster, the official historian of the NHS, never saw the Stone critique and consequently assumed that the hospital service was given a clean bill of health by all interested parties. 'No part of this powerful investigative process', according to Webster, 'discovered evidence of waste within the NHS; the investigators were generally satisfied that the service was delivering a high quality of service in an economical manner.'[75]

Despite the growth of partnerships, which often dulls the candour of charitable officialdom, there remains a historic tension between the voluntary and state sectors. But it commands little attention in government circles, where a democracy operating outside the parameters of ministerial control can hardly be imagined. A minister for the voluntary sector would have seemed a contradiction in terms in the nineteenth century. As the Victorians recognized, the essence of charity, like the essence of voluntarism generally, is its independence and autonomy—it is the antithesis of collective or statutory authority.[76] Government provision depends on compulsory taxation; it is not altruistic but materialist in conception. It is largely about furthering equality. Charitable provision, on the other hand, cannot be extorted by force; its proponents have usually been driven by a liberal polity that is primarily individualist, even though it may be egalitarian. Distinctions between charity and government action are thus deeply rooted, not least in thinking about their respective roles and boundaries. The state is likely to retain its pre-eminence in the health and social services in Britain, but the perennial question remains: where should the balance lie between the 'right' to welfare and the 'virtue' of charity?[77]

Organized charity has had problems finding its place in a welfare economy dominated by government, but it has shown resilience in recent decades, as the rise in the number of institutions registered with the Charity Commission in England and Wales, currently standing at about 180,000, attests.[78] There have been gains in membership in some societies, especially those that support the environment. On the other hand, there has been a decline in membership of Christian associations and women's organizations, groups that provided so much of the personal service in the past.[79] In the Mothers' Union, membership figures plummeted from over 600,000 in 1938 to 122,000 in 2005.[80] Membership in the National Federation of Women's Institutes dropped from 446,700 in 1950 to 215,000 in 2005.[81] Volunteers recognize the need for personal ministration, but few modern charities have been able to maintain such a high level of face-to face interaction as in the nineteenth century. Informal carers and neighbourhood schemes, such as lunch clubs, playgroups, and youth projects carry on in a way reminiscent of Victorian Britain, but they attract little attention and are chronically short of funds.[82] And while foundations and non-profit agencies have grown in prominence in recent years, they have largely done so without mass membership or roots in the locality.

Charity is as much about the contributors as the recipients. And in the British voluntary sector, as in its American equivalent, there has been a shift of mass participation from *member* to *client*, with a consequent loss of institutional democracy.[83] Geared to clients, contemporary voluntary societies offer fewer opportunities for personal service than local institutions did in the past. The growth of government bureaucracy has encouraged greater professionalism and largeness of scale in those charities that have formed partnerships with the state, but not without cost. In the King's Fund, for example, the employment of officers and staff from the public sector, combined with the linking of pay and pensions to NHS scales, eroded the institution's voluntary ethos.[84] What was taking place in the Fund was a cultural shift of some significance, which mirrored what was happening elsewhere in the charitable sector. Those charities that work closely with the local or central government are more likely to shape their priorities to suit available grants, to create their own bureaucracies, to distance charitable campaigners from beneficiaries, and to play down religion.

Although Christianity continues to have a role in philanthropic work, locally, nationally, and internationally, the recent charitable revival, encouraged by government funding, does not reflect a religious revival. With reduced memberships, most Christian churches no longer serve as vital centres of community life as in the past. (In America, over 300,000 active congregations serve as 'the most ubiquitous and important voluntary bodies'.)[85] Most of the leading British charities founded in the mid-twentieth century, including Oxfam (1942), Mind (1946), and War on Want (1951), are wholly secular. Moreover, the state's ascendancy in welfare has encouraged the further secularization of religious charities, which have found it difficult to navigate the hazards of partnership and the contract culture without jettisoning former principles. Some, like the Shaftesbury Society and Barnardo's, have sacrificed their once ardent independence and now accept large sums from government sources.[86] Other religious institutions have shifted their priorities and avoided partnerships, for they are uneasy about greater government regulation and find it difficult to work with an officialdom that is impersonal and insensitive to spiritual issues.

The growth of government welfare has encouraged a more professional and statistical approach in the charitable sector, and this has told on religious institutions. When the Wolfenden Committee reported on the state of voluntary organizations in 1978, it observed that charities were increasingly 'secular and materialist in outlook rather than inspired by the desire to rescue or evangelise'.[87] There are individuals in Britain today whose religious zeal is reminiscent of Sarah Martin or Josephine Butler, but they are rare outside the Pentecostal churches. More exceptional still are Christian charities that are reminiscent of the Ranyard Mission or the Religious Tract

Society. Even Christian Aid and CAFOD do not carry forward the old proselytizing spirit. The Christian-inspired hospice movement, which recalls those Victorian nursing societies that sought to help the dying face death, pioneered a frontier where the state was largely ineffective. It is a prime example of the continuing capacity of religion to address an issue of great significance. But in a secular and centralized Britain, where religious enthusiasm is subject to doubt and disdain, Victorian charity seems a world away, though from time to time churchmen look back on it with nostalgia as they lament the egotism and greed of contemporary society.[88]

Whether they receive government funding or not, many Christian charities have watered down their religious image in recent decades. The Church of England Children's Society dropped 'Church of England' from its title in 1982. Barnardo's described itself as 'a Christian childcare organization' in 1990, but welcomed recruits 'from all world faiths'.[89] Avowedly Christian charity, though far from exhausted, is a pale shadow of its former self, as the decline of institutions such as the Bible Society or the Lord's Day Observance Society will attest. In a secular culture, the churches, weakened by falling memberships, have lost their traditional clarity and sense of direction. Between 1980 and 2000, 300 churches closed *each year* in England.[90] Today, charitable campaigners are more likely to rely on charity shops than churches for support.[91] Meanwhile, sectarian discipline, crucial to charitable expansion in the past, has given way to ecumenicalism, which to devout Victorians would seem like no religion at all. The religious denominations, once a mainspring of charity and public spirit, have become distracted and self-absorbed. In Christian circles and in the media, the hubbub over gay rights and women priests has drowned out reports of the social work carried out by the churches.

In contemporary Britain it is normal to be charitable without religious motivation. Typically, British volunteers cite altruism, filling spare time, or the need for a more imposing CV as reasons for participation. Religious concerns, though not insignificant, are no longer uppermost in the minds of the millions of volunteers.[92] A study by the Voluntary Centre in London in 1981 put the percentage of those motivated by religion at 10 per cent. A more recent MORI survey suggests that even those who belong to churches and other religious institutions are volunteering less and less.[93] As the bishop of Wakefield, Eric Treacy, said in 1974: 'We are still living on our capital of Christian inheritance. Today, there remain in our national attitudes, traditions and standards which are part of our Christian inheritance, but the capital is running out. The next generation will inherit less than we did in the way of Christian values.'[94] Only time will tell whether contemporary charitable campaigners who have discarded the faith of their parents and grandparents will pass on to their own children an obligation to support voluntary causes.

America has also seen a decline in commitment to voluntarism since the Progressive Era.[95] But there, where the provision of government welfare is relatively modest, religion remains much more buoyant. In a recent American survey, religion accounted for over 60 per cent of US charitable donations.[96] Competing, unestablished churches continue to stimulate religious institutions to seek a prominent role in social reform. Because of the Bush administration's support from the religious right and its hostility to federal programmes, faith-based initiatives are high on the political agenda in the United States. In 2004 the government awarded $2 billion in grants to religious groups for social projects.[97] Whether such institutions will have a major impact is open to question.[98] In Britain, the idea of giving a more prominent role to religious activists in the delivery of welfare has been under discussion in political circles, but it would seem even less likely to succeed, if only because the churches are relatively weak, as are the tax incentives to giving.[99]

Federal funding for charity in America has not, as yet, much undermined the autonomy of American charities because of their low level of accountability to government.[100] But this may change should religious charities take on greater responsibility for what are seen as community *needs*. Charities are held more accountable in Britain because the public commonly expects government to be responsible for such needs. In the United States, concern about religion intruding into the sphere of government has opened up the constitutional issue of the separation of church and state. In Britain, Christians who promote faith-based projects also often want the state to provide funding and support.[101] But state sponsorship of overtly religious voluntary social work is a sensitive issue in Britain as in America, not only because many people assume that government has the primary obligation for social services but because a secular public has become suspicious of mixing religion and politics.

Christian institutions in Britain have declined or diluted their religious message, but does it matter for the future of the nation's civic and political life? Is religion necessary to check the growth of democratic tyranny, as Tocqueville claimed when he pronounced that Christianity was essential to modern democracies? The Victorians commonly believed that Christianity and liberty, faith and freedom, marched heroically side by side. But who today would second the argument put by Thomas Stephenson in 1869, that 'good citizens can only be found in good Christians'?[102] A Gallup poll in 1981 revealed that only 13 per cent of the respondents believed Britain to be a Christian society, and only 23 per cent thought the disappearance of Christianity as the dominant culture unfortunate.[103] Given the prevalence of such attitudes, it seems doubtful that most contemporary Britons, unlike American Tocquevillians, would accept the proposition that Christianity is essential to western democracy. It is a measure of how far secularization has taken hold in Britain since the nineteenth century.

In any appraisal of British social democracy, much depends on whether one thinks, like Tocqueville, that state entitlements turn citizens into dependent clients with a consequent loss of freedom. This in turn often depends on whether one puts a premium on freedom from oppression or freedom from want. The former was more widely esteemed before the advent of universal suffrage, the latter in an era of representative democracy and expanding government. The resurgence of interest in civil society since 1989 reflects the growing sense that central government, under Labour or Conservative leadership, has become imperious and undemocratic, and that free associations with their traditions of grass-roots democracy are needed to keep it in check. It represents a return not to associational religion as such, but to the liberal Victorian belief in the diffusion of power as a guarantor of freedom. Whether a voluntary sector increasingly funded and regulated by government will promote freedom remains at issue.

In the audit of religion in Britain, many would say that the decline of Christian culture has led not to a loss of liberty but to a loss of civility, what the Victorians called 'manners and morals', those essential signs of respectability. The contemporary preoccupation with hooliganism among the young might suggest that incivility is on the rise.[104] But the high level of boorishness in the past should be remembered. There was a 'panic' over hooliganism in the late Victorian years, and much energy was spent trying to eliminate it.[105] But in contemporary Britain people are often bemused by the idea of respectability and the source of its authority. Respectability to a Victorian was largely a function of religion, a secular expression of Christian discipline. Clearly, respectability was a binding force in nineteenth-century society, fortified by the ubiquitous biblical teaching in local schools and charities. It has lost its potency with the waning of Christian sensibilities. In a diverse, market-driven culture, in which individuals often feel adrift, what is there to restrain behaviour beyond the fading residue of religious morality and the criminal law?

Few dissent from the view that the British have entered an era when the bonds that hold the nation together have loosened. The weakening of the cultural consensus founded on Christianity has played its part in the process. Secularism, the global economy, and multiculturalism do not, it seems, make for social cohesion or encourage high levels of social capital. Nor does 'believing without belonging' to institutions encourage human interaction.[106] In the nineteenth century, as noted, those parts of Britain with the most uniform denominational populations had the highest levels of religious observance and charitable activity. Recent research by the General Household Survey in Britain confirms that the more prosperous, settled, and socially homogeneous the neighbourhood the higher the levels of trust and cooperation.[107] A study of the pattern of social capital in contemporary American communities suggests that people living in diverse neighbourhoods are more suspicious of their neighbours and less likely to join community organizations.[108]

Whatever the future of civil society in Britain, a tantalizing question remains in the audit of Christianity. Was it simply fortuitous that Britain reached the apogee of its prestige and power between the evangelical revival in the eighteenth century and the waning of Christianity in the twentieth? The causes of the rise and fall of Britain are highly contentious and fraught with complexity. Secularism, materialism, and greater tolerance have led to advances and benefits, opportunities and innovations in British society that would astonish the Victorians. Few citizens would wish to return to Sabbatarianism, missionary medicine, or an education centred on the Bible. On the other hand, the buoyancy and assurance of nineteenth-century Britain was a reflection of the nation's self-esteem and standing in the world. Few nations have been so confident. To Victorians, Protestantism and liberalism were the pillars of Britain's prosperity, political stability, and imperial grandeur, and they came together in the doctrine of self-help, which, in the words of Samuel Smiles, was 'the true source of national vigour and strength'.[109] Such faith and self-confidence, whether a delusion or not, evaporated in the twentieth century.

The mid-Victorians were perhaps the last generation of Britons to take undiluted comfort from Christianity, and whose self-belief was not overshadowed by national self-doubt and discontent. Since their day, the rationalism, detachment, and insatiable appetite for change have led to doubts and uncertainties that would leave them aghast. Modernity, despite all the benefits and advances, as Max Weber observed, brought in its wake a narrowing of imagination, the isolation of the individual, and disenchantment.[110] In his powerful essay 'A Free Man's Worship' (1903), Bertrand Russell, no friend to Christianity, expressed the 'materialist' view of the 'tragic isolation' of the individual in a world without religion, in which a 'sure doom falls pitiless and dark' as 'omnipotent matter rolls on its relentless way'.[111] The loss of Christian conviction in Britain—and with it often went a sense of the nation in retreat—has been a principal cause of disenchantment and anomie, for little beyond distractions and material possessions have filled the emptiness left by its departure. Socialism as a substitute religion proved a chimera. And as Christian conviction waned, so too did a tradition of charitable ministration, without which humanity became, at least to the faithful, nothing but a 'sounding brass or a tinkling cymbal'.[112]

The melancholy G. M. Young, who mourned the cost of certainties lost, observed that the Victorians themselves contributed mightily to the doubts that have afflicted modern Britain. 'The function of the nineteenth century', he wrote, 'was to disengage the disinterested intelligence, to release it from party and sect . . . and to set it operating over the whole range of human life and circumstance.'[113] In the ferment of minds unshackled from former loyalties, people increasingly discarded the tenets of religion. In Christianity's decline, the spirit of critical inquiry played a part, to be sure, but so too did democratic advance, the growth of government, world wars, greater social mobility, secular education, medical progress, an ever-widening universe of entertainments and recreations, and expanding opportunities for women. Religion, however earnest and vital, was ill equipped to meet so many challenges. The great Christian culture of Victorian Britain, built on a revered and historic narrative of liberty and faith, was overtaken by events. But at the beginning of the new millennium, it takes some effort to think of our secular state at ease with the disinterested mind; and we may, like Young years ago, still see 'in the daily clamour for leadership, for faith, for a new heart or a new cause . . . the ghost of late Victorian England whimpering on the grave thereof'.[114]

Notes

CHAPTER 1

1. *A Brief Sketch of the Life of the Late Miss Sarah Martin* (Yarmouth, 1845), 3–9.
2. Steve Bruce, 'The Demise of Christianity in Britain', in *Predicting Religion: Christian, Secular and Alternative Futures*, ed. Grace Davie, Paul Heelas, and Linda Woodhead (Aldershot, 2003), 54; Alan D. Gilbert, 'Secularization and the Future', in *A History of Religion in Britain: Practice and Belief from Pre-Roman Times to the Present*, ed. Sheriden Gilley and W. J. Sheils (Oxford, 1994), 512; Callum G. Brown, *The Death of Christian Britain: Understanding Secularization 1800–2000* (London, 2001), 3.
3. *1891 Census of England and Wales*, III, p. xxx.
4. James Obelkevich, 'Religion', *The Cambridge Social History of Britain 1750–1950*, ed. F. M. L. Thompson, 3 vols. (Cambridge, 1990), iii. 328.
5. 'Preliminary Address', *Reports of the Society for Bettering the Condition and Increasing the Comforts of the Poor* (Dublin, 1800), p. viii.
6. A Lady, *The Whole Duty of Woman or, a Guide to the female sex, from the age of sixteen to sixty* (Stourbridge, 1815), 23.
7. Quoted in David McCullough, *John Adams* (New York, 2001), 619.
8. Ian Bradley, *The Call to Seriousness: The Evangelical Impact on the Victorians* (London, 1976), 21.
9. Edmund Gosse, *Father and Son: A Study of Two Temperaments* (New York, 1907), 290.
10. See e.g. Robert Putnam, *Bowling Alone: The Collapse and Revival of American Community* (New York, 2000). On Britain, see Peter A. Hall, 'Social Capital in Britain', *British Journal of Political Science*, 29: 3 (July 1999), 417–59.
11. Philip Larkin, 'Church Going', in *Collected Poems*, ed. Anthony Thwaite (London, 1988), 98.
12. R. J. Morris, 'Clubs, societies and associations', *Cambridge Social History of Britain 1750–1950*, iii. 443.

13. G. P. Gooch, *English Democratic Ideas in the Seventeenth Century* (Cambridge, 1954; first pub. 1898), 7.
14. Jean S. Heywood, *Children in Care: The Development of the Service for the Deprived Child* (London, 1978), 13.
15. *Voluntary Social Services: Their Place in the Modern World*, ed. A. F. C. Bourdillon (London, 1945), 303.
16. Quentin Skinner, *Liberty Before Liberalism* (Cambridge, 1998), 17. For a stimulating discussion of the protean nature of civil society see *Civil Society in British History: Ideas, Identities, Institutions*, ed. Jose Harris (Oxford, 2003).
17. Geoffrey Finlayson, *Citizen, State, and Social Welfare in Britain, 1830–1990* (Oxford, 1994), 40.
18. Hilda Jennings, *The Private Citizen in Public Social Work* (London, 1930), 18.
19. Quoted in Bernard Semmel, *The Methodist Revolution* (New York, 1973), 91.
20. Manuscript diary of a Victorian woman, 1860s, in the author's possession.
21. Bradley, *The Call to Seriousness*, 14–15.
22. Margaret McMillan, *The Life of Rachel McMillan* (London, 1927), 89.
23. H. Stuart Hughes, *Consciousness and Society: The Reorientation of European Social Thought 1890–1930* (New York, 1958), 320.
24. Quoted in Semmel, *The Methodist Revolution*, 75.
25. McMillan, *The Life of Rachel McMillan*, 89.
26. S. J. D. Green, *Religion in the Age of Decline: Organisation and Experience in Industrial Yorkshire, 1870–1920* (Cambridge, 1996), 182.
27. Jose Harris, 'Victorian Values and the Founders of the Welfare State', in *Victorian Values*, ed. T. C. Smout (Oxford, 1992), 174–5.
28. Brian Harrison, 'Civil Society by Accident? Paradoxes of Voluntarism and Pluralism in the Nineteenth and Twentieth Centuries', in *Civil Society in British History*, ed. Harris, 91–3.
29. Arthur Schlesinger Jr., 'Biography of a Nation of Joiners', *American Historical Review*, 50 (1944), 24.
30. David Owen, *English Philanthropy, 1660–1960*, (Cambridge, Mass., 1964), 481–82.
31. John Stuart Mill, *Principles of Political Economy* (Harmondsworth, 1970), 312–13.
32. Samuel Smiles, *Self-Help with Illustrations of Conduct & Perseverance* (Repr. London, 1958), 36.

33. Joanna Innes, 'Central Government "Interference": Changing Conceptions, Practices and Concerns, c. 1700–1850', in *Civil Society in British History*, ed. Harris, 39.

34. Revd Archer Gurney, *Loyalty and Church and State: A Sermon Preached . . . on the occasion of the National Thanksgiving for the Recovery of H.R.H. the Prince of Wales* (1872), 6.

35. Owen, *English Philanthropy, 1660–1969*, 20.

36. See W. O. B. Allen and Edmund McClure, *Two Hundred Years: The History of the Society for Promoting Christian Knowledge, 1698–1898* (London, 1898).

37. S. C. Williams, *Religious Belief and Popular Culture in Southwark c.1880–1939* (Oxford, 1999), ch. 4.

38. Boyd Hilton, *The Age of Atonement: The Influence of Evangelicalism on Social and Economic Thought, 1785–1865* (Oxford, 1988), 103.

39. Kathleen Heasman, *Evangelicals in Action* (London, 1962), 14.

40. Owen, *English Philanthropy, 1660–1960*, 95.

41. D. W. Bebbington, *Evangelicalism in Modern Britain: A History from the 1730s to the 1980s* (London, 1989), 149.

42. Brian Harrison, *Drink and The Victorians: The Temperance Question in England 1815–1872* (London, 1971), ch. 8.

43. J. D. Gay, *The Geography of Religion in England* (London, 1971), 89, 97. On Catholicism see also K. D. M. Snell and Paul S. Ell, *Rival Jerusalems: The Geography of Victorian Religion* (Cambridge, 2000), ch. 5.

44. Quoted in Owen, *English Philanthropy*, 1660–1960, 1.

45. George Macaulay Trevelyan, *History of England* (London and New York, 1929), 617.

46. *Essays in Ecclesiastical Biography*, 2 vols. (London, 1849), i. 382.

47. *Nonconformist*, 27 (Apr. 1842), 265. Quoted in Britain Harrison, *Peaceable Kingdom: Stability and Change in Modern Britain* (Oxford, 1982), 217.

48. Geoffrey Best, *Mid-Victorian Britain 1851–75* (London, 1971), 159–60.

49. Walter Bagehot, *Physics and Politics* (London, 1872), 188–9.

50. Elizabeth Barrett Browning, *Aurora Leigh* (London, 1857), 349.

51. *Octavia Hill's Letters to Fellow-Workers 1872–1911*, ed. Robert Whelan (London, 2005), 422.

52. James Grant, *Sketches In London* (London, 1838), 4.

53. This case was cited in an advertisement from the Spitalfields' Benevolent Society, *The Times*, 28 Dec. 1820.

54. *Ragged School Union Magazine*, 1 (1849), 165

55. Gen. William Booth, *In Darkest England and the Way Out* (London, 1890), 191.

56. Ibid. 158.

57. Ibid. 79–80.

58. William Canton, *History of the British and Foreign Bible Society*, 5 vols. (London, 1904–10), i. 354.

59. On the working-class contribution to the voluntary hospitals see Keir Waddington, *Charity and the London Hospitals, 1850–1898* (Royal Historical Society, 2000).

60. Bebbington, *Evangelicalism in Modern Britain*, 128–9.

61. For more detailed figures on gender and religiosity see Brown, *The Death of Christian Britain*, 156–61.

62. See F. K. Prochaska, *Women and Philanthropy in Nineteenth-Century England* (Oxford, 1980).

63. Samuel Green, *The Story of the Religious Tract Society* (London, 1899), 24, 28, 45.

64. *Forty-Fourth Annual Report of the Reformatory and Refuge Union* (London, 1900), 8.

65. Brian Heeney, *The Women's Movement in the Church of England 1850–1930* (Oxford, 1988), 40.

66. Thomas Walter Laqueur, *Religion and Respectability: Sunday Schools and Working-Class Culture 1780–1850* (New Haven and London, 1976), 246.

67. See Prochaska, *Women and Philanthropy in Nineteenth-Century England*, ch. 3.

68. Eugene Stock, *The History of the Church Missionary Society*, 4 vols. (1899–1916), iii. 664; iv. 522.

69. Mrs G. S. Reaney, *Our Daughters: Their Lives Here and Hereafter* (London, 1891), p. vi.

70. Mrs Pember Reeves, *Round About a Pound a Week* (London, 1914), 39–40.

71. See e.g. William Conybeare, *Charity of the Poor to the Poor* (London, 1908).

72. Friedrich Engels, *The Condition of the Working Class in England*, ed. W. O. Henderson and W. H. Chaloner (Stanford, 1958), 102, 140.

73. *Family Budgets: Being the Income and Expenses of Twenty-Eight British Households, 1891–1894* (1896), 75.

74. B. Abel-Smith, *The Hospitals, 1800–1948* (London, 1964), 250–1.

75. Richard M. Titmuss, *Problems of Social Policy* (London, 1976), 67.

76. F. K. Prochaska, *Philanthropy and the Hospitals of London: The King's Fund 1897–1990* (Oxford, 1992), 10.

77. Frank Prochaska, *Royal Bounty: The Making of a Welfare Monarchy* (New Haven and London, 1995), 159.

78. See Martin Gorsky, *Patterns of Philanthropy: Charity and Society in Nineteenth-Century Bristol* (Royal Historical Society, 1999), 184–5.

79. *The Christian Mother's Magazine*, 2 (Oct. 1845), 640.

80. Prochaska, *Women and Philanthropy in Nineteenth-Century England*, 83.

81. *The Evangelical Magazine*, 29, N.S. (Apr. 1851), 226.

82. See Frank Prochaska, *The Voluntary Impulse* (London, 1988), 27–31, *passim*.

83. *Man's Duty to his Neighbour* (London, 1859), 71.

84. The phrase comes from Parliamentary Papers, *Committee on Charitable Trusts*, Cmd. 8710, (1952), par. 53.

85. Jerry White, *Rothschild Buildings: Life in an East End Tenement Block 1887–1920* (London, 1980), 148, *passim*.

86. Laura E. Stuart, *In Memoriam Caroline Colman* (Norwich, 1896), 56 and *passim*. See also *Carrow Works Magazine*, 1 (1907).

87. Recent scholarship is beginning to change perceptions. See e.g. R. J. Morris, *Class, Sect and Party: The Making of the British Middle Class, Leeds 1820–50* (London, 1990).

88. Elizabeth Gaskell, *North and South* (Harmondsworth, 1995), 326.

89. *The Times*, 9 Jan. 1885, 9.

90. *Forty-Second Report of the Charity Commissioners* (1895), 17.

91. Various sociologists think Christianity is in terminal decline. See e.g. *Predicting Religion*; see also Brown, *The Death of Christian Britain*.

92. Peter Brierly, 'Religion', in *Twentieth-Century British Social Trends*, ed. A. H. Halsey and Josephine Webb (London, 2000), 650–74.

93. See Grace Davie, *Religion in Britain Since 1945: Believing Without Belonging* (Oxford, 1994).

94. On the current state of the secularization debate see Jeremy Morris, 'The Strange Death of Christian Britain: Another Look at the Secularization Debate', *The Historical Journal*, 46: 4 (2003), 963–76.

95. Pat Thane, 'Government and Society in England and Wales, 1750–1950', in *The Cambridge Social History of Britain 1750–1950*, iii. 2.

96. Owen, *English Philanthropy, 1660–1960*, 225.

97. Quoted in Robert Whelan, *The Corrosion of Charity: From Moral Renewal to Contract Culture* (IEA Health and Welfare Unit, London, 1996), 47.
98. Alexis de Tocqueville, *Democracy in America*, Modern Library edition (New York, 1981), 440. On Tocqueville and religion see Doris S. Goldstein, *Trial of Faith: Religion and Politics in Tocqueville's Thought* (New York, 1975).
99. *Alexis de Tocqueville's Memoir on Pauperism*, trans. by Seymour Drescher, with an Introduction by Gertrude Himmelfarb (London, 1997), 25, 31.
100. *From Max Weber: Essays in Sociology*, ed. H. H. Gerth and C. Wright Mills (New York, 1946), 18.
101. de Tocqueville, *Democracy in America*, 584–5.
102. Hall, 'Social Capital in Britain', 453.
103. See e.g. *The Times*, 11 Jan. 2001.

CHAPTER 2

1. Alan D. Gilbert, *The Making of Post-Christian Britain: A History of the Secularization of Modern Society* (London and New York, 1980) 34.
2. Quoted in John Lawson and Harold Silver, *A Social History of Education in England* (London, 1973), 188.
3. Hannah More, *Moral Sketches of Prevailing Opinions and Manners* (London, 1819), 214.
4. M. G. Jones, *The Charity School Movement: A Study of Eighteenth Century Puritanism in Action* (Cambridge, 1938), 28.
5. Quoted ibid. 35.
6. Robert Nelson, *Address to Persons of Quality and Estate* (London, 1715), 239, quoted in David Owen, *English Philanthropy, 1660–1960* (Cambridge, Mass., 1964), 34.
7. Quoted in Jones, *The Charity School Movement*, 59.
8. W. O. B. Allen and Edmund McClure, *Two Hundred Years: The History of the Society for Promoting Christian Knowledge*, 1698–1898 (London, 1898), 136.
9. Owen, *English Philanthropy, 1660–1960*, 27.
10. Ibid. 23.
11. Jones, *The Charity School Movement*, 176–82.
12. Ibid. 345.

13. Ibid. 35.

14. Christabel Coleridge, *Charlotte Mary Yonge: Her Life and Letters* (London, 1903), 161.

15. Jones, *The Charity School Movement*, 346.

16. For an excellent recent discussion of Sunday Schools see K. D. M. Snell and Paul S. Ell, *Rival Jerusalems: The Geography of Victorian Religion* (Cambridge, 2000), ch. 9.

17. Owen, *English Philanthropy, 1660–1960*, 113.

18. For a discussion of early Sunday schools and a thorough treatment of Raikes's place in the movement see Philip B. Cliff, *The Rise and Development of the Sunday School Movement in England 1780–1980*, National Christian Education Council (Redhill, Surrey, 1986).

19. Ibid. 27.

20. R. A. Houston and W. W. J. Knox, *The New Penguin History of Scotland: From the Earliest Times to the Present* (London, 2001), 314.

21. Owen, *English Philanthropy, 1660–1960*, 115.

22. Snell and Ell, *Rival Jerusalems*, 319.

23. Sir Llewellyn Woodward, *The Age of Reform 1815–1870* (Oxford, 1962), 474–7.

24. More, *Moral Sketches of Prevailing Opinions and Manners*, 85.

25. John Watkins, *Memoirs of Her Most Excellent Majesty Sophia-Charlotte, Queen of Great Britain* (London, 1819), 314–15.

26. Quoted in F. M. L. Thompson, *The Rise of Respectable Society: A Social History of Victorian Britain 1830–1900* (London, 1988), 141.

27. *Gentleman's Magazine* (Nov. 1800), 1076.

28. For a discussion of this issue see Bernard Semmel, 'Elie Halévy, Methodism, and Revolution', introduction to Elie Halévy, *The Birth of Methodism in England* (Chicago, 1971).

29. Thomas Walter Lacqueur, *Religion and Respectability: Sunday Schools and Working-Class Culture 1780–1850* (New Haven, 1976), 179–86.

30. On this issue see W. R. Ward, *Religion and Society in England 1790–1850* (New York, 1973).

31. Snell and Ell, *Rival Jerusalems*, 288–9, 317–18.

32. W. H. Watson, *The First Fifty Years of the Sunday School* (London, [n.d.]), 138–9, 147–9.

33. On finances see Cliff, *The Rise and Development of the Sunday School Movement in England*, 99–100.

34. Snell and Ell, *Rival Jerusalems*, 274, 293.

35. Ibid. 303–4, 318.

36. Laqueur, *Religion and Respectability*, 252–4. See also Malcolm Dick, 'The Myth of the Working-class Sunday School', *History of Education*, 9 (1980), 27–41.

37. *A Brief Sketch of the Life of the Late Sarah Martin* (Yarmouth, 1845), 8.

38. Agnes Weston, *My Life Among the Bluejackets* (London, 1912), 62.

39. Quoted in Ferdinand Mount, *Mind the Gap* (London, 2004), 175.

40. A detailed set of rules for Sunday schools can be found in Cliff, *The Rise and Development of the Sunday School Movement in England*, 35–6.

41. Laqueur, *Religion and Respectability*, 44.

42. Snell and Ell, *Rival Jerusalems*, 277–8.

43. Cliff, *The Rise and Development of the Sunday School Movement in England*, 100–13, 150–2.

44. Coleridge, *Charlotte Mary Yonge*, 95.

45. Ibid.

46. Cliff, *The Rise and Development of the Sunday School Movement in England*, 122.

47. Edmund Gosse, *Father and Son: A Study of Two Temperaments* (New York, 1907), 225.

48. *The Fourth Report of the British and Foreign Bible Society* (London, 1818), p. lxxv; Eugene Stock, *The History of the Church Missionary Society*, 4 vols. (London, 1899–1916), iii. 820.

49. *The Children's Missionary Meeting in Exeter Hall, on Easter Tuesday, 1842* (London, 1842).

50. F. K. Prochaska, *Women and Philanthropy in Nineteenth-Century England* (Oxford, 1980), ch. 3.

51. Laqueur, *Religion and Respectability*, 172–3.

52. Snell and Ell, *Rival Jerusalems*, 282.

53. For details, see Owen, *English Philanthropy, 1660–1960*, 119.

54. Henry James Burgess, *Enterprise in Education: The Story of the Work of the Established Church in the Education of the People Prior to 1870* (London, 1958), 212.

55. Maurice J. Quinlan, *Victorian Prelude: A History of English Manners 1700–1830* (New York, 1941), 171; Laqueur, *Religion and Respectability*, 44.

56. Data compiled from English parish registers put the number of men unable to sign the marriage register at 33 % in 1840. Fewer than 50 % of women were unable to sign by that time. R. S. Schofield, 'Dimensions of

Illiteracy, 1750–1850', *Explorations in Economic History*, 10 (1973), 437. R. K. Webb also gives a figure of two-thirds to three-quarters of the working classes being able to read in the 1830s, *The English Working Class Reader* (London, 1955), 22. See also Gertrude Himmelfarb, *The Idea of Poverty: England in the Early Industrial Age* (London, 1984), 374.

57. *Sunday School Repository or Teacher's Magazine*, 3 (1816), 217–18.

58. Lord Mahon, *History of England from the Peace of Utrecht to the Peace of Versailles 1713–1783*, 7 vols. (Boston, 1853), vii. 333.

59. British Library, Add. Mss 27,828, fo. 61.

60. *The Autobiography of Francis Place 1771–1854*, ed. Mary Thale (Cambridge, 1972), 44.

61. G. M. Young, *Victorian England: Portrait of an Age* (London, 1936), 5.

62. Revd Thomas Guthrie, *A Plea for Ragged Schools; or, Prevention is better than Cure* (Edinburgh, 1847), 9.

63. See Mary Carpenter, *Reformatory Schools for the Children of the Perishing and Dangerous Classes and for Juvenile Offenders* (London, 1851).

64. An Old Potter, *When I was a Child* (London, 1903), 134, quoted in Cliff, *The Rise and Development of the Sunday School Movement in England*, 142.

65. C. J. Montague, *Sixty Years in Waifdom Or, The Ragged School Movement in English History* (London, 1904), 29, 35.

66. Norris Pope, *Dickens and Charity* (London, 1978), 153.

67. Owen, *English Philanthropy, 1660–1960*, 147.

68. Montague, *Sixty Years in Waifdom*, 34.

69. Quoted in Pope, *Dickens and Charity*, 166.

70. *Ragged School Union Magazine*, 2 (1850), 61.

71. Carpenter, *Reformatory Schools for the Children of the Perishing and Dangerous Classes*, 62.

72. Ibid. 136, 150.

73. Owen, *English Philanthropy, 1660–1960*, 148.

74. *Edinburgh Review*, 222 (1865), 355.

75. George K. Behlmer, *Child Abuse and Moral Reform in England, 1870–1908* (Stanford, 1982), 66.

76. *Ragged School Union Magazine*, 8 (1856), 232.

77. See e.g. [Caroline Frances Cornwallis], *The Philosophy of the Ragged Schools* (London, 1851), 1–2.

78. Quoted in Georgina Battiscombe, *Shaftesbury: A Biography of the Seventh Earl 1801–1885* (London, 1974), 302.

79. *Ragged School Union Magazine*, 15 (1863), 57.

80. *Edinburgh Review*, 222 (1865), 355.

81. Edwin Hodder, *The Life and Work of the Seventh Earl of Shaftesbury*, 3 vols. (London, 1887), ii. 342. Montague, *Sixty Years in Waifdom*, 196.

82. Himmelfarb, *The Idea of Poverty*, 376–7.

83. Thompson, *The Rise of Respectable Society*, 145.

84. Quoted in E. G. West, *Education and the State A Study in Political Economy* (London, 1970), 86.

85. *Life and Struggles of William Lovett* (London, 1876; 1967 edn.), 111. See also Gillian Sutherland, 'Education', in *The Cambridge Social History of Britain* 1750–1850, ed. F. M. L. Thompson, 3 vols. (Cambridge, 1990), iii. 130–1.

86. *Commentaries on British Parliamentary Papers: Education*, ed. Celina Fox, *et al.* (Dublin, 1977), 58.

87. D. W. Bebbington, *The Nonconformist Conscience: Chapel and Politics, 1870–1914* (London, 1982), 127.

88. Geoffrey Best, *Mid-Victorian Britain 1851–1875*, (London, 1971), 173.

89. Burgess, *Enterprise in Education*, 187.

90. Quoted in ibid. 190, from F. Close, *The Spirit of the Debate in the House of Commons on Education*, 21.

91. Hodder, *The Life and Work of the Seventh Earl of Shaftesbury*, ii. 522.

92. Allen and McClure, *Two Hundred Years*, 158.

93. W. B. Stephens, *Education in Britain, 1750–1914* (Basingstoke, 1998), 78.

94. Eric E. Rich, *The Education Act of 1870: A Study of Public Opinion* (London, 1970), pp. vii–viii.

95. *Parliamentary Debates*, 188, 15 July 1867, cols. 1540, 1549.

96. Quoted in Young, *Victorian England*, 115.

97. The Act, 33 & 34 Vict. c. 75, is included in James Murphy, *The Education Act 1870: Text and Commentary* (New York, 1972).

98. For details on school attendance and literacy see Stephens, *Education in Britain*, ch. 2.

99. H. C. Dent, *1870–1970: Century of Growth in English Education*, (London, 1970), 14.

100. J. S. Hurt, *Elementary Schooling and the Working Classes 1860–1918* (London, 1979), 25.

101. Young, *Victorian England*, 115.

102. Hodder, *The Life and Work of the Seventh Earl of Shaftesbury*, iii. 267.

103. Quoted in Owen Chadwick, *The Victorian Church* (London, 1970), part II, 301.

104. Quoted in Burgess, *Enterprise in Education*, 190.

105. Quoted in Geoffrey B. A. M. Finlayson, *The Seventh Earl of Shaftesbury 1801–1885* (London, 1981), 490.

106. Murphy, *The Education Act of 1870: Text and Commentary*, 66.

107. Sir James Kay Shuttleworth, *Public Education as Affected by the Minutes of the Committee of Privy Council from 1846 to 1852 with Suggestions as to Future Policy* (London, 1853), 36.

108. Chadwick, *The Victorian Church*, part II, 304–5.

109. For a case study of this process see J. C. Tyson, 'The Church and School Education', in *A Social History of the Diocese of Newcastle 1882–1982* (Stocksfield, Northumberland, 1981), 270–90.

110. Rich, *The Education Act of 1870: A Study of Public Opinion*, p. vii.

111. Lawson and Silver, *A Social History of Education in England*, 321.

112. Hugh McLeod, *Secularisation in Western Europe, 1848–1914* (London, 2000), 72–3.

113. Chadwick, *The Victorian Church*, part II, 300–1.

114. Burgess, *Enterprise in Education*, 215.

115. Hodder, *The Life and Work of the Seventh Earl of Shaftesbury*, iii. 265.

116. Ibid. 266.

117. Lawson and Silver, *A Social History of Education in England*, 345.

118. For a discussion of this transition see Montague, *Sixty Years in Waifdom*.

119. Tyson, 'The Church and School Education', 286.

120. *The Lambeth Conference 1948: The Encyclical Letter from the Bishops; together with Resolutions and Reports* (London, 1948), part II, 19.

121. Pat Thane, *Foundations of the Welfare State* (London, 1996), 190.

122. A. J. P. Taylor, *English History 1914–1945* (Oxford, 1965), 568.

123. Lawson and Silver, *A Social History of Education in England*, 419.

124. Peter Pilkington, 'The Church in Education', *Faith in Education*, Civitas e-book (London, 2001), 55.

125. Jon Davies, 'Re-sacrilising Education and Re-criminalising Childhood: An Agenda for the Year 2132', in *Teaching Right and Wrong: Have the Churches Failed?*, ed. R. Whelan (London, IEA Health and Welfare Unit, 1994), 9.

126. John Marks, 'Standards in Church of England, Catholic and LEA Schools in England', *Faith in Education*, 8, 10.

127. Davies, 'Re-sacrilising Education and Re-criminalising Childhood', 9.

128. Penny Thompson, 'How the Will of Parliament on Religious Education was Diluted by Civil Servants and the Religious Education Profession', *Faith in Education*, 58.

129. Quoted in S. J. D. Green, *Religion in the Age of Decline: Organisation and Experience in Industrial Yorkshire, 1870–1920* (Cambridge, 1996), 221.

130. Cliff, *The Rise and Development of the Sunday School Movement in England*, 202.

131. Laqueur, *Religion and Respectability*, 246. For further statistics on this issue see Cliff, *The Rise and Development of the Sunday School Movement in England*, passim.

132. *Official Year-book of the Church of England 1910* (London, SPCK), p. xxxii.

133. *Official Year-book of the Church of England 1941* (London, SPCK), 6.

134. Callum G. Brown, *The Death of Christian Britain: Understanding Secularization 1800–2000* (London, 2001), 163.

135. John Stevenson, *British Society 1914–45* (Harmondsworth, 1984), 361–2.

136. Gilbert, *The Making of Post-Christian Britain*, 95. On Sabbatarianism see J. Wigley, *The Rise and Fall of the Victorian Sunday* (Manchester, 1980).

137. Brian Harrison, *Peaceable Kingdom: Stability and Change in Modern Britain* (Oxford, 1982), 240.

138. E. R. Norman, *Church and Society in England, 1770–1970* (Oxford, 1976), 152.

139. Quoted in Brown, *The Death of Christian Britain*, 87.

140. Ibid. 104.

141. Cliff, *The Rise and Development of the Sunday School Movement in England*, 211.

142. Quoted ibid. 215.

143. In 1939 voluntary contributions to Church of England Sunday schools stood at £107,000; in 1940 it stood at £80,000. *Official Year-book of the Church of England 1942* (London, SPCK), 272.

144. Cliff, *The Rise and Development of the Sunday School Movement in England*, chs. 15–16.

145. From *Sunday Schools Today* (Free Church Federal Council, 1957), 8, quoted in ibid. 279.

146. Peter Brierley, *UK: Christian Handbook Religious Trends 2000/01* (London, 1999), Table 2.15. R. Currie, A. Gilbert, and L. Horsley, *Churches and Churchgoers: Patterns of Church Growth in the British Isles*

since 1700 (Oxford, 1977). See also Brown, *The Death of Christian Britain*, 168, 188.

147. Brown, *The Death of Christian Britain*, 188.

148. G. K. Chesterton, *What's Wrong with the World* (London, 1910), 194.

149. Friedrich Nietzsche, *On the Genealogy of Morality*, ed. Keith Ansell-Pearson (Cambridge, 1994), 101.

CHAPTER 3

1. For a good introduction to visiting practices see Charles B. P. Bosanquet, *A Handy-book for Visitors of the Poor in London* (London, 1874).

2. Eric McCoy North, *Early Methodist Philanthropy* (New York, 1914), 36–40.

3. Sampson Low, *The Charities of London* (London, 1850), 117, cited the Strangers' Friend Society of London as the oldest institution of its kind in England.

4. Quoted in North, *Early Methodist Philanthropy*, 47–8.

5. *The Nature, Design, and Rules of the Benevolent or Strangers' Friend Society* (London, 1803), 6–7, 47.

6. *The Wesleyan Methodist Magazine*, 1 (1845), 661–8.

7. Martin Hewitt, 'The Travails of Domestic Visiting: Manchester, 1830–70', *Historical Research: Bulletin of the Institute of Historical Research*, 71: 175 (June 1998), 204, 225.

8. See e.g. the objects of the West Street Chapel Benevolent Society cited in Anthony Highmore, *Pietas Londinensis*, 2 vols. (London, 1810), ii. 920–1.

9. A. F. Young and E. T. Ashton, *British Social Work in the Nineteenth Century* (London, 1956), 188.

10. The London City Mission was a pioneer of visiting employees in their places of employment. See www.lcm.org.uk.

11. *The Harbinger* (Sept. 1853), 283.

12. Constance Battersea, *Reminiscences* (London, 1922), 414–17. On Jewish charity generally, see Modechai Rozin, *The Rich and the Poor: Jewish Philanthropy and Social Control in Nineteenth-Century London* (Brighton, 1999).

13. George Behlmer, *Friends of the Family: The English Home and its Guardians, 1850–1940* (Stanford, 1998), 44.

14. Quoted ibid. 37.

15. *The Thirty-Fifth Report of the London City Mission* (London, 1870), pp. vii–viii.

16. Low, *The Charities of London*, 127–8.

17. J. C. Pringle, *Social Work of the London Churches* (London, 1937), 190–1.

18. Margaret Goodman, *Sisterhoods in the Church of England* (London, 1863), 236–42.

19. *Handbook of Catholic Charitable and Social Works* (London, 1905), 12–14.

20. See e.g. *Bedford Institute, First-Day School and Home Mission Association. Report* (London, 1867), 14.

21. Quoted in Ronald G. Walton, *Women in Social Work* (London and Boston, 1975), 57.

22. See e.g. Charles Loch, *How to Help Cases of Distress* (London, 1883), 16–17.

23. Brian Heeney, *The Women's Movement in the Church of England 1850–1930* (Oxford, 1988), 27; Behlmer, *Friends of the Family*, 34. The figures come from *The Official Year-book of the Church of England*.

24. Heeney, *The Women's Movement in the Church of England*, 27.

25. Behlmer, *Friends of the Family*, 34.

26. G. A. Campbell, *The Civil Service in Britain* (London, 1965), 56, 69.

27. Hewitt, 'The Travails of Domestic Visiting: Manchester, 1830–70', 209.

28. Royal Commission on the Aged Poor, *Parliamentary Papers* (1895), vol. 14, 222.

29. Raphael Samuel (ed.), *East End Underworld: Chapters in the Life of Arthur Harding* (London, 1981), 24.

30. [Mrs J. B. Wightman] *Annals of the Rescued* (London, 1861), 242–4. For other letters of this type see F. K. Prochaska, *Women and Philanthropy in Nineteenth-Century England* (Oxford, 1980), 116.

31. The Revd Buckley Yates, *Miss Shepherd, of Cheadle, Staffordshire* (Manchester, 1876), 111.

32. Francis A. West, *Memoirs of Mrs. Jane Gibson* (London, 1837), 334–5.

33. *Meliora*, 7 (1864), 242.

34. *A Brief Sketch of the Life of the Late Miss Sarah Martin* (Yarmouth, 1845), 8.

35. Beatrice Webb, *My Apprenticeship* (London, 1926), 21.

36. John Dungett, *Life and Correspondence of the Late Mrs. Margaret Burton* (Darlington, 1832), 27–8.

37. Ibid. 73–4.

38. Ibid. 191.

39. The Revd Alfred Barrett, *Holy Living: Exemplified in the Life of Mrs Mary Cryer* (London, 1845), 4, 9.

40. *The Devotional Remains of Mrs. Cryer* (London, 1854), 102–4.

41. *The Autobiography of Francis Place*, ed. Mary Thale (Cambridge, 1972), 47.

42. George Brown, *The History of the British and Foreign Bible Society* (London, 1850), ii. 540.

43. S. C. Williams, *Religious Belief and Popular Culture in Southwark, c.1880–1939* (Oxford, 1999), 66–7.

44. M. J. Quinlan, *Victorian Prelude: A History of English Manners, 1700–1830* (New York, 1941), 183.

45. Quoted in Heeney, *The Women's Movement in the Church of England*, 29.

46. Octavia Hill, *District Visiting* (London, 1877), 14.

47. Octavia Hill, *Our Common Land* (and Other Short Essays) (London, 1877), 61.

48. The Revd Charles Neil, *The Christian Visitor's Handbook* (London, 1882).

49. Quoted in Heeney, *The Women's Movement in the Church of England*, 29.

50. Arthur Jephson, *Some Hints for Parish Workers in London* (London, 1904), 4–5.

51. Seth Koven, *Slumming: Sexual and Social Politics in Victorian London* (Princeton, 2004), 8.

52. *Dear Miss Nightingale: A Selection of Benjamin Jowett's Letters to Florence Nightingale, 1860–1893*, ed. Vincent Quinn and John Prest (Oxford, 1987), 88.

53. Quoted in Margaret B. Simey, *Charitable Effort in Liverpool in the Nineteenth Century* (Liverpool, 1951), 65.

54. *The Correspondence of William Ellery Channing, D.D, and Lucy Aikin*, ed. Anna Letitia le Breton (Boston, 1874), 90.

55. [Ellen Ranyard], *London, and Ten Years Work in It* (London, 1868), 7.

56. Kathleen Heasman, *Evangelicals in Action* (London, 1962), 37. From its inception the London City Mission used paid visitors, but they were prohibited from giving temporal relief.

57. See *Meliora*, 12: 45, (1869), 89–91.

58. Ellen Ranyard, *The True Institution of Sisterhood: or a Message and its Messengers* (London, 1862), 16.

59. Jane Lewis, *The Voluntary Sector, the State and Social Work in Britain: The Charity Organisation Society/Family Welfare Association since 1869* (Aldershot, 1995), 11.

60. Kathleen Woodroofe, *From Charity to Social Work in England and the United States* (London, 1968), 31.

61. For a critical study of the impact of the COS see Robert Humphreys, *Sin, Organized Charity and the Poor Law in Victorian England* (London, 1995).

62. Robert Whelan, *Helping the Poor: Friendly Visiting, Dole Charities and Dole Queues* (London, 2001), 15.

63. C. S. Loch, *How to Help Cases of Distress* (London, 1883), 16.

64. For a list of these inquiries see W. A. Bailward, 'The Charity Organisation Society: A New Historical Sketch', *Quarterly Review*, 206 (Jan. 1907), 55–76.

65. Woodroffe, *From Charity to Social Work in England and the United States*, 53–4.

66. Walton, *Women in Social Work*, 147.

67. Behlmer, *Friends of the Family*, 46.

68. Webb, *My Apprenticeship*, 221, quoted in David Owen, *English Philanthropy 1660–1960* (Cambridge, Mass., 1964), 504.

69. William Beveridge, *Voluntary Action: A Report on Methods of Social Advance* (London, 1948), 224.

70. D. W. Bebbington, *The Nonconformist Conscience: Chapel and Politics, 1870–1914* (London, 1982), 59.

71. [Mrs H. O. Barnett], *Canon Barnett: His Life, Work and Friends*, 2 vols (London, 1918), i. 37.

72. K. D. M. Snell and Paul S. Ell, *Rival Jerusalems: The Geography of Victorian Religion* (Cambridge, 2000), 418.

73. Owen, *English Philanthropy, 1660–1960*, 525.

74. Sidney Webb, 'Social Movements', in *The Cambridge Modern History*, ed., A. W. Ward, G. W. Prothero, and Stanley Leathes, 13 vols. (Cambridge, 1902–11), xii. 765. See also Jose Harris, *Private Lives, Public Spirit: Britain 1870–1914* (London, 1994), 17.

75. Lloyd George to Alan Anderson, 1 June 1922; a copy of this letter can be found in the King's Fund file entitled '1922 Appeal', London Metropolitan Archives.

76. Quoted in Geoffrey Finlayson, *Citizen, State and Social Welfare in Britain 1830–1990* (Oxford, 1994), 101.

77. Quoted in Margaret Brasnett, *Voluntary Social Action: A History of the National Council of Social Service* (London, 1969), 2.

78. *Westminster Review*, 135 (1891), 373.

79. Virginia Woolf, *To The Lighthouse* (London, 1927), 10.

80. Investigation by the Royal Commission on the Poor Laws and Relief of Distress, *Parliamentary Papers* (1909), vol. 43, appendix.

81. Quoted in Brian Harrison, *Peaceable Kingdom: Stability and Change in Modern Britain* (Oxford, 1982), 258.

82. See Theresa Mary Deane, 'The Professionalisation of Philanthropy: The Case of Louisa Twining', Ph.D thesis, Sussex University (2005).

83. George Eliot, *Middlemarch: A Study of Provincial Life* (Edinburgh and London, 1990), 66.

84. See e.g. 'Claims of Women', *Fortnightly Review*, 15 (1871), 109.

85. Prochaska, *Women and Philanthropy in Nineteenth-Century England*, 172–3, 180–1.

86. Ibid. 227–30.

87. See Susan Pedersen, *Eleanor Rathbone and the Politics of Conscience* (New Haven and London, 2004).

88. *Correspondence of William Ellery Channing, D.D., and Lucy Aikin*, 397.

89. Walton, *Women in Social Work*, 31.

90. On women and local government see Patricia Hollis, *Ladies Elect: Women in English Local Government 1865–1914* (Oxford, 1987).

91. C. R. Attlee, *The Social Worker* (London, 1920), 124.

92. Quoted in Heeney, *The Women's Movement in the Church of England*, 18, 138.

93. *The Lambeth Conference, 1920: Encyclical Letter from the Bishops with Resolutions and Reports* (London, 1920), 93–4.

94. See e.g. Louisa Hubbard, 'Statistics of Women's Work', in *Woman's Mission*, ed. Baroness Burdett-Coutts (London, 1893).

95. There were 74,647 district visitors listed for the Church in 1918 and 64,173 in 1928. Heeney, *The Women's Movement in the Church of England*, 27.

96. Constance Braithwaite, *The Voluntary Citizen: An Enquiry into the Place of Philanthropy in the Community* (London, 1938), 94.

97. For an introduction to some of these war funds, see Diana Condell, 'A Gift for Christmas: The Story of Princess Mary's Gift Fund, 1914', *Imperial War Museum Review*, 4 (1989), 77.

98. *Final Report of the Administration of the National Relief Fund*, Cmd. 1272 (HMSO), 3. See also Frank Prochaska, *Royal Bounty: The Making of a Welfare Monarchy* (New Haven and London, 1995), 180.

99. *Voluntary Social Services: Their Place in the Modern State*, ed. A. F. C. Bourdillon (London, 1945), 213–14.

100. Maggie Andrews, *The Acceptable Face of Feminism: The Women's Institute as a Social Movement* (London, 1997), 26, 101.

101. Finlayson, *Citizen, State, and Social Welfare in Britain*, 205.

102. Heeney, *The Women's Movement in the Church of England*, 27; *The Official Year-Book of the National Assembly of the Church of England 1941*, 284.

103. Pat Thane, *Foundations of the Welfare State* (London, 1996), 203–4.

104. Campbell, *The Civil Service in Britain*, 69; John Stevenson, *British Society 1914–45* (Harmondsworth, 1984), 462.

105. M. J. Daunton, 'Payment and Participation: Welfare and State Formation in Britain 1900–1951', *Past & Present* (Feb. 1996), 170.

106. Thane, *Foundations of the Welfare State*, 161.

107. Quoted in Finlayson, *Citizen, State and Social Welfare in Britain*, 279.

108. Thane, *Foundations of the Welfare State*, 161; Robert Humphreys, *Poor Relief and Charity 1869–1945: The London Charity Organization Society* (Houndsmill, Basingstoke, 2001), 180.

109. Braithwaite, *The Voluntary Citizen*, 171. See also Owen, *English Philanthropy, 1660–1960*, 527–8.

110. See Brasnett, *Voluntary Social Action*, 67, *passim*.

111. See Elizabeth Macadam, *The New Philanthropy* (London, 1934).

112. Richard M. Titmuss, *Problems of Social Policy* (London, 1976), 373–4.

113. For a stimulating discussion of the WVS, which sees it as an institution that upheld the continuities of class, see James Hinton, *Women, Social Leadership, and the Second World War* (Oxford, 2002).

114. Philip S. Bagwell, *Outcast London: A Christian Response: The West London Mission of the Methodist Church 1887–1987* (London, 1987), 113.

115. Ibid. 112–14.

116. Titmuss, *Problems of Social Policy*, 330. See also Stevenson, *British Society 1914–45*, 448.

117. Nicholas Timmins, *The Five Giants: A Biography of the Welfare State* (London, 1995), 31.

118. Titmuss, *Problems of Social Policy*, 331.

119. King's Fund, *Forty-Fifth Annual Report*, 16. See also George C. Curnock, *Hospitals Under Fire* (London, 1941). On the issue of bomb damage and the formation of the National Health Service see F. K. Prochaska, *Philanthropy and the Hospitals of London: The King's Fund 1897–1990* (Oxford, 1992), ch. 6.

120. *The Official Year-Book of the National Assembly of the Church of England 1942*, 3.

121. *The Official Year-Book of the National Assembly of the Church of England 1944*, 3.

122. G. Stephen Spinks, *Religion in Britain since 1900* (London, 1952), 217.

123. Ibid. 224.

124. Angus Calder, *The People's War: Britain—1939–1945* (New York, 1965), 479.

125. Cyril Garbett, *Church and State in England* (London, 1950), 278–9, 286.

126. On the issue of reconstruction see *The Churches and War Damage: Payments for War Damage to Ecclesiastical Buildings under Section 69 of the War Damage Act, 1943* (London, 1944).

127. A. J. P. Taylor, *English History 1914–45* (Oxford, 1965), 455.

128. The experience of Bethnal Green was typical. See *Voluntary Social Services*, 257–62.

129. *The Times*, 27 Oct. 1933, quoted in Elizabeth Macadam, *The New Philanthropy* (London, 1934), 304.

130. Sir William H. Beveridge, *The Pillars of Security and Other War-time Essays and Addresses* (New York, 1943), 119.

131. Thane, *Foundations of the Welfare State*, 204.

132. Bagwell, *Outcast London: A Christian Response*, 56–7, 127.

133. See John Oliver, *The Church and the Social Order: Social Thought in the Church of England 1918–1939* (London, 1968).

134. William Temple, *Citizen and Churchman* (London, 1941), 35–6.

135. Ibid. 31.

136. *The Lambeth Conference 1948: The Encyclical Letter from the Bishops; together with Resolutions and Reports* (London, 1948), part II, 17.

137. Ibid.

138. Ibid., part I, 32.

139. Stuart Mews, 'Religious Life Between the Wars, 1920–1940', in *A History of Religion in Britain: Practice & Belief from Pre-Roman Times to the Present*, ed. Sheridan Gilley and W. J. Sheils (Oxford, 1994), 471.

140. Garbett, *Church and State in England*, 279.

141. Temple, *Citizen and Churchman*, 36.
142. Edward Norman, 'Church and State since 1800', in *A History of Religion in Britain*, ed. Gilley and Sheils, 286.
143. Jeffrey Cox, *The English Churches in a Secular Society: Lambeth, 1870–1930* (Oxford, 1982), 275.
144. Quoted in Spinks, *Religion in Britain since 1900*, 225.
145. Callum G. Brown, *The Death of Christian Britain: Understanding Secularization 1800–2000* (London, 2001), 170–3.
146. Ibid. 179.
147. See the series of pamphlets under the general title *Visitation Evangelism in Scotland*, ed. by D. P. Thomson (Edinburgh, 1946–56).
148. Walton, *Women in Social Work*, 222.
149. The London City Mission employs about 100 'evangelists' today, who run clubs and classes and carry out household visits. See www.lcm.org.uk.

CHAPTER 4

1. Samuel Smiles, *Self-Help with Illustrations of Conduct & Perseverance* (repr. London, 1958), 341.
2. C. J. Montague, *Sixty Years in Waifdom Or, The Ragged School Movement in English History* (London, 1904), 256.
3. John Matthias Weylland, *These Fifty Years: Being the Jubilee Volume of the London City Mission* (London, [1884]), 137–8.
4. Mary Bayly, *Ragged Homes and How to Mend Them* (London, 1860), 112.
5. See the annual reports of the Ragged School Union and Shaftesbury Society.
6. [Ellen Ranyard], *London and Ten Years Work in It* (London, 1868), 16.
7. George K. Behlmer, *Friends of the Family: The English Home and Its Guardians, 1850–1940* (Stanford, 1998), 63.
8. Jeffrey Cox, *The English Churches in a Secular Society, Lambeth 1870–1930* (New York and Oxford, 1982), 71.
9. Quoted in Behlmer, *Friends of the Family*, 68.
10. Brian Heeney, *The Women's Movement in the Church of England 1850–1930* (Oxford, 1988), 44. For the annual figures of membership see the *Mothers' Union Handbook and Central Report*.
11. The mothers' meeting abroad is a large subject in itself. The periodicals of the Mothers' Union and the Ranyard Mission provide much useful material.

12. *Ranyard Magazine*, 46 (Jan. 1929), 3.
13. *Woman's Mission*, ed. Baroness Burdett-Coutts (London, 1893), app. 412.
14. Weylland, *These Fifty Years*, 138.
15. *The Fathers' Meeting: Half-an-Hour's Reading for Working Men* (London, [1873]), 4.
16. Quoted in Heeney, *The Women's Movement in the Church of England*, 44.
17. Gen. Booth, *In Darkest England and the Way Out* (London, 1890), 219.
18. In 1916 the Mothers' Union, the largest society running mothers' meetings, had 415,354 members and 8,266 branches, an average of 50 members per branch. See *Mothers' Union Handbook and Central Report* (1916), p. xxx. In 1895 the Ragged School Union and Shaftesbury Society had 9,580 members enrolled in 133 meetings, an average of 72 per meeting. See the *Fifty-First Annual Report of the Ragged School Union and Shaftesbury Society* (London, 1895), 13.
19. *Biblewomen and Nurses*, 13 (Aug. 1879), 156–7.
20. Bayly, *Ragged Homes and How to Mend Them*, 118.
21. For examples of this see *Life As We Have Known It*, ed. Margaret Llewelyn Davies (London, 1931), 40.
22. Quoted in Joyce Coombs, *George and Mary Sumner: Their Life and Times* (London, 1965), 120.
23. Ibid. 188.
24. See e.g. *The Mothers' Union Workers' Paper* (Sept. 1914), 134–5; *Mothers' Union Handbook and Central Report* (London, 1903), 33.
25. Heeney, *The Women's Movement in the Church of England*, 45.
26. *Biblewomen and Nurses*, 6 (Oct. 1889), 192.
27. [Mrs H. O. Barnett], *Canon Barnet: His Life, Work, and Friends*, 2 vols. (London, 1918), i. 100.
28. Bayley, *Ragged Homes and How to Mend Them*, 120.
29. *Missing Link Magazine*, 1 (Mar. 1865), 77; *Biblewomen and Nurses*, 15 (June 1898), 11.
30. [Barnett], *Canon Barnett*, i. 101.
31. [Ellen Ranyard], *Nurses for the Needy or Bible-Women in the Homes of the London Poor* (London, 1875), 212–14.
32. Bayly, *Ragged Homes and How to Mend Them*, 254–5.
33. See Rozsika Parker, *The Subversive Stitch: Embroidery and the Making of the Feminine* (London, 1984).
34. Ibid. 15.

35. Bayly, *Ragged Homes and How to Mend Them*, 198.
36. Louisa Twining, *Recollections of Life and Work* (London, 1893), 208–9. See also *Bible Work at Home and Abroad*, 2 (Aug. 1885), 235–6.
37. Charles Booth, *Life and Labour of the People in London*, 17 vols. (London, 1903), viii. 18–19.
38. *Missing Link Magazine*, 17 (Sept. 1881), 263; Bayly, *Ragged Homes and How to Mend Them*, 253.
39. *Ranyard Magazine*, 46 (Jan. 1929), 2.
40. *Correspondence of William Ellery Channing, D.D., and Lucy Aikin*, ed. Anna Letitia le Breton (Boston, 1874), 398.
41. Brian Harrison, *Drink and the Victorians: The Temperance Question in England 1815–1872* (London, 1971), 315.
42. Booth, *In Darkest England and the Way Out*, 47.
43. *Report on the Visitation of Females at their own Homes in the City of Westminster* (London, 1854), 4.
44. A Mother, *Bright Glimpses for Mothers' Meetings* (London, 1868), 2.
45. See *The North London Training Home: What is it Doing?* (London, n.d.).
46. *The Twenty-Ninth Annual Report of the London City Mission* (London, 1864), 8.
47. *Missing Link Magazine*, 18 (May 1882), 130.
48. *The Fifty First Annual Report of the Ragged School Union and Shaftesbury Society*, 13.
49. *Advance*, 8 (Feb. 1909), 27 and *passim*.
50. See F. K. Prochaska, *Women and Philanthropy in Nineteenth-Century England* (Oxford, 1980), 214–16.
51. *The Fathers' Meeting*. 32.
52. L. Sapsworth, *The Emancipation of Women* (London, 1913), 16–17.
53. See e.g. *Biblewomen and Nurses*, 13 (Aug. 1896), 157–8.
54. See Melanie Tebbutt, *Making Ends Meet: Pawnbroking and Working-Class Credit* (Leicester and New York, 1983), ch. 2. The problems of family expenditure that reduced wives to pawnshops are poignantly described in Lady Bell, *At the Works* (London, 1969), ch. 2.
55. See Paul Johnson, *Saving and Spending: The Working-Class Economy in Britain, 1870–1939* (Oxford, 1985), 225–7.
56. [Ranyard], *London, and Ten Years Work in It*, 8–10.
57. *Advance*, 5 (Oct. 1906), 92.
58. *Biblewomen and Nurses*, 9 (May 1892), 94–5; 13 (Aug. 1896), 156–7.

59. Ibid., 22 (Mar. 1905), 59. See also Booth, *Life and Labour of the People of London*, vii. 18–19.

60. Olive Parker, *For the Family's Sake: A History of the Mothers' Union 1876–1976* (Folkestone, 1975), 32–3

61. S. R. P. [Miss S. R. Powers], *Remarks on Woman's Work in Sanitary Reform* (London, [1862]), 3rd edn. 19.

62. [Barnett], *Canon Barnett*, i. 100.

63. See e.g. *Advance*, 7 (Apr. 1908), 77. The periodicals of the Mothers' Union, particularly the *Mothers' Union Journal*, provide an excellent guide to the wide range of topics discussed by that society.

64. Bayly, *Ragged Homes and How to Mend Them*, 244–6.

65. On education see Parker, *For the Family's Sake*, 35–9. On housing see the *Mothers' Union Journal* (Apr. 1919), 19.

66. Bayly, *Ragged Homes and How to Mend Them*, 89.

67. Twining, *Recollections of Life and Work*, 207.

68. [Barnett], *Canon Barnett*, i. 100.

69. *Biblewomen and Nurses*, 25 (July 1908), 125; (Aug. 1908), 133–4.

70. On the Infant Welfare Movement see Deborah Dwork, *War is Good for Babies and other Young Children: A History of the Child Welfare Movement in England 1898–1918* (London and New York, 1987). See also G. F. McCleary, *The Early History of the Infant Welfare Movement* (London, 1933); Jane Lewis, *The Politics of Motherhood: Child and Maternal Welfare in England 1900–1939* (London, 1980).

71. *Ranyard Magazine*, 34 (February 1917), 37.

72. See details at the back of the reports of the Ragged School Union and Shaftesbury Society.

73. [Barnett], *Canon Barnett*, i. 100.

74. See e.g. M. Penelope Hall, *The Social Services of Modern England*, 4th edn. (London, 1959), part III.

75. Mrs Harold Gorst, 'Down the Abyss', *Sketches of the Salvation Army Social Work* (London, 1906), 87.

76. Simon Szreter, *Fertility, Class and Gender in Britain, 1860–1940* (Cambridge, 1996), 1.

77. *Missing Link Magazine*, 17 (Sept. 1881), 263; *Biblewomen and Nurses*, 7 (May, 1891), 92–3.

78. *Biblewomen and Nurses*, 32 (July 1915), 122.

79. *The Mothers' Union Workers' Paper* (Sep. 1914), 134–5; (July 1918), 89.

80. Sidney and Beatrice Webb, *The Consumers Co-operative Movement* (London, 1921), 168.
81. *The Mothers' Union Official Handbook 1916* (London, 1916), p. xxxii.
82. See Anna Davin, 'Imperialism and Motherhood', *History Workshop*, 5 (Spring 1978), 9–65.
83. *Toward the Sunrise. The Story of the Shaftesbury Society and Ragged School Union. 72ⁿᵈ Annual Report 1915–1916 (1916)*, 6. See also *Friendly Leaves*, 44 (Aug. 1919), 115.
84. *The National League for Physical Education and Improvement. Annual Reports, 1918* (London, 1918), 12.
85. *The Mothers' Union Official Handbook 1919* (London, 1919), p. xxxv.
86. Heeney, *The Women's Movement in the Church of England*, 44.
87. See the illustration in Behlmer, *Friends of the Family*, 69.
88. *In the Making. 94ᵗʰ Annual Report 1937–1938 of the Shaftesbury Society and R.S.U.* (1938), 24.
89. *Shaftesbury Magazine*, 97 (June 1945), 11.
90. *Friendly Leaves*, 44 (Aug. 1919), 115.
91. See the Mothers' Union website, www.themothersunion.org. The London City Mission also sponsors women's meetings that retain something of a Victorian spirit. See www.lcm.org.uk.

CHAPTER 5

1. See e.g. L. Clayton, *The London Medical Mission: What Is It Doing?* (London, 1873) 2; *Missing Link Magazine*, 4 (May, 1868), 133.
2. For a wide-ranging discussion of this theme see *The Church and Healing*, ed. W. J. Sheils (Oxford, 1982).
3. See M. M. Gordon, *The Double Cure: or, What is a Medical Mission* (1869).
4. A. Wood, *An Address to Students* (Edinburgh, 1854), 7.
5. Elizabeth Gaskell, *North and South* (Harmondsworth, 1995), 167.
6. Gen. Booth, *In Darkest England and the Way Out* (London, 1890), 171.
7. Ibid.
8. [E. Ranyard], *Nurses for the Needy, or, Bible-Women in the Homes of the London Poor* (London, 1875), 45.
9. Anne Summers, *Female Lives, Moral States: Women, Religion and Public Life in Britain 1800–1930* (Newbury, Berks., 2000), 86.

10. See [C. M. Marsh], *Death and Life: A Record of the Cholera Wards in the London Hospital* (London, 1867), 33–43.

11. See C. E. Rosenberg 'Florence Nightingale on Contagion: The Hospital as Moral Universe', in *Healing and History*, ed. C. E. Rosenberg (New York and Folkestone, 1979), 116–36.

12. Martha Kenney, *Charity: a Poem* (London, 1823).

13. Sarah Robinson, *Light in Darkness* (London, 1859), 5–6.

14. *Lectures on Medical Missions* (Edinburgh, 1849), 227.

15. Florence Nightingale, *Notes on Nursing: What It Is, and What It Is Not* (London, 1860), preface.

16. Robert Southey, *Sir Thomas More: or, Colloquies on the Progress and Prospects of Society*. 2. vols., 2nd edn. (London, 1831), ii. 227–8.

17. M. Adelaide Nutting and Lavinia L. Dock, *A History of Nursing*, 2 vols. (New York and London, 1907), ii. 80–1.

18. Charles Dickens, *The Life and Adventures of Martin Chuzzlewit* (London, 1843–4), ch. 19.

19. On the history of these institutions see Mary Stocks, *A Hundred Years of District Nursing* (London, 1960); Robert Dingwall, Anne Marie Rafferty, and Charles Webster, *An Introduction to the Social History of Nursing* (London, 1988), ch. 9.

20. Nutting and Dock, *A History of Nursing*, ii. 80–1.

21. Gwen Hardy, *William Rathbone and the Early History of Nursing* (Ormskirk, 1981), 49.

22. Summers, *Female Lives, Moral States*, 87, 92.

23. [Ranyard], *Nurses for the Needy*, 33.

24. *Missing Link Magazine*, 9 (Dec. 1875), 384.

25. Stocks, *A Hundred Years of District Nursing*, 25.

26. [E. Ranyard], *Life Work; or, the Link and the Rivet* (London, 1861), 281.

27. [Ranyard], *Nurses for the Needy*, 304. In the 1890s trained staff nurses in hospitals received £20–30 a year plus room and board worth about £20. See L. Holcombe, *Victorian Ladies at Work: Middle-Class Working Women in England and Wales, 1850–1914* (Newton Abbot, 1973), 79.

28. Quoted in E. Platt, *The Story of the Ranyard Mission, 1857–1937* (London, 1937), 21.

29. [Ranyard], *Nurses for the Needy*, 251.

30. Quoted ibid. 43.

31. Ibid. 251.

32. See the letter from Miss Nightingale, Ranyard Collection, London Metropolitan Archives.

33. [Ranyard], *Nurses for the Needy*, 42.

34. Ibid. 52–3.

35. Quoted in G. M. Young, *Victorian England: Portrait of an Age* (London, 1936), 24.

36. For detailed information on nineteenth-century diets for the sick see J. Pereira, *A Treatise on Food and Diet* (London, 1843) and F. W. Pavy, *A Treatise on Food and Dietetics* (London, 1874).

37. Platt, *The Story of the Ranyard Mission, 1857–1937*, 124.

38. *London Biblewomen and Nurses Mission* (London, 1912), 22.

39. J. Woodward, 'Medicine and The City: The 19th-century experience', in *Urban Disease and Mortality in 19th-century England*, ed. R. Woods and J. Woodward (London, 1984), 69.

40. *Census of England and Wales 1901: County of London, Area, Houses and Population* (London, 1902), 102, 126.

41. R. E. Selfe, *Light Amid London Shadows* (London, 1906), 139.

42. Booth, *In Darkest England and the Way Out*, 170.

43. [Ranyard], *Nurses for the Needy*, 249–50.

44. *Biblewomen and Nurses*, 11 (Dec. 1894), 221, 241.

45. There is an example of a nurse's visiting card in [Ranyard], *Nurses for the Needy*, 55–6.

46. *Biblewomen and Nurses*, 11 (Dec. 1894), 241.

47. [Ranyard], *Nurses for the Needy*, 172.

48. Ibid. 250.

49. *Correspondence of William Ellery Channing, D.D., and Lucy Aikin*, ed. Anna Letitia le Breton (Boston, 1874), 397.

50. On this issue, see John M. Eyler, *Victorian Social Medicine: The Ideas and Methods of William Farr* (Baltimore and London, 1979), ch. 6.

51. Eleanor F. Rathbone, *William Rathbone: A Memoir* (London, 1905), 155. Quoted in David Owen, *English Philanthropy, 1660–1960* (Cambridge, Mass., 1964), 458.

52. [Ranyard], *Nurses for the Needy*, 67–8.

53. Ibid. 250.

54. These changes are discussed in the *Missing Link Magazine*, which was continued under different titles after 1884.

55. Platt, *The Story of the Ranyard Mission, 1857–1937*, 37–40.

56. *Biblewomen and Nurses*, NS 32 (1916), 40, 152–3.

57. Rosenberg, 'Florence Nightingale on Contagion', 129.

58. Platt, *The Ranyard Mission, 1857–1937*, 56.

59. For the figures on visitation see the *Annual Reports* of the Ranyard Mission.

60. See Geoffrey Gorer, *Death, Grief, and Mourning* (New York, 1965), 126–7.

61. See A. D. Gilbert, *The Making of Post-Christian Britain* (London, 1980), 60–1.

62. Francis Watson, *Dawson of Penn* (London, 1951), 130.

63. J. M. Winter, *The Great War and the British People* (London, 1986), 305.

64. A. J. P. Taylor, *English History 1914–1945* (Oxford, 1965), 120.

65. John Stevenson, *British Society 1914–45* (Harmondsworth, 1984), 124.

66. See Martin Gorsky, John Mohan, and Martin Powell, 'The Financial Health of Voluntary Hospitals in Interwar Britain', *Economic History Review*, 55: 3 (2002), 533–57.

67. Dingwall, Rafferty, and Webster, *An Introduction to the Social History of Nursing*, 99.

68. Richard M. Titmuss, *Problems of Social Policy* (London, 1976), 331.

69. MH, *Hospital Survey: The Hospital Services of London and the Surrounding Area* (1945), 62.

70. F. K. Prochaska, *Philanthropy and the Hospitals of London: The King's Fund, 1897–1990* (Oxford, 1992), 136–8, 151.

71. Titmuss, *Problems of Social Policy*, 449, n.

72. National Archives, MH/80/24. See also MH/77/76.

73. Quoted in John E. Pater, *The Making of the National Health Service* (London, 1981), 122.

74. Brian Abel-Smith, *A History of the Nursing Profession* (London, 1960), 161.

75. Stocks, *A Century of District Nursing*, 145.

76. *Parliamentary Debates*, 5th ser., vol. 422 (30 Apr. 1946), col. 47.

77. John Trevelyan, *Voluntary Service and the State: A Study of the Needs of the Hospital Service* (London, 1952), 32.

78. Dingwall, Rafferty, and Webster, *An Introduction to the Social History of Nursing*, 182.

79. *The Ranyard Mission and the Ranyard Nurses Annual Report for the Year ending 31ˢᵗ March 1954* (London, 1954), 3.

80. *The Ranyard Mission and the Ranyard Nurses Annual Report for the Year ending 31ˢᵗ March 1964* (London, 1964), 2.

81. The only surviving institution that retains the Ranyard name today is the Ranyard Memorial Home, Blessington Road, SE13, in which the last secretary of the mission died in the 1970s. Mrs Ranyard is also commemorated in a window in St Mark's Church, Kennington Park Road, SE11. I am grateful to the members of the staff of the Ranyard Memorial Home and St Mark's Church for this information.

82. *Nursing in the Community* (London, 1970), 18.

83. Stocks, *A Hundred Years of District Nursing*, 46.

84. Ibid., see the photograph opp. 161.

CHAPTER 6

1. G. M. Young, *Victorian England: Portrait of an Age* (Oxford, 1936), p. vi.

2. Jose Harris, 'Society and the State in Twentieth-century Britain', in *The Cambridge Social History of Britain, 1750–1950*, ed. F. M. L. Thompson, 3 vols. (Cambridge, 1990), iii. 64.

3. Beth Breeze, 'The Return of Philanthropy' *Prospect* (Jan. 2005), 53.

4. Harris, 'Society and the State in Twentieth-century Britain', 63.

5. This is an issue that might be given more treatment by theorists of modernization. See Grace Davie, *Europe: The Exceptional Case: Parameters of Faith in the Modern World* (London, 2002).

6. See above, 95.

7. Jeffrey Cox, *The English Churches in a Secular Society: Lambeth, 1870–1930* (Oxford, 1982), 275.

8. M. Penelope Hall and Ismene V. Howes, *The Church in Social Work* (London, 1965), 272.

9. Alexis de Tocqueville, *Democracy in America*, Modern Library edn., (New York, 1981), 440.

10. W. H. Beveridge, *Social Insurance and Allied Services* (London, 1942), 17. See also Derek Fraser, *The Evolution of the British Welfare State* (London, 1973), 200.

11. National Archives, MH/80/29.

12. William Henry McMenemey, *A History of the Worcester Royal Infirmary* (Worcester, 1947), p. viii.

13. Richard Crossman, 'The Role of the Volunteer in the Modern Social Service', in *Traditions of Social Policy*, ed. A. H. Halsey (Oxford, 1976), 265, 279, 283.

14. F. K. Prochaska, *Philanthropy and the Hospitals of London: The King's Fund, 1897–1990* (Oxford, 1992), 166.
15. Ibid.
16. David Selbourne, *The Principle of Duty: An Essay on the Foundations of the Civic Order* (London, 1994), 38.
17. Richard Crossman, *Planning for Freedom* (London, 1965), 58.
18. Douglas Jay, *The Socialist Case* (London, 1937), 317.
19. Quoted in David Owen, *English Philanthropy, 1660–1960* (London, 1964), 537.
20. Quoted in Asa Briggs and Anne Macartney, *Toynbee Hall: The First Hundred Years* (London, 1984), 35–6.
21. M. Penelope Hall, *The Social Services of Modern England*, 4th edn. (London, 1959), 357.
22. See David Green, *Reinventing Civil Society: The Rediscovery of Welfare Without Politics* (London, 1993), ch. 10.
23. Ferdinand Mount, *The British Constitution Now: Recovery or Decline* (London, 1992), 168.
24. *From Max Weber: Essays in Sociology*, ed. H. H. Gerth and C. Wright Mills (New York, 1946), 224.
25. John and Sylvia Jewkes, *The Genesis of the British National Health Service* (Oxford, 1962), 20–1. See also, Prochaska, *Philanthropy and the Hospitals of London*, 130–1.
26. See Prochaska, *Philanthropy and the Hospitals of London*, 187.
27. Jose Harris, *William Beveridge: A Biography* (Oxford, 1997), 461.
28. Michael Oakeshott, 'The Political Economy of Freedom' (1949), repr. in *Rationalism in Politics and Other Essays* (New York, 1962), 37–58.
29. Malcolm Muggeridge, *Things Past*, ed. Ian Hunter (London, 1978), 111.
30. Hilaire Belloc, *The Servile State* (London, 1927), pp. x, xiv, 136, 183.
31. G. K. Chesterton, *What's Wrong with the World* (London, 1910), 76, 78.
32. Tocqueville, *Democracy in America*, 556, 578. See also Larry Siedentop, *Tocqueville* (Oxford, 1994), 92–5.
33. *Parliamentary Debates*, 5th ser. (Lords), vol. 163, cols. 89, 105.
34. Ibid., col. 119.
35. Prochaska, *Philanthropy and the Hospitals of London*, 122–3.
36. William Beveridge, *Voluntary Action: A Report on Methods of Social Advance* (London, 1948), 10, 318, 320.
37. *Parliamentary Debates*, 5th ser. (Lords), vol. 163, cols. 95–6.

38. Harris, 'Society and the State in Twentieth-century Britain', 104.
39. Beveridge, *Voluntary Action*, 225.
40. Ibid., 322–3.
41. Harris, *William Beveridge*, 460.
42. Maggie Andrews, *The Acceptable Face of Feminism: The Women's Institute as a Social Movement* (London, 1997), 146–7.
43. Madeline Kerr, *The People of Ship Street* (London, 1958), 102–3.
44. Mary Morris, *Voluntary Work in the Welfare State* (London, 1969), 257.
45. Parliamentary Papers, *Committee on Charitable Trusts*, Cmd. 8710 (1952), par. 53.
46. See e.g. Eleanor Rathbone, *The Disinherited Family* (London, 1924).
47. Geoffrey Finlayson, *Citizen, State, and Social Welfare in Britain 1830–1990* (Oxford, 1994), 366.
48. Quoted in Maria Brenton, *The Voluntary Sector in British Social Services* (London, 1985), 143–4.
49. Finlayson, *Citizen, State, and Social Welfare in Britain*, 375–6.
50. Prochaska, *Philanthropy and the Hospitals of London*, 228.
51. Simon Jenkins, *Accountable to None: The Tory Nationalization of Britain* (London, 1995), 214.
52. See e.g. *Faith in the City: A Call for Action by Church and Nation: The Report of the Archbishop of Canterbury's Commission on Urban Priority Areas* (London, 1985), 25.
53. Raphael Samuel, 'Mrs. Thatcher's Return to Victorian Values', in *Victorian Values*, ed. T. C. Smout (Oxford, 1992), 22–3.
54. Jenkins, *Accountable to None*, 268.
55. Brian Harrison and Josephine Webb, 'Volunteers and Voluntarism' in *Twentieth-Century British Social Trends*, ed. A. H. Halsey and Josephine Webb (London, 2000), 615–16.
56. *Independent*, 3 Nov. 1994.
57. Quoted in Brian Harrison, 'Civil Society by Accident? Paradoxes of Voluntarism and Pluralism in the Nineteenth and Twentieth Centuries', in *Civil Society in British History: Ideas, Identities, Institutions*, ed. Jose Harris (Oxford, 2003), 79. See also Blair's speech at the NCVO conference, July 1999, quoted in Jeremy Kendall, *The Voluntary Sector: Comparative Perspectives in the UK* (London, 2003), 128.
58. *The Times*, 3 May 1988.
59. Ibid., 11 Jan. 2001.
60. House of Lords, Internet Publications, Charities Bill (HL), Session 2004–5.

61. For a discussion of state-sponsored voluntarism see Paul Hirst, *Associative Democracy: New Forms of Economic and Social Governance* (Cambridge, 1994), ch. 6.

62. Quoted in Brenton, *The Voluntary Sector in British Social Services*, 68.

63. Quoted in Finlayson, *Citizen, State, and Social Welfare in Britain*, 376.

64. Quoted in Robert Whelan, *Involuntary Action: How Voluntary is the 'Voluntary' Sector?* (London, 1999), 20.

65. *The Times*, 17 Dec. 1984.

66. Kendall, *The Voluntary Sector*, 25. Another study put the percentage of government funding at 35%. *The Report of the Commission on the Future of the Voluntary Sector Summary of Evidence*, (London, NCVO, 1996), 18.

67. www.lotterygoodcauses.org.uk.

68. Whelan, *Involuntary Action*, 17.

69. Quoted in Jane Lewis, *The Voluntary Sector, the State and Social Work in Britain: The Charity Organisation Society/Family Welfare Association since 1869* (Aldershot, 1995), 85.

70. For a positive approach to partnership, see Nicholas Deakin, 'Voluntary Inaction', in *Involuntary Action*, 27–34.

71. Quoted in Prochaska, *Philanthropy and the Hospitals of London*, 174.

72. Owen, *English Philanthropy, 1660–1960*, 527.

73. London Metropolitan Archive, KF, Division of Hospital Facilities, Guillebaud Committee. First Draft Memorandum, section I, pp. 1, 12, in file entitled 'Guillebaud Enquiry', quoted in Prochaska, *Philanthropy and the Hospitals of London*, 181–2.

74. A copy of the submission, dated 14 May 1954, is in the above-mentioned file.

75. Charles Webster, *The National Health Service: A Political History* (Oxford, 1998), 32.

76. Francis J. Gladstone, *Voluntary Action in a Changing World* (London, 1979), 3–4.

77. On this issue see D. J. Den Uyl, 'The Right to Welfare and the Virtue of Charity', *Social Philosophy & Policy*, 10: 1, (1993), 192–224.

78. Harrison and Webb, 'Volunteers and Voluntarism' in *Twentieth-Century British Social Trends*, 589; www.charity-commission.gov.uk.

79. Helen Cameron, 'The Decline of the Church of England as a Local Membership Organization: Predicting the Nature of Civil Society in 2050', in *Predicting Religion: Christian, Secular and Alternative Futures*,

109–119. Philip A. Hall, 'Social Capital in Britain', *British Journal of Political Science*, part 3 (July 1999), 421, 457.

80. Brian Heeney, *The Women's Movement in the Church of England 1850–1930* (Oxford, 1988), 44; www.themothersunion.org.

81. Harrison and Webb, 'Volunteers and Voluntarism' in *Twentieth-Century British Social Trends*, 597; www.womens-institute.co.uk.

82. Bob Holman, 'The Voluntaries: Another Perspective', in *Involuntary Action*, 41–44.

83. On American non-profit institutions see Douglas W. Rae, *Urbanism and Its End* (New Haven and London, 2003), 380.

84. Prochaska, *Philanthropy and the Hospitals of London*, 214.

85. *Times Literary Supplement*, 19 Nov. 2004, 12. See also Mark Chaves, *Congregations in America* (Cambridge, Mass., 2003), 3.

86. Whelan, *Involuntary Action*, 23.

87. *The Future of Voluntary Organisations: Report of the Wolfenden Committee* (London, 1978), 185.

88. See *Faith in the City: A Call for Action by Church and Nation. The Report of the Archbishop of Canterbury's Commission on Urban Priority Areas*, 359, *passim*.

89. Finlayson, *Citizen, State and Social Welfare in Britain*, 331–2.

90. Doreen Rosman, *The Evolution of the English Churches 1500–2000* (Cambridge, 2003), 313.

91. The Association of Charity Shops alone has nearly 6,000 member shops. See www.charityshops.org.uk.

92. Estimates of the number of volunteers to voluntary institutions vary considerably. A recent survey by the Charity Commissioners found that over 4 million adults had given time to charities in the previous month. *Meeting the Challenge of Change: Voluntary Action into the 21st Century: The Report of the Commission on the Future of the Voluntary Sector* (London, 1996), 31. See also Hall, 'Social Capital in Britain', 421, 427.

93. Justin Davis Smith, 'What We Know About Volunteering: Information from the Surveys', *Volunteering & Society: Principles and Practice*, ed. Rodney Hedley and Justin Davis Smith (London, 1992), 83. Kendall, *The Voluntary Sector*, 22–3, sees volunteering in religious congregations as still quite significant.

94. *C. of E. Newspaper*, 29 Mar. 1974, quoted in Alan D. Gilbert, *The Making of Post-Christian Britain: A History of the Secularization of Modern Society* (London and New York, 1980), p. ix.

95. See Robert D. Putnam, *Bowling Alone: The Collapse and Revival of American Communities* (New York, 2000).

96. *Economist* (31 Aug. 2004), 58.

97. *New York Times*, 2 Mar. 2005, A17.

98. See the discussion of social-service activities in American congregations in Chaves, *Congregations in America*, ch.3.

99. Melanie Phillips, *America's Social Revolution* (London, 2001), 8–9. See the websites of Faithworks and the Conservative Christian Fellowship.

100. Neil Gilbert, *Capitalism and the Welfare State: Dilemmas of Social Benevolence* (New Haven and London, 1983), 8.

101. see e.g. the activities of Faithworks.

102. See above, 26.

103. Alan D. Gilbert, 'Secularization and the Future', in *A History of Religion in Britain: Practice and Belief from Pre-Roman Times to the Present*, ed. Sheriden Gilley and W. J. Sheils (Oxford, 1994), 513.

104. *Economist*, (13 Sept. 2003), 54.

105. See George K. Behlmer, *Friends of the Family: The English Home and its Guardians, 1850–1940* (Stanford, 1998), 239.

106. See Grace Davie, *Religion in Britain since 1945: Believing Without Belonging* (Oxford, 1994).

107. *People's Perceptions of their Neighbourhood and Community Involvement: Results from the Social Capital Module of the General Household Survey 2000* (London, HMSO, 2002); *Economist*, (28 Feb. 2004), 52. See also Smith, 'What We Know About Volunteering, 76–8.

108. This is a point emphasized by Robert Putnam in a paper delivered to the Social Policy Seminar at Rhodes House, Oxford, in Feb. 2003. See also *Economist* (28 Feb. 2004), 52.

109. Samuel Smiles, *Self-Help with Illustrations of Conduct & Perseverance* (repr. London, 1958), 35.

110. Gilbert, *The Making of Post-Christian Britain*, 14. See also *From Max Weber: Essays in Sociology*, 128.

111. Bertrand Russell, *Why I Am Not a Christian and Other Essays on Religion and Related Subjects* (New York, 1957), 104, 115.

112. 1 Corinthians, 13: 1.

113. Young, *Victorian England*, 187.

114. Ibid.

Index